American Poetry in Performance

American Poetry in Performance

FROM WALT WHITMAN TO HIP HOP

Tyler Hoffman

The University of Michigan Press
Ann Arbor

Published in the United States of America by
The University of Michigan Press
Manufactured in the United States of America
⊗ Printed on acid-free paper

2014 2013 2012 2011   4   3   2   1

A CIP catalog record for this book is available from the British Library.

Library of Congress Cataloging-in-Publication Data

Hoffman, Tyler.
    American poetry in performance : from Walt Whitman to hip hop / Tyler Hoffman.
        p. cm.
    Includes bibliographical references and index.
    ISBN 978-0-472-11781-9 (cloth : alk. paper)
        1. Performance poetry—United States—History and criticism.
    2. Oral interpretation of poetry. 3. American poetry—History and criticism. 4. American poetry—African American authors—History and criticism. 5. Poetry slams—United States—History. I. Title.
    PN4151.H64   2011
    811—d   2011014824

for my parents
Donald Lee Hoffman
and
Nancy Jane Hoffman
and
my children
Noah Joseph Hoffman
Samuel Robert Hoffman
Lili Dare Hoffman

Acknowledgments

THANKS TO THE FOLLOWING READERS for their judiciousness: Howard Marchitello, Bill Pannapacker, Ken Price, and Michael Robertson. Thanks also to Stephen Cushman, Ed Folsom, and Jay Parini, for whose continuing support I am deeply grateful. I am indebted too to my colleagues in the Dean's Office (you know who you are) for their company and encouragement as the project came to its conclusion, and to Lisa Zeidner, John Lafont, and Joe Rively for being there. My book is dedicated to those whom I owe the most.

I also am extremely thankful to Phil Pochoda and Tom Dwyer at the University of Michigan Press for their belief in this project and stewardship of it.

Finally, I wish to acknowledge support from the Rutgers University Research Council and extend my appreciation to the editors of *Studies in American Humor, The Wallace Stevens Journal,* and the *Walt Whitman Quarterly Review* in which versions of parts of the following chapters originally appeared.

Contents

Introduction

All the arts are capable of duende, but where it finds its greatest range, naturally, is in music, dance, and spoken poetry, for these arts require a living body to interpret them, being forms that are born, die, and open their contours against an exact present.

—FEDERICO GARCÍA LORCA

To study performance is not to study completed forms . . . [but to] become aware of performance itself as a contested space, where meanings and desires are generated, occluded, and of course multiply interpreted.

—ELIN DIAMOND

IN 1882 IN HIS BOOK *Specimen Days and Collect,* Walt Whitman published a short reiterative prose piece called "Ventures, on an Old Theme." In it, he makes his case again for an American poetry free of meter and rhyme, insisting, "In these States, beyond all precedent, poetry will have to do with actual facts, with the concrete States, and—for we have not much more than begun—with the definitive getting into shape of the Union." He calls on a new breed of lofty poet to cement the states together, to divert the danger of crass materialism and instill the virtues of "nationality and patriotism." Whitman ends by announcing his belief in the reciprocal relationship that must exist between the artist and the public in a democracy, with the epigrammatic assertion, "To have great poets, there must be great audiences, too."[1]

That sentence has echoed through the ages, and served as both a foil and a rallying cry for American poets who have sought to understand and articulate the cultural dynamic of popularity. In a 1914 issue of *Poetry,* the editor, Harriet Monroe, and her foreign correspondent, Ezra Pound, debated the motto taken from Whitman on the cover of the magazine: "To have great poets, there must be great audiences, too." Pound opened fire first, protesting, "The artist is *not* dependent upon his audience," and judging that "this sentence is Whitman tired. You have only to compare Whitman to my mutton-headed ninth cousin, or to any other American of his time who had the 'great audience,' to see the difference." He goes on to compare Whitman unfavorably to Dante, who "never gave way" to a desire to capture a large public, and whose terms for that public—"the rabble"; "the *vulgo*"—make clear his distaste and distinct sense of superiority: "The artist is not dependent upon the multitude of his listeners. Humanity is the rich effluvium, it is the waste and the manure of the soil, and from it grows the tree of the arts." Monroe argues conversely that modern democracy demands a different conception of the relationship between the artist and the masses: "Modern inventions, forcing international travel, inter-racial thought, upon the world, have done away with Dante's little audience, with his contempt for the crowd, a contempt which, however, disregarded the fact that his epic, like all the greatest art, was based upon the whole life of his time, the common thought and feeling of all the people. No small group today can suffice for the poet's immediate audience, as such groups did in the stay-at-home aristocratic ages; and the greatest danger which besets modern art is that of slighting the 'great audience' whose response alone can give it authority and volume, and of magnifying the importance of a coterie."[2] She finds that there must be an "energy of sympathy" reciprocal to the "energy of creation" to invigorate a democracy, and thereby validate the art of the "poet-prophet." The Whitman motto continued to appear on the cover of *Poetry* until 1950 when the editor, Karl Shapiro, removed it at T. S. Eliot's suggestion, much to his later regret.[3]

Other poets and poetry commentators have wielded Whitman's message to express their views on the popularization of poetry and its effects. The African American poet Sterling Brown in an essay entitled "Our Literary Audience," published in *Opportunity* in 1930, had this to say: "'Without great audiences we cannot have great poets.' Whitman's trenchant commentary needs stressing today, universally. But particularly do we as a racial group need it." He makes his case for the vital need of the black artist to write realistically about all of black life, including the most common elements of it, and the consequent need for the black audience to be receptive to representations of the race that are truthful even if they are not "idealistic, optimistic tracts for race advertisement."[4] Brown ends his essay in reaffirmation of Whitman: "Without great audiences we cannot have great literature." On the other hand, a number of years later, in 1962, the poet Louis Simpson reacted with abhorrence to Whitman's formulation, con-

tending, "This tag from Whitman, which adorns or used to adorn every issue of *Poetry,* is about as close to the opposite of the truth as you can get. To
have great poetry all that is needed is great talent."[5] Simpson's elitist sense
is in line with Pound's and Eliot's, and suggests that the cultivation of a
public in fact may be an impediment to producing a lasting literature.

More recently, an article in *Time* (December 16, 1991) on the emergent
poetry slam scene ran Whitman's sentence as its epigraph, teeing up its discussion of "the new generation of defiantly populist poets" intent on communicating poetry to as large an audience as possible, with the idea being
to effect a cultural revolution. In an article in Toronto's *National Post* (February 28, 2006) Whitman's formulation is once again cited, this time as
preface to the announcement of the North American tour of rapper Saul
Williams and the industrial rock band Nine Inch Nails and the exploration
of Williams's decision to expand his reach by performing for the "white
kids wearing all black" that largely comprise the audience for Trent Reznor,
founder of Nine Inch Nails. As these sitings demonstrate, Whitman's epi-
gram increasingly is deployed in discussions about poetry in performance
off the page, framing tensions between page and stage—that is, between
textuality and orality—that shape so many of the discussions around poetry performance in the modern period and debates surrounding the merits of publicness.

In "The Peril of the Poetry Reading: The Page Versus the Performance"
published on the website of the American Academy of Poets, David Groff,
who concedes that "public poetry events bring people together, creating
a community for the most intimidating of the verbal arts," expresses
reservations about the embodiment of poetry and its public appeal: "But
even if the poem takes on a fresh life when it's delivered in the voice of
its maker, it loses more than it gains. . . . Only when we acknowledge that
a poem performed is no substitute for a poem read in private will we truly
advance the cause of the poetic word." Many assumptions about poetry
and its cultural prestige are packed into that statement, and many of
them are contested in this book. Groff goes on to ask the loaded question: "In the effort to make poetry popular, is poetry-making itself de-
based?" He answers his own question with lament: "There's no chance
for the poet or listener's eye to pause, slow down, or linger over a line.
How many times have you wanted to ask a poet to decelerate or reread a
poem? A recited poem vanishes faster than a vapor trail." The evanes-
cence of performance is seen here as a failing, with no distinction made

between a poem read well and a poem read poorly (who *would* enjoy the latter?).

In his keynote address at the 1996 PEN Literary Awards, Richard Howard sounds the same note as Groff, offering up "a modest proposal that may yet restore an art that was once the glory and the consolation of our race to something like its ulterior status. My proposal is simply this: to make poetry, once again, a secret": "We have failed . . . to make poetry known; we have merely made it public. If we are to save poetry, which means if we are to savor it, we must restore poetry to that status of seclusion and even secrecy that characterizes our authentic pleasures and identifies only our intimately valued actions." On the other side stands future poet laureate Robert Pinsky, who, in reply to Howard, asserts that poetry is "part of our shared communal life, as surely as is the Internet," and that the participation of poets in the public sphere is "part of the civic life of art, a part of the way society held onto the art of poetry, thereby preserving it for the unborn."[6]

In the following pages I explore the civics of American performance poetry and the nexus of its oral and print modalities in the light of shifting political and cultural formations in the nation over the last century and a half. In many ways, my book is as much a study of public performance poetry in the United States as it is a study of the cultures that give rise to it and the performance of cultures and cultural identities within it. For too long we have not paid close enough attention to the meanings that emerge in particular performance contexts; we have not questioned fully enough the situatedness of public performance poetry or sought to understand the ramifications of certain poems as first and foremost to be read aloud, to be staged for a live audience. In an effort to help correct the balance, I analyze a range of materials, many of which have not garnered much in the way of critical attention before, including multiple printed and recorded versions of poems. Keeping in mind the dialectic of performance and text, I seek to show how performance on the page often seeks to authenticate performance off the page, and vice versa. As the anthropologist Dennis Tedlock reminds us, "There is nothing about writing, in and of itself, that requires a text to be fixed for all times and places. Writing, like speaking, is a performance." That is to say, writing, like speaking, can resist reproduction ("Performance's only life is in the present") such that even if it is performed again, "this repetition itself marks it as 'different.'"[7] Often it is the case with the poets taken up in the following chapters that no single performance in print, just as no single oral performance by them, is definitive. By parsing individual performance styles, I reveal the semantic value of extralexical, or paralinguistic, features, and submit to a rehearing certain poems that we thought we knew well.

In addition to these prosodic concerns, I am also interested in how audiences responded to poets in performance both on and off the page, whether live or electronically, and how those responses are shaped by the pressures of American mass culture. The politics surrounding poets' negotiations of the cultural economy and the rise of new communications technologies within it are crucial to a thorough understanding of how a public performance poetry is sounded and heard in the modern period. Often, these politics inflect the fictions of performance that poets construct in and about their work, in tropes of utterance and audition that often are imbued with national significance.

John Miles Foley, refusing the oral/written dichotomy, proposes a four-part taxonomy of oral poetry: material composed and transmitted entirely without writing; works written for oral performance ("voiced texts"); poems transmitted in writing from preliterary times, such as Homeric epic, *Beowulf,* and Mahabharata; and, finally, poetry like James Macpherson's Ossianic poetry and Elias Lönnrot's *Kalevala* that is written to be experienced as oral, although read by literate audiences ("written oral poetry"). The poetry I address falls primarily under the categories of "voiced texts" (scripts) and "written oral poetry" (poetry that seeks to encode in it a quality of oralness). In many cases, a poem that is performed aloud subsequently is written down, serving as a kind of transcript, and I examine closely these transpositions as well. It is important to note that Foley does not consider at any length the impact of mediatization on his types of oral poetry. Of course, writing is a medium, and so a performance that exists in printed form is always "mediated," but when I speak of a "mediatized" performance I mean, as performance theorist Philip Auslander points out (by way of Jean Baudrillard), "to indicate that a particular cultural object is a product of the mass media or media technology," that is, produced by electric amplification: " 'Mediatized performance' is performance that is circulated on television, as audio or video recordings, and in other forms in technologies of reproduction."[8] This condition of mediatization affects in essential ways our reception of performance poetry and its cultural work.

Related to mediatization is the critical concept of "liveness," which has been the subject of much lively debate within the field of performance studies of late. In opposition to Peggy Phelan, who finds that one of the

defining features of performance is that it stands outside the cultural economy, Auslander (I think correctly) "doubt[s] very strongly that any cultural
discourse can actually stand outside the ideologies of capital and reproduction that define a mediatized culture or should be expected to do so, even
to assume an oppositional stance."[9] Theirs is a debate over the ontology of
performance, with Phelan taking the view that "performance's only life is
in the present," that by its very nature it "cannot be saved, recorded, documented, or otherwise participate in the circulation of representations *of*
representations," and, on the other hand, Auslander asserting that there
exist no significant ontological distinctions between live and mediatized
cultural forms, that "in our period of history, and in our Western societies,
there is no performance that is not always already a commodity."[10] While
Auslander takes aim at those who would valorize live performance over the
mediatized, he recognizes that many poets "impute to live performance the
social, perhaps even political, function of opposing the oppressive regime
of 'electronic noise' imposed upon us by the mass media" and celebrate the
"ostensible curative powers" of live performance as well as its "putative
ability to create community"; as he sees, "Concepts such as these do have
value for performers and partisans of live performance. Indeed, it may even
be necessary for performers, especially, to believe in them."[11] That observation, along with his comments on authenticity and simulation in a digital
age, will figure in my discussion, as I document the evolution of spoken poetry in a modern consumerist America and the politically freighted
mythologies that attend it.

    Federico García Lorca identifies spoken poetry as among those arts that
"require a living body to interpret them," one of the "forms that are born,
die, and open their contours against an exact present." In that exact present, we can speak of "performance" in two ways: bodies bring poems into
being—that is, they enact poems—through a dramatic entertainment; and
bodies bring subjectivity into being. Lately, in a range of disciplines, a great
deal of attention has been paid to the nature of the self and the ways in
which identity is constructed in the world. The sociologist Erving Goff-
man, for example, shed much needed light on the cultural performance of
the self, showing that in everyday life we are always performing roles. Judith Butler similarly contends that identity categories such as gender, race,
class, and sexuality are performed rather than essential, that they are socially and culturally constructed and thus are always contested and in flux.
She refers to the daily reproduction (or re-citation) of acts and practices

that affirm gender and other social norms that we inherit as "the performativity of identity." Her notion of performativity is based on her reading of philosophers J. L. Austin and Jacques Derrida. Drawing a distinction between performative utterance and constative utterance, Austin contends that the former are not true or false and actually perform the utterance to which they refer; thus, performative utterances perform the action they designate. Derrida finds that identities are reproduced, or "cited," as repetitions of normative injunctions; these repeated iterations both consolidate the force of identity and, as Butler believes, provide the occasion for its subversion. I will seek to show the ways in which poets acknowledge, either implicitly or explicitly, this truth about identity formation (and deformation) in their performance poetry and poetics. Thus, although Charles Bernstein argues that "the poetry reading enacts the poem not the poet; it materializes the text not the author," my strong sense is that what is performed at a poetry reading is necessarily both the poet *and* the poem.[12]

It is perhaps not surprising, then, that what is at stake in so much public performance poetry is cultural identity itself—markers of gender, sexuality, race, ethnicity, class, and nationality. Just as with these categories, which are socially and culturally constructed and which thus evolve continually, the poetry that I examine in this book is also shifting. With respect to the construct of nation, which, as Benedict Anderson observes, is not tangible or palpable—it represents "an imaginary community"—orality offers a means by which to incarnate abstract values and ideals; it helps make "nation" feel real. Otto Bauer relatedly argues that national character is "changeable," and declares that "ego" is intimately bound up in nation and the idea of nation; as the thinking goes: "If someone slights the nation they slight me too . . . [F]or the nation is nowhere but in me and my kind." The egos on display in public performance poetry either go in for this thinking or strenuously resist such chauvinism, sometimes even as they undertake their own alternative nation-building.

This study stands at the crossroads of the humanities and social sciences, and the importance of anthropology and sociology not only to the performance of identity but to the textual performance of poetry in the United States cannot be overstated. In recent years, much work has been done in these fields to articulate a set of best practices for dealing with oral performance and its transcriptions. In his essay "Breakthrough into Performance" (1975), the anthropologist Dell Hymes called for a more thorough study of "variation in performance," citing the "virtual absence of serious stylistic analysis of native American Indian traditions and of individual performers." In essays in the early 1960s, Hymes laid out an approach that he called "the ethnography of speaking," which sought to discover the patterns and functions of speaking within specific cultural contexts in terms of setting, participants, ends, act sequence, key (tone), instrumentalities (communication channels), norms of interaction and interpretation, and genre. Through this model, Hymes helped pioneer a linguistic anthropological approach to ethnopoetics, and the various patterns and functions that he identifies will underlie discussion in subsequent chapters.

Elizabeth Fine in *The Folklore Text* (1984) discusses the history of what she calls, via the linguist Roman Jakobson, "the 'intersemiotic' translation of performance to print," and her insights shape my readings. Fine draws on a range of anthropologists and sociolinguists in her theorizing of how to handle the movement of speech into writing, to construct a "performance-centered text," that is, a transcript of a performance that would convey contextual and stylistic information, in part through typography and layout. Believing that performance is situated behavior, Fine illustrates how one would go about rendering "the oral-physical symbols of artistic verbal performance" through "the two-dimensional, visual symbols of the printed page."[13] Although in this book I am not myself attempting to create performance-centered texts, her examination of the implications of performance theory for re-creating oral poetry in a print medium, and of the scoring methods to do so, bears importantly on the construction of performance-centered texts by American public poets themselves.

Of course, performance presumes an activated audience, and performance poetry presents itself as one of the most persistently dialogic of forms, embracing polyvocality and resisting as it does finality and closure, with the work not to be identified with any single graphical or performative realization of it. Although Bakhtin stamped poetry as monologic and the novel as dialogic, his poetics of utterance, where the only way to understand the self is in relation to an addressee, very much applies to poetry, and, in particular, to orally performed poetry, where the social and political value of intonation sounds literally. As we will see, Bakhtin's theory of the emancipatory potential of carnival also can help clarify the sometimes subversive enactments of performance poetry in the public sphere.

That phrase, *the public sphere,* also calls for comment. According to the social philosopher Jürgen Habermas, in the eighteenth century the public sphere consisted of organs of information and political debate such as newspapers and journals, as well as institutions of political discussion such as parliaments, political clubs, literary salons, public assemblies, pubs and coffeehouses, meeting halls, and other public spaces where sociopolitical discourse took place. For the first time in history, individuals and groups could shape public opinion, giving direct expression to their needs and interests while influencing political practice. As Habermas's critics have noted, and Habermas since has conceded, the liberal public sphere that he describes was not as diverse or as tolerant as he imagined; thus, working-class, plebeian, and women's public spheres developed alongside the bourgeois public sphere to represent voices and interests excluded in this forum. Sometimes these public spheres overlap; other times, they conflict. One interest of this study is to plot the involvement of public performance poetry in emergent counterpublic spheres. Nancy Fraser defines a counterpublic sphere as a place "where members of subordinated social groups invent and circulate counterdiscourses, which in turn permit them to formulate oppositional interpretations of their identities, interests, and needs."[14] As Gerard Hauser further explains, such a sphere is by definition "a site of resistance," and "its rhetorical identity is as an arena for hearing proscribed voices, expressing proscribed ideas, and entertaining the alternative reality they advance to the existing order." Whether the resistance is militant or not, the discourse of a counterpublic sphere "speaks . . . of an alternative reality to that of the majority culture and their exclusion from its processes of decision making that bear on their lives."[15]

Central to this matter of publicness or counterpublicness are the related concepts of aura and artistic reproducibility, with the rise of new technologies and of increasingly media-dominated public spheres impacting in important ways on public poetry and its sitings. Walter Benjamin notes that, at one time, artistic works had an "aura" deriving from their uniqueness, and that the new media shattered this quasi-religious ethos. The reproduction of works of art (by means of photography or radio transmission) means that they are actually designed for reproducibility; in cinema, for instance, we have copies without an original. Benjamin does not mourn the aura destroyed by mechanical reproduction, believing that art is thereby liberated from a "parasitical dependence on ritual" and authenticity, and so can participate in history and politics.[16] The quality of *duende* (emotion, expression, authenticity) prized by most spoken word poets leads some to take a dim view of the mechanics of reproduction; in other instances, though, such technologies are embraced by these poets in an effort to forge community on a grand scale, to catalyze widespread social and political change, typically with the idea that aura, authenticity, and cult value are not routed thereby.

Roland Barthes's 1967 pronouncement of the "death of the author" also rings differently in the situation of the artist performing live, a figure who can be seen and heard as not dead, a palpable presence. When this same poet turns to the pen (or keyboard) to craft performance-centered texts, she simultaneously affirms and challenges Barthes's view that "writing is the destruction of every voice," as she works against writing's lack in an effort to preserve and reproduce the charismatic poetic voice.[17] If the presence of the poet in performance does impose some limit on the performed text, since to separate the work from its creator would seem an impossibility, we might argue that it is not always the same voice's body on display, a condition that thereby offers another form of plenitude. Indeed, if we do not identify any one performance of the poem as authoritative, we could say that there as many meanings to the poem as there are performances of it. Thus, we do not need to deconstruct the author, as Barthes would have us do, to appreciate the multiplicities of public performance poetry.

It is important to state that in this book my focus is on poets committed to an oral poetics (as opposed to poets who, while they may read their poetry on occasion, are perfectly content on the page) and who are, at the same time, public poets, by which I mean poets interested in reaching and cultivating a mass audience, not an elite coterie. So while it may be true, as a writer in the slam poetry anthology *The Spoken Word Revolution* (2003) notes, that "Robert Frost was probably the twentieth century's greatest U.S. performance poet," he is not taken up here because, although he is intensely interested in the sounds of poetry (and in "the sound of sense"—or intonation—in poetry) and performed famously on many occasions, including John F. Kennedy's inauguration, he did not compose (and recompose) for performance primarily; his poetry sits comfortably on the printed page.[18] At issue in these pages is poetry made with an awareness of a live audience to whom the work could be read aloud, or of a distant reader-audience who would perform it out loud themselves.

It also is crucial to note at the outset a few other boundaries of this study. First, in these pages I primarily examine what has been termed "oral poetry," a form Richard Kostelanetz defines as "syntactically standard language written to be read aloud," rather than "text-sound art," or pure sound poetry, which "extends back to primitive chanting" and is not syntactically standard.[19] Second, I focus on types of lyric poetry as opposed to verse drama, where performativity is more obviously at issue. Third, my intention throughout is to read American public performance poetry and its rhetoric in the context of a technologically advanced (mass-mediated) society, a condition that Walter Ong refers to as "secondary orality," which (as opposed to "primary orality," that is, the orality of preliterate cultures) is "essentially a more deliberate and self-conscious orality, based permanently on the use of writing and print."[20] Therefore, I do not explore aboriginal oral poetry, where understandings and constructions of speech are far different from what they are in a literate society.

It is necessary to state, too, that the mantle of "oral poet" has not always been happily worn by some of the artists represented here, despite the fact that these same artists clearly often are writing toward performance off the page. Sonia Sanchez, for one, bristles at being labeled in this way, finding that it is "much easier to relegate our [African American] form to being always oral form," that a double standard is at play, with a white poet like Allen Ginsberg, who often "chants" his work, not marginalized as "an oral poet" in the same way that she or Amiri Baraka, whom she claims Ginsberg based his delivery style on anyway, would be. Indeed, she has gone so far as to deny being a "performance poet," a designation that she feels is meant "to limit us [African Americans]," "to keep us out of the arena of being poets."[21] I will carefully weigh the racial implications of these remarks, and my twin focus on the poem in the mouth and in print—and on the interplay between them—is intended not to relegate any of the poets discussed in the pages that follow to an inferior position, but to see them as participating in a major, though often overlooked, tradition—indeed, as squarely at the center of American literature from the 1850s to the present.

Bob Holman, whose work I address in my final chapter, refers to the oral poetic tradition as "the Hidden Book,"[22] one, that is, that has rarely been read and contains within it a richness worth knowing. It is the purpose of this critical study to recover that Book and attend to its performativities. Tracing a history of performance poetry in the United States from Whitman through the rap-meets-poetry scene, I argue that the country itself and its publics and counterpublics have spoken themselves into being in the act of poetry performance, whether through registers of resonance or dissonance.

The title of my first chapter, "Walt Whitman 'Live,'" intends to position

Whitman as modern America's first performance poet. Although he was not a widely or wildly popular poet-performer of his day, as others, like James Whitcomb Riley, were, Whitman was thoroughly committed to the idea of performance and a public poetics of voice, to the aesthetic ideals of improvisation and open-endedness. Others have pointed up the "profound significance of the voice in Whitman's thinking," but have not viewed that item in light of his poetic revisioning, which I tie to his urge to "liveness."[23] "Voice" in his work has been framed as "a crucial mediating trope," but it has not been shown yet how in his work voice serves as a metonym for nation, and for Whitman's performance of self and nation.[24] Indeed, too often discussions of presence in Whitman studies are separated out from the cultural work that Whitman seeks to perform through his poetry, left unconnected to the political events of his day.

As I argue, Whitman's poetry is founded on the masculine politics of the "launch'd voice" as formulated in the nineteenth century in America, and the textual instability of *Leaves of Grass* stands as a sign of his essential performativity. It is noteworthy that he would appear to be one of the first poets to record his poetry via the phonograph; moreover, his meditations on vocalism in his notebooks significantly shape his concept of a public performance poetry. While several critics have noted Whitman's debt to oratorical media, they have not examined in relation to it his typographical inscriptions or his practice of poetic revision. I show how Whitman embodies myriad cultural identities in multiple editions of *Leaves* and how his performances respond to the nuances of shifting ideologies and express his desire to forge, in the face of great odds, a national polity. Whitman's encounter with emergent sound recording technologies and with the culture of celebrity (and the issues of aura and presence that obtain there) further shape his mythologies of the spoken word and their corresponding notions about America and Americanness.

Ambivalent heir to Whitman, Vachel Lindsay cultivated a peculiar performance style that he sought to score in marginal reading directions in the performance-centered texts of *The Congo and Other Poems* (1915) and later works. In performance, Lindsay put on the forms of "blackness" through a complex affair of mimicry, trying to redeem the figure of the public poet at a time when literary popularity (and mass culture itself) was deemed feminizing. His "higher vaudeville" performance pieces stage related cultural anxieties and encode vocalization in strongly gendered terms. I read his performance of a masculine working-class identity against the performances of other male modernists and of Edna St. Vincent Millay's famous performance of femininity in her popular recitals, and link that performance to his civic ideology. I also examine Lindsay's stage presence with respect to the rise of the radio and other communications technologies saturating middle America, interrogating his advocacy of directness and liveness, of all things unmediatized. In the end, I interrogate Lindsay's disenchantment with the commodification of the spoken word and point up his predicament, the "ordeal" that he endured as a result of his bid for publicity in a fast-industrializing cultural economy.

The so-called New Negro poets demonstrate both on and off the page the vexed question of "authenticity" as it relates to vocal reproduction and an emergent racial politics. When James Weldon Johnson published his book of sermonic poetry *God's Trombones* (1927), a rescue of Reconstruction-era preaching, he chose not to include marginal reading instructions or expressive typography, as Lindsay had done. Johnson's decision not to compose performance-centered texts cuts two ways: first, it suggests his view that only those familiar with the figure of the black preacher will hear the poem properly, that it is a racially closed system; second, it insists that the black poet must refuse dissonant sound effects (dialects) that would fail to uplift the race. In addition to Johnson's sermonic poetry, Zora Neale Hurston's transcriptions of the black preaching voice in *Mules and Men* (1935) and the white southern writer Dr. Edward Clarkson Leverett (Ned) Adams's in *Congaree Sketches* (1927) illustrate the racial problematics of rehearing. The chapter goes on to consider the career of Langston Hughes and his effort to perform African American citizenship in his social poetry. I "listen fluently" (Hughes's character Simple's words) to his print and recorded voice in light of the politics of the Left (socialism and black nationalism), and against the grain of the poet Sterling Brown's voice, and end by examining Hughes's remodelings of his own previously published poetry as part of his evolving performance of a black public sphere.

In the chapter following, the curtain opens on the landmark reading of six Beat poets at the Six Gallery in San Francisco on October 13, 1955, a siting that represents a new phase in the history of American poetry as performance art, if not a beginning. Drawing on Bakhtin's concept of the "carnivalesque," I show how the Six Gallery reading, where Allen Ginsberg performed "Howl" for the first time, sought to challenge the dominant culture and its social hierarchies and effect "communitas." In the process, I explore the ideology of voice that crystallizes during the Cold War, with per-

14   AMERICAN POETRY IN PERFORMANCE

sonal audibility imagined as a potent resistance to U.S. imperialist aggression. In reading Ginsberg's divergent oral performances (and subcultural and mainstream reactions to those performances) as soundings of race and gender, I also find that the content and style of certain poems change in response to shifts in national and Ginsberg's own sexual politics. Anne Waldman, who offers a fiercely gendered reading of ritual vocalization and event in line with contemporaneous feminist performance art, provides a compelling counterpoint. I also investigate the phenomenon of jazz poetry in the late 1950s and early 1960s, with special attention to a section of Ferlinghetti's *A Coney Island of the Mind* (1958) and its subversive performance of American commodity culture and personal identity within it.

With the full flowering of black cultural nationalism in the 1960s, poets began to worry about and insist on the full integration of the black artist in the black community. Amiri Baraka (formerly Leroi Jones) communicates an aggressive subaltern politics in his poetry, and his performance aesthetic underscores the changeableness of gender, race, and nation. Don L. Lee (later Haki Madhubuti), in step with Baraka, develops a delivery style and scripted vocal presence that are meant to publicize poetry to the black community in a wider way, using rap to dissolve distinctions between high and low culture. Through audiotexts and the soundscapes surrounding their production, I explore as well prominent women poets of the movement, notably Nikki Giovanni and Sonia Sanchez, and their chants of a new black womanhood, some of which were performed with gospel choirs and blues bands in an attempt to bring poetry—and the black nationalist message—to an expanded cross-section of African Americans. Throughout the chapter I weigh the politics of amplitude in Black Arts movement poetry and the cultural effects of the mediatization of the grain of the voice.

In my final chapter, "Slam Nation," which re-cites the title of a 1998 documentary film on the slam poetry scene (*SlamNation*), I respond to one of the most interesting and controversial new poetic forms to erupt onto the U.S. cultural scene in recent years. The poetry performed at the slam has been dismissed by some as nothing more than a sideshow attraction; however, as this cultural form has spread, making poetry more accessible to more people, slammers have continued to theorize their aesthetic in serious terms, and the form has begun to be taken much more seriously. Drawing on statements about the slam by its organizers, poets, and audiences, I trace the American roots of its participatory poetics and show how it seeks to construct what Bakhtin calls a "second culture," an alternative to the dominant culture from whose values the poets largely dissent. I also demonstrate how a vulgar humor incites a treacherous laughter that temporarily suspends the official hierarchies of the dominant culture in effecting the participants' own identitarian politics. My chapter ends with an analysis of virtual performances of public poetry, its multimediatic extensions, and on the simulation of liveness in a digital age.

The performance theorist Elin Diamond has stated that performance is "a contested space, where meanings and desires are generated, occluded, and of course multiply interpreted." This definition is consistent with Judith Butler's contention that identity itself is a contested construct. The idea of the performance space as *agon* stands out, with poets vying in public with themselves, with other poets, with their audiences, and with American culture. Whitman observed that "the place of the orator and his hearers is truly an agonistic arena. There he wrestles and contends with them—he suffers, sweats, undergoes his great toil and extasy. Perhaps it is a greater battle than any fought by contending forces on land and sea." The person who wins, he observes, is capable of establishing the "mightiest rule."[25] In the chapters to come, we will assess how Whitman and descendant poets amplify this expressed ideology of the spoken word as they map for themselves a quintessentially American history and theory of public poetry.

CHAPTER I

Walt Whitman "Live":
Performing the Public Sphere

Others take finish, but the Republic is ever constructive and ever keeps vista.

—WHITMAN, FROM "BY BLUE ONTARIO'S SHORE"

The want for something finished, completed, and technically beautiful will certainly not be supplied by this writer, as it is by existing esthetic works.

—WHITMAN IN CONVERSATION, VIA TRAUBEL

WHITMAN IS NOT WELL KNOWN for having recited his poetry out loud to others, and is on record as saying that he was "nothing of a reader," that, in fact, he preferred not to read his own work and couldn't *recite* it in any event, since he didn't have it memorized (*WWWC*, 9:124). Despite such claims, he did perform on numerous occasions, both in private and in public, and attached great significance to those exercises. From his memoranda we know that he was in the habit of reading poetry aloud to himself from his youth, riding omnibuses up and down Broadway "declaiming some stormy passage from Julius Caesar or Richard, (you could roar as loudly as you chose in that heavy, dense, uninterrupted street-bass.)" (*PP*, 727). To his friend Horace Traubel in 1889 he recalled, "I did my best reading when I was alone that way—off in the woods or on the shore. Long ago, when I was a young man, Coney Island was a favorite spot. At that time Coney Island had not the reputation it has now—it was then a desert island—nobody went there. Oh yes! When I read, it was in solitude, never in frequented places, except perhaps, Broadway, on the stage-coaches, where a little noise more or less made no difference." Earlier that year, again to Traubel, he recounted of his lyric "A Voice Out of the Sea," "I always enjoyed saying it—saying it to the winds, the waters, the noisy streets—on stagecoaches. And one has love for the sound of his own voice—somehow it's always magnetic" (*WWWC*, 5:321, 463).

In discussion with Traubel about the practice of reading aloud, Whitman cites Ernest Legouvé's *The Art of Reading* (translated into English in 1879), a copy of which he owned, explaining that in one of the chapters an actress named Rachel is described as being "aroused when going to her room and reading aloud her plays, whatnot," in part under the spell of her own voice; he concludes that "there are some who contend that no one can get a full or adequate idea of a poem till it is heard rendered aloud—the human voice to give it its free scope ring!" and adds, "I don't know but there's a vast deal to be said to that effect" (*WWWC*, 5:321). Although Whitman does not say so, in this remark he picks up another thread in Legouvé's book, from the chapter "How Reading Reveals," where that author contends that "even reading aloud is not without its delusions. If it discovers beauties, it detects faults as well. . . . How many writers and writings that I used to admire passionately, that possibly you admire passionately now, I have found totally unable to stand this terrible test!" Whitman tells Traubel that he always had tried his own poems-in-progress out by reading them aloud to himself "in a palpable voice" and by doing so was able "to get a new angle on them—see things I could not see in any other way" (*WWWC*, 3:375). In another conversation with his friend he notes, "The great French writer Legouvé says this is the final, the supreme, test, after all else is tried—how will a poem read, recite, deliver: with what effect? How will it hold its own when repeated? That is the court in which it must justify itself." While he says he would not give such a theory his "radical endorsement," Whitman regards it as one "not to be rejected scornfully" (*WWWC*, 4:116).

In his early years, Whitman shaped by hand his texts for ultimate portability, creating reading copies that he could take with him on site to declaim. On the cover of a reading copy of Shakespeare's *Richard the Second* that he made by tearing the leaves of the play out of a complete volume and binding them in wrapping paper, he wrote: "Had it put this shape to take in my pocket to Coney Island on my seashore jaunts—read it & 'spouted' it there."[1] Whitman also bundled together late in life a set of poems that he deemed "favorite" pieces for "spouting," and, pointing to the package of poems sitting on a chair, told Traubel, "I was a great spouter in my early days—even later on—had my favorite pieces—these among them" (*WWWC*, 5:463). He imagined the same fate for *Leaves of Grass*, saying on August 21, 1888, "I have long teased my brain with visions of a handsome little book at last . . . for the pocket. That would tend to induce people to take me along with them and read me in the open air: I am nearly always successful with the reader in the open air" (*WWWC*, 2:175). This imagined pocket edition anticipates *Gems from Walt Whitman* (1889), in whose compilation Whitman assisted, Haldeman-Julius's Little Blue Books, and the beat poet Lawrence Ferlinghetti's populist City Lights "Pocket Books" series—a series that includes Allen Ginsberg's *Howl*.[2]

In a review of the 1855 edition of *Leaves* that he penned himself, Whitman, speaking of himself in the third person, explains the importance of the spoken word to his art, stating, "In the scheme this man has built for himself the writing of poems is but a proportionate part of the whole. It is plain that public and private performance . . . have their equal call upon him and receive equal attention."[3] Clearly, Whitman was not content to appear merely as a writer, wanting to make an impression upon us as an oral performer, to simulate a live vocal presence. As he felt, the printed voice does not measure up to the "launch'd" voice and is, in the end, a sign of the artist's failure to prove his publicity, his complexion literally "pallid" from the lack of sunlight that comes of too much privacy: "Poets here [in America], literats here, are to rest on organic different bases from other countries; not a class set apart, circling only in the circle of themselves, modest and pretty, desperately scratching for rhymes, pallid with white paper, shut off, aware of the old pictures and traditions of the race, but unaware of the actual race around them—not breeding in and among each other till they all have the scrofula. Lands of ensemble, bards of ensemble!" (*PP*, 1357). Indeed, the affective force of Whitman's verse, his desire to reach people directly, led him so far as to assert the importance of understanding his poetry as essentially not "literary," by which he means not figuratively dense but also not static and self-contained: "No one will get at my verses who insist upon viewing them as a literary performance . . . or as aiming mainly toward aestheticism" (*PP*, 671). Whitman tied his rejection of the "literary" to oral performance more conspicuously in 1888, at the same time disavowing the title of "poet" as he made his goal plain: "If they call me no poet then no-poet it may be. I don't care what they call me—by one name or another name—it is all one—so that I produce the result—so that I get my word spoken and heard—maybe move men and women" (*WWWC*, 2:150).

Although certain reviewers of *Leaves* warned against reading the poems aloud, especially to a mixed audience, many have found his verse ripe for recitation.[4] Abraham Lincoln is reported to have read aloud from the book—an "unusual" occurrence apparently, as it is reported that Lincoln rarely vocalized anything in his Springfield law office but newspaper extracts; *Leaves*, though, we are told, he "read with sympathetic emphasis verse after verse," hailing them for their "virility, freshness."[5] The former slave Sojourner Truth also was struck by the oracularity of *Leaves* read aloud, exclaiming, "It was God who wrote it."[6] Henry James, despite writing some unsympathetic reviews of Whitman's work, nonetheless, according to Edith Wharton, was cured of his stammer when reciting Whitman, whose lines poured fluidly from his lips.[7] Much later, Doc Searls, senior editor of *Linux Journal*, a leading technology magazine, reported on his popular blog that Whitman's poetry came alive for him in the voice of *The Prairie Home Companion*'s Garrison Keillor, whom he heard on the radio reciting Whitman: "I was so knocked out by what I heard that I had to pull over and stop the car. Here, I knew, was Truth with a capital T."[8]

In light of this sense of the clarifying and transformative power of utterance, Whitman himself is not always sanguine about the communicative capacity of the printed page, despairing at times, as he does in "The Unexpress'd," that "in poesy's voice or print—[there is] something lacking" (*PP*, 653). Often ironically he would distance himself from the material conditions of print in his poems, referring to them as obstacles to be surmounted, impediments to his ability to communicate with "power and pathos" (*WWWC*, 6:365). The 1855 version of "A Song for Occupations" announces his distaste for the printed word, even as he must succumb to it: "I was chilled with the cold types and cylinder and wet paper between us. / I pass so poorly with paper and types. . . . I must pass with the contact of bodies and souls" (*LGV*, 1:84n). In "Now Precedent Songs, Farewell" he finds that some of the best of himself is left unremarked on the printed page: "From fibre heart of mine—from throat and tongue—(My life's hot pulsing blood, / The personal urge and form for me—not merely paper, automatic type and ink,) / Each song of mine—each utterance in the past—having its long, long history" (*LVG*, 3:728). In "Song of the Open Road" he concedes that much simply is "untransmissible by print" and confesses in a hushed tone that "I and mine do not convince by arguments, similes, rhymes, / We convince by our presence" (*PP*, 303). Indeed, Whitman favors terms such as "song," "chant," and "utterance" throughout his writings when describing his poetry.

Whitman's ambivalence was keen: He knows that he has little choice but to rely on the page to express his message to America, despite the reticence of the page, and so adopts strategies to breach the divide between script and speech. What we have in the case of *Leaves* is a text that promotes the fiction of its own liveness at every turn: we encounter as readers the presence of a physical speaker where we would expect absence. For Whitman, there was to be no difference between the book of poems and his own body and its voice: "Who touches this [*Leaves*] touches a man"; "this is no book, but more a man, within whose breast the common heart is throbbing so much. These are no printed leaves, human lips O friend for your sake freely speaking" (*PP*, 611; *NUPM*, 4:1467). At the same time, no matter how often or how closely we read the poem on the page, Whitman insists, there are always other possible performances of it, with no two performances identical.

Whitman's insertion of bodily self-images in his books speaks to his concern for performance as well as his ambivalence with respect to emergent technologies of reproduction. As we see in various versions of *Leaves*, beginning with the 1855 edition, photographic portraiture helps him to define his presence to an audience. Peggy Phelan has remarked that "all portrait photography is fundamentally performative," as it "tries to make an inner form, a (negative) shadow, expressive: a developed image which renders the corporeal, a body-real, as a real body. Uncertain about what this body looks like or how substantial it is, we perform an image of it by imitating what we think we look like. We imagine what people might see when they look at us, and then we try to perform (and conform to) those images."[9] Whitman tried to live up to certain photographic images of himself and worked to deny the validity of others: as a photographic subject, he was the consummate performer.

Ed Folsom has shown how photographic images of Whitman in his books point to his desire to construct "an illusion of presence," and yet to expose at the same time the "constructedness" of identity, as in the 1855 frontispiece engraving: "Instead of seeking an engraving that pretended to be a copy of a daguerreotype, he had Samuel Hollyer . . . engrave Gabriel Harrison's daguerreotype in a way that did not attempt to *disguise* but rather *emphasized* the artificial and constructed nature of the steel-cut image." Photographs had to be engraved in books for most of Whitman's life, and Whitman reprinted the 1855 engraving in the 1856, 1876, 1881–82, 1884, 1888, 1889, and 1892 printings of *Leaves*. Once it became possible to reproduce photos in books, Whitman continued to highlight the contingency of identity, staging "a retreat from advancing technologies" with the woodcut portrait by William J. Linton in his 1876 issue of *Leaves*. As Folsom observes: "Whitman's retrogression from steel engraving to woodcut, then, serves to intensify the sense of artifice and to indicate ways that inked words and inked portraits could mutually support each other as they advertised themselves as artists' constructions of identity."[10]

As he was doing this, Whitman also was tipping into his books portraits of himself. In 1876 he included an actual photo in *Leaves,* and in his 1882–83 *Specimen Days* and then in 1888 he used one of the new halftone processes of photo reproduction that allowed the mass printings of photographs on specially treated paper. On the one hand, Whitman handled each book himself, and so in that sense did not yield completely to the economy of mass production; on the other hand, he tried to reach as many people as he could, lamenting at the end of his career that he and his poetry had not been "absorbed" as fully as he had hoped they would be early on. Beginning with the 1876 edition of *Leaves,* Whitman is one of the first poets to include a facsimile of his signature in his books. While the reproduction of a signature served as an act of authentication of person*hood* for someone like Frederick Douglass, it served as an act of authentication of person*ality* for Whitman, since what was at stake for Whitman was not his credibility as a writer (as it was for Douglass), but rather his credibility as an affective writer. As Whitman put it tenderly in an 1888 note in *Leaves:* "I have wanted to leave something markedly *personal.* I have put my name with pen-and-ink with my own hand in the present volume. And from engraved or photo'd portraits taken from life, I have selected some, of different stages, which please me best, (or at any rate that displease me least,) and bequeath them at a venture to you, reader, with my love" (*PP,* 1365). He designates the 1888 *Complete Poems and Prose* an "authenticated and personal book," one that has been touched and signed by the poet himself. The illusion of the book as unmediated object stands as proof of Whitman's concern for cultivating an intimate relationship with his audience, for dissolving distance and coming into direct personal contact.

As I argue, Whitman is the first American poet in a condition of "secondary orality" to prize liveness *and* to theorize and authorize a public poetry based on the phenomenology of liveness. Coming of age with the phonograph and other sound-recording technologies, Whitman wanted his poems to be "felt, like the magnetism of a presence," but sometimes worried about the vulnerability of the printed word to inauthenticity and manipulation in a mass-mediated society.[11] In his performances on the page, through successive editions of *Leaves*, he foregrounds the communicative media of writing and voice, aligning and realigning his Americanism in provocative ways as he goes. I aim to show that Whitman's poetic texts—texts that exist in a state of change—intend to establish the poet's publicness through the performance of gender, political authority, and social relations for a nation in crisis.

"POWER AND PATHOS": AUDIBILIZING MASCULINE SENTIMENT

Whitman's desire to declaim in public was not unique; it was informed by a culture caught up in the enthusiasms of the spoken word. Whitman's contemporary, Mark Twain, wrote from Philadelphia that he had taken part in "what is called a free-and-easy," an event that occurs "at the saloons on Saturday night, at which a chairman is appointed, who calls on any of the assembled company for a song or recitation, and as there are plenty of singers and spouters, one may laugh himself to fits at very small expense."[12] The saloon was established by midcentury as the social center for workers and the single men of boardinghouses, and the entertainment that it offered enacted the camaraderie that built group identity. The "free-and-easy" exemplifies the performative culture in which Whitman partook. While there is no evidence that Whitman performed at a free-and-easy, Justin Kaplan reports that "At Pfaff's [a beer cellar on Broadway] during the first September of the war Walt read aloud from the manuscript of a new poem ("Beat! Beat! Drums!") that was about to be published, almost simultaneously, in the Boston *Evening Transcript,* the New York *Leader,* and *Harper's Weekly*" (263). After the war, Whitman remembered fondly the close association he had had with the young men at Pfaff's, remarking, "We all loved each other more than we supposed." Although in retrospect he claimed that "my own great pleasure at Pfaff's was to look on—to see, talk little, absorb," his performance as both auditor and orator there predicts his desire to construct and participate in a larger fraternal public sphere on the Pfaff's model (*WWWC,* 1:417).[13]

During the Civil War, Whitman performed in the intimacy of hospital wards, making a record of his recitals in his diary: "October 1st, 1863. Among other things in my visits to hospitals, I commence reading pieces"

(*NUPM,* 2:537). Ten days later he wrote to Abby Price: "Then I read to the boys—the whole ward that can walk gathers round me & listens."[14] In *Specimen Days* he recalls, "In camp and everywhere, I was in the habit of reading or giving recitations to the men. They were very fond of it, and liked declamatory poetical pieces. We would gather in a large group by ourselves, after supper, and spend the time in such readings" (*PP,* 767). In this setting, he found another way to connect with men in sympathetic terms. For the first time in the 1871 version of "As I Sat Alone by Blue Ontario's Shore" Whitman tells of his ministrations in the camps and the power of "personal presence," or what he calls "magnetism," in an entry in *Specimen Days:* "Upon this breast has many a dying soldier lean'd to breathe his last, / This arm, this hand, this voice, have nourish'd, rais'd, restored, / To life recalling many a prostrate form" (*PP,* 751; *LGV,* 1:205). In these lines we not only hear, but hear about, the salvific "voice," an appendage every bit as tangible as arm or hand, with the ability to resurrect dead soldiers.

Whitman kept up this practice of reading to small groups, though in a far different context, once the war was over. Herbert Gilchrist documented Whitman's visits to Gilchrist's mother's house in Philadelphia in 1876–77, on one occasion noting, "In the evening Sunday he recited Tennyson's *Ulysses* grandly, and at my request the *Mystic Trumpeter* [one of Whitman's poems]. He said it exercised his lungs, the animal part—but that he did mostly this, and seldom entered into the spiritual part."[15] Whitman's friend, Maurice Bucke, reported that he had heard Whitman read "Mystic Trumpeter" "in a manner which singularly combined strong emphasis with the very realization of self-composure, simplicity and ease," further noting,

His voice is firm, magnetic, and with a certain peculiar quality we heard an admiring auditor call unaffectedness. Its range is baritone, merging into bass. He reads very leisurely, makes frequent pauses or gaps, enunciates with distinctness, and uses few gestures, but those very significant. Is he eloquent and dramatic? No, not in the conventional sense, as illustrated by the best known stars of the pulpit, court-room, or the stage—for the bent of his reading, in fact the whole idea of it, is evidently to first form an enormous mental fund, as it were, within the regions of the chest, and heart, and lungs— a sort of interior battery—out of which, charged to the full with such emotional impetus only, and without ranting or any of the usual accessories or clap-trap of the actor or singer, he launches what he has to say, free of noise or strain, yet with a power that makes one almost tremble.[16]

The poetics of naturalness that Bucke posits here—one that is without affectation but powerfully affective, demonstrating a "sincerity of voice and manner"—is a sign of the times, as Whitman proposes to bring oratory in line with intimate conversation (the poet not "ranting," but "leisurely" speaking), to insist on the centrality of passionate speech as embodied in delivery to the project of persuasion and the communication of moral truths.[17]

As Whitman's fame grew, he was invited to perform his poetry at official celebrations and commemorations. He "spouted" his poem "After All Not to Create Only" (later titled "Song of the Exposition") at the American Institute Exhibition in New York City in 1871 for $100; the published text of that poem states that Whitman recited it to "2–3,000 people and 5–600 hushed workmen," and the preamble suggests another instance of Whitman's magnificent ability to puff himself:

> His manner was at first sight coldly quiet, but you soon felt a magnetism and felt stirred. His great figure was clothed in gray, with white vest, no necktie, and his beard was unshorn as ever. His voice is magnificent, and is to be mentioned with Nature's oceans and the music of forests and hills. His gestures are few, but significant. Sometimes he stands with his hands in his breast pockets; once or twice he walked a few steps to and fro.

Just as Whitman imagined his unrhymed and unmetered verse to be as "liquid, billowy waves," so his auditors in this instance sensed (or were imagined to have sensed) in his vocalism a poet without affectation or a stultifying formality (*WWWC*, 1:414). In that performance, we are told he was "perfectly self-possessed," and his overall delivery ("A few allusions of his poem were in a playful tone, but the main impression of markedly serious, animated, and earnest") met with hearty approval.

Later in life, Whitman did make a name for himself as an orator, in particular through his Lincoln lecture, which was delivered nineteen times in eleven years and concluded with a recital of his popular elegy "O Captain! My Captain!" The speaking bureau manager James Pond records in *Eccentricities of Genius* (1900) that Whitman "gave a few readings under my management during his life," with one bringing in $1,800 in receipts; of another event, at Madison Square Theatre on the anniversary of Lincoln's birthday, Pond notes, "Just as he [Whitman] was about to recite 'My Captain,' a little girl, the granddaughter of [the poet] Edmund Clarence Sted-

man, walked out upon the stage and presented him with a beautiful bou-
quet."[18] Traubel described his reading of the poem at the conclusion of his
final lecture as done "with greatest effect—power and pathos," no doubt re-
strained in gesture as was the lecture, which was billed in 1887 as itself a
"prose poem."[19] Through his performance of his elegy for the slain president,
he was in effect performing patriotism. In the 1880s, when Whitman gave
public lectures and readings, he was asked to recite the poem so often that he
exclaimed (in 1888), "Damn My Captain. . . . I'm almost sorry I ever wrote
the poem," though, he admitted, it had "certain emotional immediate reasons for being" (*WWWC*, 2:304). This frustration of the public poet in the
face of repeated requests to recite a standard is a thread that we will find running throughout the history of modern American poetry performance.

Published to immediate acclaim in the *New York Saturday Press*, "O Captain! My Captain!" was widely anthologized during Whitman's lifetime.
The poet was distressed, though, to find the punctuation of "O Captain!
My Captain!" deranged in the initial printing. On page proofs for a second
publication, Whitman crossed out the exclamation point at the end of the
first line, replacing it with a semicolon; other punctuation marks at line
ends also are emended. The editors apparently had erred by picking up earlier versions (what Whitman calls "bad perversions") of punctuation and
whole lines that had appeared in the poem prior to Whitman's 1871 revision of it. (Whitman revised the poem in 1866 and again in 1871.)[20] His revisions suggest the care with which Whitman composed paralinguistic features on the page, trying to enforce particular vocal effects in order to carry
through the urgencies of the personality behind the scripted word. In "A
Font of Type" Whitman refers to the printer's arsenal as "This latent
mine—these unlaunch'd voices—passionate powers, / Wrath, argument, or
praise, or comic leer, or prayer devout." When he states parenthetically,
"(Not nonpareil, brevier, bourgeois, long primer merely)," he means that
these points of type (listed in ascending order of size: six-, eight-, nine-, and
ten-point) are to be regarded as more than inert characters, "pallid slivers"
though they may be; they are expressive *of* character, and must be enlisted
by the page-bound poet as part of a carefully orchestrated system of vocal
notation (*PP*, 614).

As late as 1879, Whitman still was projecting into the future an image of
himself on the stump: "I intend to go up and down the land (in moderation) seeking whom I may devour, with lectures, and reading of my own
poems" (*PP*, 1301). The parenthetical qualifier "in moderation" suggests

Whitman's understanding of the nervous exhaustion that such vocal expenditure could cause. The American neurologist George M. Beard noted in
1881 that "American oratory is partly the product of American nervousness.
For success in the loftier phases of oratory, fineness of organization, a touch
of the nervous diathesis are essential"; he concluded that "this delicacy of
organization, united with Saxon force, makes America a nation of orators."[21] Beard makes plain, then, that if American oratory relies on a certain
fineness of temper, it also relies on a racial robustness. Whitman's use of
the verb "devour" suggests his vision of oratory as a consuming of the audience, as the incorporation of many into one: "Notwithstanding the diversity of minds in such a multitude, by the lightning of eloquence, they
are melted into one mass, the whole assembly actuated into one and the
same way, become as it were but one man, and have but one voice" (*NUPM*,
6:2239). The political dream of the masses congealed into a single voice, a
single nation, lies at the heart of his republican performance aesthetic.

Indeed, the conjunction of oral performance and nationhood hearkens
back to the textual foundation of the American republic itself, as do fictions
of oral performance, with utterance standing as a figure for the making of
the United States, a political entity that is imagined as "spoken into being."[22] Jay Fliegelman notes the ambivalence at the heart of understandings of orality in the eighteenth century: "In one view orality was 'an inner
voice of emotion' and an expression of subjectivity. In another it was 'pub-
lic-oriented oratorical communication,' a mode of expression in which national values and a common sensibility were to be articulated and reinforced or (if romanticized as preliterate) recovered." He also has shown that
the Declaration of Independence is a document made to be "heard as performance" rather than "read silently," coming as it does with recital directions: "The locations of the marks on the rough draft of the Declaration as
well as the locations of the 'quotation marks' on the proof copy of the Dun-
lap broadside represent not breath or punctuational pauses but precisely
what Jefferson discusses: rhythmical pauses of emphatical stress that divide
the piece into units comparable to musical bars or poetic lines." With the
text operating as score, telling the reader how to position the voice at any
given moment, he finds that, "rather than merely standing in opposition
to print, orality can also be, and in the eighteenth century often was, a
defining characteristic of print, a set of cues within a text that signal it is to
be heard by the ear (as performance) as much as it is to be read by the eye."
Such recital cues are designed to compensate for "the anonymity (the ab-

sence of a physical speaker) of written prose, and for whatever ambiguity was occasioned by that anonymity."[23]

In early editions of *Leaves* Whitman, in an effort to get his word heard, employs dots to separate words and phrases to instruct the reader in how to hear the work and how to perform it when reading it aloud.[24] These dots are not unlike those throughout the Declaration of Independence that attempt to instruct the voice in how to posture in a public reading of it. Of the Declaration of Independence and its vocal markers, Fliegelman finds that such inscriptions of the body on the page "serve as print culture's compensation for the loss of an expressive oral mode, a compensation for the inadequacy of print culture to rise to the challenge of demonstrating rather than merely representing the affective." He further notes that the oral readings of the Declaration that Jefferson's markings overtly contemplated made it "an event rather than a document. They [i.e., the readings] gave it a voice, which . . . was experienced emotionally and responded to vocally. Read out loud, the document that denounced a false community would galvanize the bond of a true one."[25] The Irish stage actor Thomas Sheridan's prosodic criticism *Lectures on the Art of Reading* (the second part, *The Art of Reading Verse*, first published in 1775), where he advocates the elocutionary use of a natural language of the heart, influenced Jefferson's notation of the Declaration of Independence as well as Whitman's idea of oratory and his scoring of the voice in the poem on the page, a scoring that similarly constructs vocalization as performing political power. (That these dot-devices, a common feature of the 1855 edition of *Leaves*, substantially recede after that initial publication—many of them replaced by a dash—I will take up later on.)

Whitman believed that it was through the thrilling directness of "live" performance—as opposed to some secondhand notation or recording of it—that a democratic society best could be substantiated. In his notebook entry of April 24, 1857, Whitman idealistically foresees himself on the national stage, "on occasion, at Washington to be, launching from public room, at the opening of the session of Congress—perhaps launching at the President, leading persons, Congressmen, or Judges of the Supreme Court," with the ambition *"always to hold the ear of the people"* (*NUPM*, 1:1554). Early in his career, when he saw himself on the lecture circuit, he imagined holding forth in the seats of political power across the country, harboring "the idea of strong *live* addresses directly to the people, adm. 10c., North and South, East and West—at Washington,—at the different State Capitols—Jef-

ferson (Mo.)—Richmond (Va.)—Albany—Washington &c—promulging
the grand ideas of American ensemble liberty, concentrativeness, individuality, spirituality &c &c" (*NUPM*, 6:2234). Whitman further observed that
"although the Lectures may be printed and sold at the end of every performance, nothing can make up for that *irresistible attraction and robust living*
treat of the vocalization of the lecture, by me,—which must defy all competition with the printed and read repetition of the Lectures" (*NUPM*,
2:407). Making a distinction between the live oration and a reproductive
representation of it, Whitman insists on the superiority of the former.

Whitman was an insatiable consumer of live performance, including
public declamation, theater, and opera. Peggy Phelan's notion that performance's only continued existence is in the spectator's memory coincides
with Whitman's, although Whitman is dismayed by the fact that a performance is undocumentable, whereas Phelan valorizes the live event that she
believes stands outside of the economy of reproduction and therefore pos-
sesses an "oppositional edge."[26] In sympathy with a Bowery reviewer's feeling of "regret that a great art should in its nature be transitory," Whitman
laments, "Well, this great thing [the live performance] has been, and all
that is now left of it is the feeble print upon my brain, the little thrill which
memory will send along my nerves, mine and my neighbors, as we live
longer the print and thrill must be feebler, and when we pass away the impress of the great artist will vanish from the world" (*PP*, 1210). Although
Philip Auslander contends that the concept of "liveness" is not applicable
to performance until the 1930s, after sound recording and motion pictures
reach maturity, believing that writing is "not . . . a form of recording in this
context," Whitman understood it as such (even if it was to his mind a pale
recording) and, moreover, set out to prove that writing itself, like speaking,
can be a performance; indeed, Phelan finds that the challenge for writing
"is to re-mark again the performative possibilities of writing itself," and advocates "the act of writing toward disappearance, rather than the act of
writing toward preservation."[27]

Whitman's fond recollection of the 1830s Bowery Theatre, his celebration of the b'hoy subculture, points to his fascination not only with participatory live performance but with the theater of masculinity as well:
"Pack'd from ceiling to pit with its audience mainly of alert, well dress'd,
full blooded young and middle-aged men, the best average of American-
born mechanics . . . the whole crowded auditorium, and what seeth'd in it,
and flush'd from its faces and eyes, to me as much a part of the show as

any—bursting forth in one of those long-kept-up tempests of hand-clapping peculiar to the Bowery—no dainty kid-glove business, but electric force and muscle from perhaps 2000 full-sinew'd men."[28] These working-class men enact their manhood as they become "a part of the show," performing a cultural identity as the actors perform a character on stage.

After hearing and seeing Emerson perform live in 1847, Whitman wrote enthusiastically in the *Brooklyn Eagle* about that event as well, sharing with Emerson a gendered vision of the forceful spoken word, which, both men believed, stood as a sign of masculine sexual and cultural potency. As David Porter says of Emerson, "To his mind the thundering affectiveness of the poet was a manly virtue to be preferred to the character of Bryant's poems, Greenough's sculpture, and Dr. Channing's preaching. Of these he said: 'They are all *feminine* or receptive and not masculine or creative.'"[29] Dismissing Dr. Channing, Emerson found himself instead "intoxicated by the ravishing pulpit eloquence of Edward Everett," noting "how joyfully & manly he spreads himself abroad."[30] In his essay "Genius" Emerson states: "I know no more striking instance of the representative character of genius than we have in the rare fact of genuine eloquence. The orator masters us by being our tongue. By simply saying what we would but cannot say, he tyrannises over our wills and affections." As Emerson imagines, the orator even has the awesome power to bridge racial, class, and religious divides, noting of Father Taylor's effect that "the whole various extremes of our little village society were for once brought together. Black & white, poet & grocer, contractor & lumberman, methodist & preacher joined with the regular congregation in rare union."[31]

Whitman also was a fan of Father Taylor and was drawn to his communitarian ideal, which, he realized, hinged on a poetics of liveness: "The mere words, (which usually play such a big part) seem'd altogether to disappear, and the live feeling advanced upon you and seiz'd you with a power before unknown" (*PP*, 1144). Also, with Emerson Whitman claimed of the Italian tenor Bettini: "None have thoroughly satisfied me, overwhelmed me, but this man. Never before did I realize what an indescribable volume of delight the recesses of the soul can bear from the sound of the honied perfection of the human voice. The *manly* voice it must be, too," for the woman's by comparison is "but as the pleasant moonlight."[32] The "perfect physique" required for oratorical performance is that of a man, too, a "representative man, with perfect power," Whitman remarks, drawing on Emerson's figure of the "representative man" who is both of his age and transcends it (*NUPM*, 6:2234). He also praises the orator Henry Ward Beecher, noting that it is "refreshing that his bold masculine discourses were *without* that prettiness and correctness of style that, say what we will, is very often accompanied by emptiness and something very akin to effeminacy."[33] In the 1856 version of his poem "Song of the Broad-Axe," this social construction of the spoken word shows again in his salute to "the brawniest breed of orators and bards," robust men endowed with the gift of prophetic speech (*LGV*, 1:181). In the poem finally titled "By Blue Ontario's Shore," the bard is more deeply sexualized, charged (in the 1856 and 1860 versions) with "Plunging his seminal muscle into its [the nation's] merits and demerits, / Making its geography, cities, beginnings, events, glories, defections, diversities, vocal in him" (*LGV*, 1:194). Each of these instances speaks to how Whitman imagines the performance of America as bound up in the performance of masculinity—a masculinity that takes the athletic and affective as indicators of nationality and patriotism.

REVISIONING AMERICA: THE PERFORMATIVE POLITICS OF PRINT

Whitman described *Leaves* as "an attempt" "from first to last, to put *a Person*, a human being (myself in the latter half of the Nineteenth Century, in America) freely, fully and truly on record" (*PP*, 671). His sense of himself as the embodiment of a particular time and place suggests that *Leaves* is in fact more than just a performance of a discrete identity; it is, as well, a performance of America in the period in which he lives. At the end of his career, he puts forth some "Last Saved Items," one of which is the statement, "Essentially my own printed records, all my volumes, are doubtless but offhand utterances f'm Personality, spontaneous"; he goes on to reiterate that his goal all along has been "to see how a Person of America, the last half of the nineteenth century, w'd appear, put quite freely and fairly in honest type" (*PP*, 1325). This last dispatch expresses his interest in the performance semiotic of speech and text, his feeling for the way that the oral and literate coexist and interact; it also attests to his belief that the truth-bearing quality of the printed word is rooted in oral "spontaneous" speech. The provisionality that we find hovering over the poems of *Leaves* directly responds to and in the end stands as a figure for the performative cultural politics in the United States in the mid-nineteenth century: "My Book and

I—what a period we have presumed to span! those thirty from 1850 to '80—and America in them!" (*PP,* 660). Whitman wanted his poetry to serve as a living document of these years, a text like the Constitution that is adaptive to changing times. In his effort "to give the personality of Walt Whitman" in *Leaves,* then, he enacts his cultural moment—or rather, a series of cultural moments of which he is a part—even as he complicates the notion of a fixed, unitary selfhood.

Some have claimed that when Whitman began to revise his work, he betrayed his early desire to produce a natural spontaneous language and with it a poetics of liveness. Mark Bauerlein marks the end of Whitman's "experimental poetics" at the moment in the 1860 edition when "upon rereading his earlier poems and finding them inadequate to his present condition, [he] revises and reorganizes them for further publication. In his attempt to improve and update his book, Whitman violates the supposedly universal, irrefutable, and immutable language of his heart, and commits the pure emotive idiom to calculated editorial amendation." But does the subsequent revising of already published poems necessarily violate their "pure emotive idiom," what Bauerlein also refers to as a "poetics of presence-feeling"?[34] Doesn't remaining true to the emotion of the moment call for improvisation, "spontaneous" response? Bauerlein seems to be troubled by the destruction of the original writing's "aura"; however, for Whitman, the sense of an original is due much less reverence, and textual emendations made easy in an age of mechanical reproduction are offset by his design of his own books, which allowed him to retain the originality of his own hand, to facilitate the presence of the aura in the mechanically reproducible work of art.

The question of authenticity is a crucial one in and for Whitman's poetry, hanging heavily over his many textual inscriptions as it does still over his purported mediatized voice—the wax cylinder recording of his poem "America" that may or may not (depending on whether the reader is in fact Whitman) preserve his presence in perpetuity. Critics have debated which edition of *Leaves* is the most "authentic," the truest to Whitman's prime intention and vision, and Whitman himself threw his weight behind the third edition (1860) at the time of its publication, going so far as to say that the two preceding editions were prototypes only, that *Leaves* had not really ever even been published before.[35] Later in life he changed his tune, allowing that he valued highly all of the iterations of his book, and so refusing to allow any one edition to override another; as he told his friend Horace Traubel, "They all count—I like all—I don't know that I like one better than any other" (*WWWC*, 1:280).

It is important to see, as Whitman himself did, that each of the editions enacts a unique self and cultural moment, that in the end what we have is (to borrow Judith Butler's phrase) "a string of performances that constitute and contest the coherence of that 'I,'" in Whitman's case an "I" famously positioned as the first word of the first poem of the first edition of *Leaves*.[36] One question that Whitman's successive editions and various performances of himself raises is whether there is indeed such a thing as an original, true, and authentic self, or whether, rather, identity is contingent, approximate, always a copy of a copy, a semblance of a self. It is my view that Whitman's provisoriness seeks to make accommodation with mass production (without violating its claim on performance) through an open-endedness that both betrays the notion of the autotelic text and flows from his understanding of the performative nature of selfhood.

If Whitman believed that each photographic portrait of him was a singular take—"one of many, only—not many in one," as he doubted the ability of the single static portrait to capture the plurality of his selves, he read "These United States" obversely, according to the motto *e pluribus unum* (out of many, one), imagining himself as a "joiner" of states into the body of a holistic nation (*WWWC*, 3:72). His public poetry registers his understanding and close monitoring of politics, in particular tensions around the contingent issues of sectionalism and slavery, as the construct of "voice" becomes a metonym for Whitman's performance of self and nation. Moreover, his view that his poems "grow of circumstances, and are evolutionary" matches his sense of the United States as in a perpetual state of becoming ("Others take finish, but the Republic is ever constructive and ever keeps vista"): his improvisations seek to shape public opinion, to assert his own relevance and the abiding soundness of his Americanism.

Particularly interesting is Whitman's work while the second edition of *Leaves* was going through the press in 1856, a year of radical political change in the United States. The election of 1856 intensified the conflict between North and South, as the major parties split along sectional lines: the Democratic party won the election by carrying a majority of slave states; the Republican party carried no slave states and all but five of the free states. This increasing sectionalism directly informs Whitman's revisions, as he struggles to heal the nation, to "fuse" it before it comes unglued. One

prime field for Whitman's retrofitting is "Song of Myself," originally untitled when it appeared in the 1855 *Leaves,* but assigned the title "Poem of
Walt Whitman, an American" in the 1856 edition. Proclaiming not only his
name but his national affiliation, Whitman seeks to defuse intensifying
sectional antagonisms spurred on by violence in Kansas over the question
of slavery, to remind his audience of their shared national identity. He
refers to himself as "Walt Whitman, an American" in the first two editions
(1855 and 1856), changing that designation later, in less nativist times, to
"Walt Whitman, . . . of mighty Manhattan" (1867–71) and "Walt Whitman,
. . . of Manhattan the son" (1881); as Reynolds reasons, the Know-Nothings
peaked in popularity in June 1855, a fact that helps explain Whitman's stri-
dent nationalism in poems of that period, although, Reynolds adds, Whitman was a nativist with a difference (that is, he did not consistently adhere
to the antiforeign and anti-Catholic bias of the Know-Nothings).[37] Whitman's Americanism is also a response to mounting sectionalism in the
country: Whitman wants to identify himself as an "American" perhaps not
primarily to repudiate the Other, but to insist on that identity in the face of
forces bent on disunion. Indeed, it is the first three editions of *Leaves*
(1855–60) that include the tag "Walt Whitman, an American," as Whitman's nationalism continues to inflect the poem past nativism's peak, in
the run-up to war.

In 1856 Whitman began the practice of dating his poems in relation to
the birth of the nation (1776, or rather "The Year I of These States"), and the
thirty-two poems within the 1856 edition of *Leaves* are meant to stand for
the thirty-two states of the Union ("There are Thirty-Two States sketched—
the population thirty millions") (*LGV,* 1:177; *PP,* 1333). (At the time, there
were only thirty-one states, but Whitman anticipates the entry of Kansas.)[38]
The poem "Resurgemus" (so-called when first published in Horace Greeley's
Tribune in 1850) became "Poem of The Dead Young Men of Europe, the 72d
and 73d Years of These States" in 1856. The title of his poem on the 1854 trial
of the returned fugitive slave Anthony Burns appears as "Poem of Appari-
tions in Boston, the 78th Year of These States" in 1856 and 1860 (changed to
"A Boston Ballad. / (1854)" in 1871). Likewise, in "Lesson Poem" (later titled
"Who Learns My Lesson Complete?"), Whitman alters the 1855 designation
that he was "born on the last day of May 1819" the next year to read that he
was "born on the last day of May in the Year 43 of America." In the same
poem, the statement, "I have become a man thirty-six years old in 1855,"
turns into "I have become a man thirty-six years old in the Year 79 of Amer-

ica" in 1856. These renditions constitute Whitman's desire to preserve the union by reminding his readers of the genius of the constitutional framework, which affiliates "These States" and yet allows for their separateness, "a simple elastic scheme" (*PP*, 472). Issuing and reissuing his own age in relation to the birth of the country signifies the extent to which he sees himself as synecdoche for the nation ("These States, what are they except myself?") (*PP*, 482). That in "Lesson Poem" Whitman's reports of his age disappear after the Civil War signifies the abatement of his need to promote himself so aggressively as "a Person of America" once the union has been secured and some sense of a collective national identity is congealing.

Another hallmark of the 1856 and 1860 *Leaves* is the extent to which the poems harp on regional diversity and sectional particularity within the expanding nation in an effort to demonstrate to states that their rights are respected under federalism. In 1856 Whitman produced a new poem called "Poem of Many in One" in which he seeks to negotiate the vexed question of the political relation of the states. Rather than foreground the poem as a romantic reverie (as he does in 1867 and 1871 with the revised title "As I Sat Alone by Blue Ontario's Shore"), Whitman in 1856 alludes to the U.S. motto *e pluribus unum* as an antidote to a mounting sectionalism, reminding his audience that America will retain its pluralism and states their due authority under the umbrella of union. In line with this view, Whitman issues in the poem a catalog of coastal states—a list dropped in all later variants of the poem—to remind Americans of the topographical variety of the country and the poet's job to take a full accounting of it: "The blue breadth over the sea off Massachusetts and Maine, or over the Virginia and Maryland sea, or over inland Champlain, Ontario, Erie, Huron, Michigan, Superior, or over the Texan, Mexican, Cuban, Floridian seas, or over the seas off California and Oregon, not tallying the breadth of the waters below, more than the breadth of above and below is tallied in him" (*LGV*, 1:194). In 1856 and 1860 only, he also includes in the poem the following citation of North American regional plenitude: "Its ample geography, the sierras, the prairies, Mississippi, Huron, Colorado, Boston, Toronto, Raleigh, Nashville, Havana, are you and me" (*LGV*, 1:207). Likewise, in "Song of Myself" geographical diversity is not articulated with the same vigor after 1860, with the line "We walk the roads of Ohio and Massachusetts and Virginia and Wisconsin and New York and New Orleans and Texas and Montreal and San Francisco and Charleston and Savannah and Mexico" cut in all future variants (*LGV*, 1:60).

Other poems that Whitman revises as part of his performative poetics are about the issue of slavery and its cultural effects, and bespeak an evolving racial politics. Most strikingly, a passage in which a slave vents his fury at his condition is excised from it, but not until the 1881–82 edition of *Leaves;* the 1855 version of the passage (largely unchanged until it is dropped) reads as follows:

> Now Lucifer was not dead. . . . or if he was I am his sorrowful terrible heir;
> I have been wronged. . . . I am oppressed. . . . I hate him that oppresses
>   me,
> I will either destroy him, or he shall release me.
>
> Damn him! how he does defile me,
> How he informs against my brother and sister and takes pay for their
>   blood,
> How he laughs when I look down the bend after the steamboat that
>   carries away my woman.
>
> Now the vast dusk bulk that is the whale's bulk. . . . it seems mine,
> Warily, sportsman! though I lie so sleepy and sluggish, my tap is death.
>
> (*LGV,* 1:116)

Why, one might wonder, would such a passage be kept so long after abolition, not simply stricken from the poetic record in 1867? The answer would seem to be that these remarks invoke a condition of oppression that has not ended with the end of slavery: while members of families are no longer being sold down the river ("I look down the bend after the steamboat that carries away my woman") circa 1871–72, the injustice with which African Americans are treated continues apace under Jim Crow. Whitman's retention of these lines suggests that it is only after black males achieve suffrage through the Fifteenth Amendment (ratified in February 1870 and so probably too late to figure in the so-called 1871–72 *Leaves,* which actually was first printed in 1870) that anything like a recuperation of their humanity is possible.[39] As Ed Folsom and Kenneth M. Price observe of the powerful deleted passage, in it Whitman is "letting his voice emerge from the black slave's mouth": "Whitman's attempt is not to speak for the black slave but to speak *as* the black slave."[40] It is no doubt the delicate situation of speaking either *for* or *as* a black slave after suffrage—of appropriating that voice, which symbolizes subjectivity and political agency—that leads Whitman no longer to want to perform his act of ventriloquy.

It is also during Reconstruction that Whitman begins to amend a number of previously published poems in order to take account of the Civil War and its aftereffects and decry the moral corruption that he sees gripping the federal government. One of the most thoroughgoing re-dressings is to his poem "Respondez!" in 1871 (its last appearance in *Leaves*), where he decries the moral turpitude into which the country has sunk, lines not present in 1856–67:

> (Stifled, O days! O lands! in every public and private corruption!
> Smother'd in thievery, impotence, shamelessness, mountain-high;
> Brazen effrontery, scheming, rolling like ocean's waves around and upon
>   you, O
> my days! my lands!
> For not even those thunderstorms, nor fiercest lightnings of the war, have
> purified the atmosphere;)
>
> (*LGV*, 1:261)

These lines significantly enlarge the tenor of the poem, which, originally addressed to the political malfeasance of 1856, is turned into one about the political and corporate mire of Reconstruction. Of course, both versions of the poem seek to expose through a series of sharp-tongued transpositions the depravity of the times—as true for 1856 as 1871, or so Whitman felt. He builds into the poem an utterance not meant to cancel out previous utterances, then, but to prove them, to reveal the self-consistency of American cultural history and his own performance of it: "As America fully and fairly construed is the legitimate result and evolutionary outcome of the past, so I would dare to claim for my verse" (*PP*, 664).

While Betsy Erkkila has documented well some of the changes that Whitman effects in these reconstructed Reconstruction-era poems, she does not comment on the poet's particular use of parentheses or on the relationship of that device to the matter of oral performance and the poet's simulation of liveness. Michael Moon refers to these marks of punctuation, abundant in the 1860 edition of *Leaves*, as "the typographical sign of utterance through 'dead lips,'" taking his cue from lines in "As I Ebb'd with the Ocean of Life": "(See! from my dead lips the ooze exuding at last! / See—the prismatic colors, glistening and rolling!)." As he finds, "This utterance emerges from between parentheses, themselves bits of 'type' which form a typographical figure or 'impression' of the 'dead lips' which enclose as they disclose what is said, encrypting the poet's voice far within the text and, indeed, launching its utterance from a posthumous position, from 'beyond' the space of ordinary human utterance which the reader presumably still occupies and from which the first two editions of *Leaves of Grass* were written."[41] As vivid as Moon's description is, it is more profitable to read parenthetical interpolation in Whitman's poetry as a sign not of a speaker with both feet in the world of the dead, but of a speaker with both feet in the world of the living, standing beside (literally, "an insertion beside") the addressee: parentheses stand as a badge of topicality, of presence, not of posthumousness, allowing Whitman to validate and authenticate truths of already uttered poems—truths that he finds to be essentially unchanged and unchanging (as the essence of all parentheses is that, without them, the sentence is complete).

In Whitman's verse after 1867 we find an increasing reliance on parentheses, as he seeks to modulate more finely his printed voice and prove the prophetic fitness of his poetry. (Of the thirty-five parenthetical statements in "Song of Myself" in the final edition of *Leaves,* only one appears as early as 1855, with two more added in 1860; the vast majority appear after the Civil War, in 1867, with twenty-three new parenthetical statements joining those three, for a total of twenty-six. In the 1871–72 edition, Whitman revises to include five more, and in the final *Leaves,* there are an additional four.) In "Song of the Banner at Daybreak," we are told for the first time in 1871 (the poem marks its first appearance in *Drum-Taps* in 1865) that "(The war is over—yet never over. . . . out of it, we are born to real life and identity;)" and, later on, that "(The war is completed, the price is paid, the title is settled beyond recall;)." The first of these statements is especially intriguing for the way that it imagines the war constructing us as citizens: our very identity as "American" is, in a continuing way, performed by the war and its legacies. Post–Civil War re-visioning of "By Blue Ontario's Shore" echoes this idea in a line added to the poem in 1867, "The war—that war so bloody and grim—the war I wish to forget—was you and me"; here, again, Whitman directly identifies us not with but *as* the war, our performance of social relations as Americans bound up in it. In 1871, the following change to the line is made: "The war, (that war so bloody and grim, the war I will henceforth forget), was you and me" (*LGV,* 1:207). The parenthetical comment is seemingly more sure here, as the speaker asserts that from this time forth he will forget the war, not just "wish" to forget it, being distant enough from it.

A final phase of Whitman's textual performance entails a shift from the unabashed nationalism so prominently on display in the Centennial (1876) edition of *Leaves* to the ethos of internationalism that inflects poems tailored for the final editions. In 1881–82 Whitman adds "Song of the Universal" to *Leaves* (the poem was first published in 1874 in the *New York Evening Post*), with the image of America "Embracing carrying welcoming all," comprehending with due respect the cultures of "other lands" (*PP*, 370). He also folds back into *Leaves* his poem "On Journeys through the States," which appears in 1860 for the first time but then is left out in 1867, interpolating two lines that transform the national procession of 1860 into an international goodwill tour "(Ay, through the world—urged by these songs, / Sailing henceforth to every land, to every sea,)" (*LGV*, 2:313). In text intended as the 1867 preface to *Leaves*, Whitman's identification of America with the world (indeed, as synecdoche for the world) resounds: "I claim that in literature, I have judged and felt everything from an American point of view which is no local standard, for America to me, includes humanity and is the universal."[42] In 1876, this attitude substantially recedes, as Whitman becomes more attuned to the charge of parochialism and arrogation, insisting that no one nation can stand for all others, that there exist legitimate multiple points of view.

In "Passage to India" Whitman hails in 1871 "The earth to be spann'd, connected by network, / The races, neighbors, to marry and be given in marriage, / The oceans to be cross'd, the distant brought near, / The lands to be welded together" (*LGV*, 3:565). Here the poet appears as a different sort of fuser—not of America, as earlier, but rather of all democratic nations. "Song of the Exposition," a poem *"Originally recited for Opening the 40th Annual Exhibition* American Institute, New York, *noon, September 7th, 1871,"* first included in *Leaves* (as an annex) in 1872, and issued again at the international Centennial exposition held in Philadelphia in 1876, likewise turns from a poem trumpeting the plenitude of America only into a multicultural celebration of the wealth of nations (*LGV*, 3:612). In a proposed 1876 preface to a foreign edition of his work, he announces that his main poetic purpose is "to suggest and help a deeper, stronger, (not now political, or business, or intellectual, but) heroic, artistic, and especially emotional, intertwining and affiliation of the Old and New Worlds": The "glory" of "These United States" is now measured "not in their geographical or republican greatness" but rather "in a vaster, saner, more splendid COMRADESHIP, typifying the People everywhere, uniting closer and closer not only The American States, but all Nations, and all Humanity. (That, O Poets! Is not *that* a theme, a Union, worth chanting, striving for? Why not fix our verses henceforth to the gauge of the round globe? the whole race?" Penning "international poems," Whitman reveals that heretofore patriotism has been defined too narrowly ("we have adhered too long to petty limits"), as he continues to take stock of the world and America's place in it, counterposing what he does ("sounded" poems) to what professional diplomats do, which is "to bind" governments together "on paper" (*NUPM,* 4:1527, 1528).

Whitman also recomposes his poem "Salut au Monde!" for the final editions of *Leaves,* removing almost all of the references to America that it had contained previously. After 1871, the author takes out lines about East Tennessee and Kentucky and the following that invoke other U.S. ethnographies:

> I hear the Virginia plantation chorus of negroes, of a harvest night, in the
>   glare of pine knots,
> I hear the strong baritone of the 'longshore-men of Manahatta—I hear the
> stevedores unlading the cargoes, and singing,
> I hear the screams of the water-fowl of solitary northwest lakes
>
> (*LGV,* 1:163)[43]

Remaining in the poem are mentions of British, Spanish, French, Italian, Australian, Egyptian, and Mexican soundscapes, however. Whitman also deletes after 1871 lines that allude to the Rocky Mountains; the Vermont hills; the "vast deserts of Western America," the "inland fresh-tasted seas of North America," Boston, Philadelphia, Baltimore, Charleston, New Orleans, Galveston, San Francisco, the Mississippi, the Columbia, the St. Lawrence, and Niagara Falls. He retains, though, all references to sites outside of North America, from the Nile to the Himalayas, as far as to the "huge dreadful Arctic and Antarctic icebergs." When he reaches section 5, he excises a line about his nation's system of railroads, "I see them welding state to state, county to county, city to city, through North America," but leaves in two other lines that originally (in 1856) followed: "I see them [railroads] in Great Britain, I see them in Europe, / I see them in Asia and in Africa." It is not sectional conflict that precipitates the changes this time, but a fervent desire to promote international understanding and equality among the races. At the close of the poem, the following lines appear in 1871:

Toward you all, in America's name,

I raise high the perpendicular hand, I make the signal,

To remain after me in sight forever,

For all the haunts and homes of men.

The democratic sign that the poet makes is similar to the one that he bran-
dishes in 1855 in "Song of Myself," but in the period 1871–81 he no longer
flashes it to fellow Americans, but to a cosmopolitan audience, as mediator,
"in America's name."

Whitman also believed, though, that Americans themselves still stood
in need of mediation. His poem "Mediums," given that title in 1867 but
first included in *Leaves* in 1860, speaks directly to his sense of the entangle-
ment of vocalism, identity, and agency, as he forecasts communicators rising up across the "States," remarking that they "shall train themselves to go
in public to become orators and oratresses, / Strong and sweet shall their
tongues be," that they "shall illustrate Democracy and the kosmos" (*LGV*,
2:312). Both men and women, their "pose" will be "brawny and supple";
they will be populists, rooted in the physical world ("They shall fully enjoy
materialism and the sight of products, the sight of the beef, lumber, bread-
stuffs, of Chicago the great city") and superior physical specimens in their
own right ("their drink water, their blood clean and clear"). The intermediary stance that these poets assume—their interpretative function—is not
unlike Whitman's own, as demonstrated through his oratorical enactment
of a range of historically marginalized identities in *Leaves*. Indeed, what
one reviewer perceived as the "mediatorial" aspect of the first edition no
doubt rests largely on the ventriloquizing effects of "Song of Myself,"
where Whitman announces that he will be speaking for those unable to
speak for themselves. Whitman is famous for saying "(I am large, I contain
multitudes)" (the parentheses are added in 1871), and he imagines his ex-
propriation of subaltern voices as an act of spiritual channeling ("Through
me many long dumb voices"; "Through me forbidden voices"). Indeed, he
assumes personalities and voices with astonishing sympathetic ease—"My
voice is the wife's voice"; 'I am the man, I suffer'd, I was there"; "I am the
hounded slave"—and performs his own multiple selfhood in the process of
doing so. He speaks on behalf of the marginalized and disenfranchised, enacting thereby their full citizenship: "My voice goes after what my eyes
cannot reach / With the twirl of my tongue I encompass worlds and volumes of worlds."

In the 1860–71 versions of the first section of what becomes in 1881 "Vo-calism," Whitman gives perhaps his fullest performance of the politics of the spoken word, maintaining that "no word spoken, but is beautiful, in its place" (*LGV*, 2:309). "Vocalism" appeared as two poems in earlier editions of *Leaves*, the first part for the first time in the section of the 1860 edition entitled "Chants Democratic" (poem 12):

To oratists—to male or female,
Vocalism, breath, measure, concentration, determination, and the divine
    power to use words.

Are you eligible?
Are you full-lung'd and limber-lipp'd from long trial? from vigorous
    practice? from physique?
Do you move in these broad lands as broad as they?
Remembering inland America, the high plateaus, stretching long?
Remembering Kanada—Remembering what edges the vast round edge of
    the Mexican Sea?
Come duly to the divine power to use words?

In this rendition Whitman characteristically reveals his high regard for those with the ability to perform vocally, and insists that American "oratists" must spread themselves throughout the nation to prove their publicity. When he asks them, "Are you eligible?" there lurks behind the question the idea of political eligibility, the idea that the orator must prove himself through vigorous citizenship. In the poem's draft form, Whitman is even more specific about the political effect of oratorical speech:

O action and
O joy! To feel the solid and turbulent masses of The States under your
    control,

Invisible within, memory, passions, judgment, all busy,
Visible without, every muscle, every nerve excited—Not a limb, not a
    feature but speaks,

Knowing in yourself You are moulding The States—the Many In One—
    people, lands, proud, friendly, equal, sensual, spiritual.[44]

It is of course in 1860 that Whitman most wants to consolidate the nation, to bring the states into "friendly, equal" relationship in an effort to avert war.

In all but the 1881 version of "Vocalism," Whitman goes on to utter the following apocalyptic lines that further delineate his fiction of performance:

> O now I see orators fit for inland America,
> And I see it is as slow to become an orator as to become a man,
> And I see that power is folded in a great vocalism.
>
> Of a great vocalism, when you hear it, the merciless light shall pour, and
>   the storm
> rage around,
> Every flash shall be a revelation, an insult,
> The glaring flame turned on depths, on heights, on suns, on stars,
> On the interior and exterior of man or woman,
> On the laws of Nature—on passive materials,
> On what you called death—and what to you therefore was death,
> As far as there can be death.

In 1881 he strikes these lines out, since they would conflict with the earlier expression (what becomes section 2) that "All waits for the right voices" and the earlier queries, "Where is the practis'd and perfect organ? where is the develop'd soul?" (*LGV*, 2:309). What he sees so clearly in the earlier versions of the poem, he no longer sees so clearly in 1881, where the "perfect physiological human voice" is held in abeyance: "Surely whoever speaks to me in the right voice, him or her I shall follow, / As the water follows the moon, silently, with fluid steps, anywhere around the globe." No doubt, he was not yet willing to rule himself out as that "right voice," still earnest in his bid to be relevant. That a poem about vocalism should betray such a high number of revisions suggests just how deeply involved the two are for Whitman, his momentariness a function of the variable twirlings of his tongue.

AUTHENTICITY, REPRODUCIBILITY, AND THE RECORDED WORD

The "electricity" and "magnetism" that Whitman ascribes to the human voice, as well as his own "magnetizing effect," take on a scientific literalness when we start to consider the impact of magnetic recording—that is, electric and electronic signaling—on the spoken word in the United States in the nineteenth century.[45] The poet's fascination with the phonograph, with the power to record and replay the human voice that it represents, led him (perhaps) to speak into that device in either 1889 or 1890, although in the early part of 1889 he still could only imagine such a system, as is revealed in this reported dialogue between Whitman and his friend and recorder Horace Traubel: Whitman states, "My thinking apparatus seems to be O.K.: it's the rest of me that gets tired. If I could talk into a machine—if I didn't have to use a pen—my troubles would be over." "No doubt we will speak into machines some day and out of them too." W. asked: "Do you mean the telephone? We have that already." I said: "No: I mean a machine with a voice." W. looked at me quizzically: "Well—who knows: having gone as far as we have with these wonders why shouldn't other wonders follow?" (*WWWC*, 4:81).

It is telling that the poem that we have been willed on wax cylinder is "America" (or part of it), as the nation somehow stands for the (recorded) voice, and vice versa. Through the grain we hear only the first four lines of the poem, but in its published form it reaches to six:

Centre of equal daughters, equal sons,
All, all alike endear'd, grown, ungrown, young or old,
Strong, ample, fair, enduring, capable, rich,
Perennial with the Earth, with Freedom, Law and Love,
A grand, sane, towering, seated Mother,
Chair'd in the adamant of Time.

(*PP*, 616)[46]

In his recorded hailing of the United States, a mediatized vocalism comes to stand for the political culture of democracy itself, the reciter's voice metonymically "enduring," "Perennial," perpetual, like the country itself. (Indeed, such a display of nationalism is perfectly in tune with Edison's agent Gouraud's display of American flags and Civil War scenes at demonstrations of the phonograph in London in the late 1880s.) The image of the democratic mother, who loves all her children equally, stands opposed to a "corporate, centralized, male-identified model of power," as Erkkila sees it, and is meant "to counteract the centralized administration of the state and the aggressively capitalist and male-powered ethos of the new market economy."[47] Of course, the invention of the phonograph ushers in a new phase in the commodification of sound recording, and thus the image of the democratic mother seated outside the "economy of repetition" would seem to be undercut by the reproducible grain of the performer's voice on record.[48] With the metaphorical mother left out of the recorded reading (mention of her is deferred until the penultimate line), we might say that the referent is the audible voice itself, preserved "in the adamant of Time," and thus very much enclosed within the cultural economy as reproducible artifact.

Whitman's desire to transcend physical boundaries, to connect with ordinary men and woman in a genuine way, and to connect ordinary men and women in and through time with each other (powerfully enacted in a poem like "Crossing Brooklyn Ferry"), helps to explain his attraction to the new technology of voice recording. As John Picker explains, "Unlike the telegraph and the telephone, the phonograph was explicitly designed for archival purposes and also ultimately to function without a specially trained and designated operator: Of the three forms, that is, only the phonograph offered a form of preservation through direct, immediate interaction with its audience." What Picker refers to as its "interactive potential" would have impressed Whitman, as would its capacity both to capture and to transcend the lineaments of the body: "Even as the phonograph rendered a speaker's voice immortal and disembodied his or her speech, it seemed to preserve in the distinct tones, accents, and breath of that voice a fragile mortality, the very corporeality that words on a page or sentiments in a poem lacked."[49] As Jacques Attali also has pointed out, the earliest forms of sound recording, such as Edison's cylinder, "were intended to serve as secondary adjuncts to live performance by preserving it. As recording technology brought the live into being, it also respected and reinforced the primacy of existing modes of performance."[50] An extension of the live, the recorded voice pointed back to a body in spontaneous performance, not replacing, but augmenting, it.

The contemporary Language poet Bob Perelman, under the letter "G" in his poem "An Alphabet of Literary History," riffs on Whitman's alleged recorded performance, poet-to-come Allen Ginsberg's response to it, and matters central to reproduction and repetition in a mechanized America. That section begins:

> For the record: Speech is writinG,
> writinG speech. That is the lesson

the body waits to hear with
every word it reads. The voice

which might still be Whitman's emerges
from the wash of static on

the old wax cylinder and names
America the center of equal daughters,

Equal sons, perennial with the earth,
With Freedom, Law and Love, and

Ginsberg noted the Brooklyn accent of
Love. But is it still really

Walt?[51]

In chiasmic equation of speech and writing at the outset, Perelman abolishes
the old Aristotelian dichotomy, on the side of Derrida, who insists that one
is not subordinate to the other, that speech does not allow a presence that
writing denies. Here Whitman (if it is him) is quite literally "on record" (note
Perelman's opening pun "For the record"), and Perelman, after enacting
some of Whitman's catalogs and pointing up that "they hardly fit into the
landscape / anymore"—a postwar, "landfill-haunted" civilization that "leads
to Newark"—jokingly takes up what is left out of the recorded reading:

But he skipped the rest of

"America": "A grand, sane, towering, seated
Mother, / Chair'd in the adamant of
Time." Perhaps there wasn't enough wax.

What's new? Very few mothers get

chairs.

"But is it still really / Walt?"—Ginsberg may have thought so, but Perelman's pointed question, raising as it does the matter of the authenticity of

the thirty-six-second recording, has not kept it from being used precisely to promote an ideal of authenticity in American popular culture. A 2009 Levi's ad campaign titled "Go Forth" features two television spots. In one, a recording of the actor Will Geer reading Whitman's poem "Pioneers! O Pioneers!" on a Folkways album released in 1957 provides the soundtrack; it focuses on the adventurous youth culture of America. The other spot trades on the putative Whitman recording in an effort to remind consumers of the company's roots: It is set to a series black-and-white images of San Francisco and post-Katrina New Orleans showing Americans of all types in bold action against a backdrop of fireworks, with the message one of self-reliance, resilience, and hope. (The ad campaign kicked off on the Fourth of July.) The vice president of brand marketing for Levi's has said that the campaign is about "reconnecting with our authentic voice—our vision for the company and for the pioneer spirit of America."[52] It also asks visitors to the website to rewrite parts of the Declaration of Independence and submit photos, video, and stories of "today's America," thereby affirming Whitman's own sense of the need to improvise to keep up with the times: "I am the new American pioneer, looking forward, never back. No longer content to wait for better times . . . I will work for better times. 'Cause no one built this country in suits."

Whitman's voice has been crucial behind the screen as well, a form of commodity in the cultural economy that has served the purpose of authentication. For Martin Scorsese's film *Gangs of New York* (2002), Daniel Day-Lewis modeled his Bowery boy speech after the alleged extant Whitman recording, in his pursuit of authenticity in his tonal re-creation of nineteenth-century New York. Dialect coach Tim Monich notes that on the wax recording, "the poet pronounces 'world' as 'woild,' and the 'a' of 'an' nasal and flat, like 'ayan'"; as he goes on to explain, "The 1840s and 1860s are too early for recordings, so I went back to period sources, humorous writings, poems, ballads, and newspaper clippings to get an idea of what New Yorkers sounded like in those days. I also listened to early recordings of people who were born and raised in the period, for instance a recording of Walt Whitman." To prepare for the part of Bill "the Butcher" Cutting, Day-Lewis not only listened to the tape but immersed himself in the poetry of Whitman and would recite "Crossing Brooklyn Ferry" to get his own speech rhythms in place.[53]

In 1891, the poet himself weighed in on the place of *Leaves* in the cultural economy, somewhat surprisingly championing copyright protection. Whitman went so far as to sign a petition for the copyright law of 1891, an act that bespeaks his desire to exert control over his body of writing, to claim ownership of it; he also realized that such a law would spur the growth of American letters generally. When the United States finally passed an international copyright law, Whitman remarked on the seeming paradox of his support for it:

> We have our international copyright at last—the bill is signed today [Thursday March 5, 1891]. The United States, which should have been the first to pass the thing, is the last. Now all civilized nations have it. It is a question of honesty—of morals—of a literature, in fact. I know it will be said by some—Here, now, how is it that you, Walt Whitman, author of "Leaves of Grass," are in favor of such a thing? Ought the world not to own the world in common? Well, when others do, we will, too. This copyright bill is the doing as we would be done by. (*WWWC*, 8:54–55)

Add to this Whitman's notion of a "Definitive edition" of *Leaves*, a notion that would look to violate the very idea of text-as-process, and one begins to wonder just what happened to Whitman in his old age.

In the so-called "death-bed edition" of *Leaves*, the author carefully recites the following publication history in his assertion of authorial rights:

> 1st ed'n 1855, Brooklyn (N.Y., South District)—renew'd (1883) 14 yrs.
> 2d ed'n 1856, Brooklyn—renew'd (1884) 14 yrs.
> 3rd ed'n 1860, Boston, Thayer & Eldridge Pub'rs.
> 4th ed'n 1867, N.Y., So. Dist.: Pub'd New York.
> 5th ed'n 1871, Washington, D.C.
> 6th ed'n 1876—Centennial issue—inc'd'g Two Rivulets: two vols.
> 7th ed'n 1881, Boston, Mass.: Osgood Pub.: [This includes in the present vol. pages 1 to 382.]
> 8th ed'n 1882, Philadelphia: McKay Pub'r.
> Sands at Seventy: Annex, 1888—November Boughs—Philadelphia.
>
> A Backward Glance, &c.: November Boughs, 1888—Philadelphia.
> Good-Bye my Fancy: 2d Annex, 1891—Philadelphia.
>   Library of Congress . . . . . Copyright Office, Washington

No. 18382 W.

To wit: Be it remembered . . . That on the 19th day of May, *anno Domini*, 1891, Walt Whitman, of Camden, N.J., has deposited in this office the title of a Book, the title or description of which is in the following words, to wit:

GOOD-BYE MY FANCY,

2d *Annex to Leaves of Grass.*

Philadelphia . . . David McKay . . . 1891.

The right whereof he claims as author, in conformity with the laws of the United States respecting copyrights.

A. R. SPOFFORD,

Librarian of Congress.

[Which last-named copyright (holding good to 1919—then, on application, continued 14 years further) expires May 19, 1933.]

As there are now several editions of L. of G., different texts and dates, I wish to say that I prefer and recommend this present one, complete, for future printing, if there should be any; a copy and fac-simile, indeed, of the text of these 438 pages.

In the prefatory poem to this final edition, Whitman uses the present participle "owning" in a way that lights up the copyright information detailed on the next page:

Come, said my Soul,
Such verses for my Body let us write, (for we are one,)
That should I after death invisibly return,
Or, long, long hence, in other spheres,
There to some group of mates the chants resuming,
(Tallying Earth's soil, trees, winds, tumultuous waves,)
Ever with pleas'd smile I may keep on,
Ever and ever yet the verses owning—as, first, I here and now,
Signing for Soul and Body, set to them my name,

(*PP,* 147)[54]

After the comma in 1876, 1882, and 1888, Whitman signs his name in black ink; in the 1891–92 edition, we get his autograph in facsimile. The mention of "fac-simile" (an exact copy or reproduction) in the copyright notice and the appearance of a facsimile signature at the end of the poem throw into relief the question of representation versus reproduction. As Peggy Phelan observes, performance is nonreproductive (that is, it cannot be saved or repeated), and throughout his career, as we have seen, Whitman essentially engaged a performative writing, not only through his use of performative (as opposed to constative) utterances, but through his radical revisioning of his poetry; he was "writing toward disappearance," and not writing toward preservation, by keeping his texts in a state of change. At the end of his life, though, Whitman would seem to be less opposed to reproduction, as he seeks to congeal the text once and for all in light of his own mortality, his bodily disappearance. Indeed, the lines, "I was chilled with the cold types and cylinder and wet paper between us. / I pass so poorly with paper and types. . . . I must pass with the contact of bodies and souls," notably disappear from the untitled second poem of the 1855 *Leaves* (later titled "A Song for Occupations" in the 1891–92 edition).

However, there is an alternate way to view this statement of ownership and his recitation (I use the term pointedly) of the publishing history of *Leaves* that squares with his long adherence to ideals of performativity. As Martin Buinicki argues, "Unlike those earlier copyright pages that highlight Whitman's identity as author of the text, here it is as though the citation of previous editions itself conveys Whitman's identity and does the work of authentication and possession once accomplished through his name alone. . . . Each edition, Whitman stresses, is a 'different text,' and his recommendation of this last edition, following as it does an exhaustive list of previous editions, highlights the unique identity of those preceding texts, each a separate embodiment of Walt Whitman."[55] In effect, Whitman is reciting (or re-siting) these editions in such a way as to confirm the authenticity of his own identity—an identity that is not fixed, but in flux, responsive to changing cultural conditions. In "Walt Whitman's Last," he vouches that "every page of my poetic or attempt at poetic utterance . . . smacks of the living physical identity, date, environment, individuality, probably beyond anything known," and some of these contextual items certainly are brought out in his copyright recitation of past editions of *Leaves* (*PP*, 1369).

Even so, the matter of reproduction and its aim of preservation does not fade away, as Whitman looks to a literary archive to keep him in memory. In his 1872 poem "Souvenirs of Democracy" (in *As a Strong Bird on Pinions Free*), which becomes, in 1881, "My Legacy," Whitman again takes advantage of the process of stereotyping by assigning a facsimile of his signature beneath the poem. The following lines appear in 1872, closing out the first stanza of the poem, in a description of the act of the "business man" bequeathing his remains: "Parceling out with care—And then, to prevent all cavil, / His name to his testament formally signs" (*LGV,* 3:633). In 1872 the poem ends with the poet arranging his affairs as well:

> Only these Souvenirs of Democracy—In them—in all my songs—behind
>   me leaving,
> To You, whoever you are, (bathing, leavening this leaf especially with my
>   breath—pressing on it a moment with my own hands;
> —Here! feel how the pulse beats in my wrists!—how my heart's-blood is
>   swelling, contracting!)
> I will You, in all, Myself, with promise to never desert you,
> To which I sign my name, / Walt Whitman [facsimile signature]

In 1881, though, these lines disappear, replaced by the following meditation: "Yet certain remembrances of the war for you, and after you, / And little souvenirs of camps and soldiers, with my love, / I bind together and bequeath in this bundle of songs" (*LGV,* 3:634). Whitman's reproduction of his signature on the page, a personal token, or souvenir, of himself, is substituted for by the war, which is meant to stand in metonymic relation to himself and his entire poetic project. As Phelan argues, performative writing is metonymic (as opposed to metaphoric) insofar as it "works to secure a horizontal axis of contiguity and displacement," and Whitman's commitment to that figure of speech in the final version of the poem suggests his fundamental ambivalence in the face of absence.[56]

This displacement may have had something to do with the poet's growing celebrity, too, with his discovery that often souvenirs of himself (as in the form of a signature) had the "heart's-blood" drained from them. Whitman increasingly worried about such tokens, bristling at the commodification of presence, as did other famous writers of his day. He spoke often to his friend Horace Traubel about the stream of autograph-seekers hounding him for signs of himself, often with consternation:

> Mrs. Keller said to him [Walt], "There is no mail today, not even an application for an autograph," he responding, "That is a rare report." (He said to me once, "It is some comfort not to get *any* mail—for, not to get *any* means *no autographers,* and it is worth almost any sacrifice to get rid of *them.*") (*WWWC,* 9:501–2)

Whitman was uncomfortable with the idea of someone collecting his autograph without having any connection to him or his work, that is, and with the idea of the reification of the self in the autograph generally. Again to Traubel, he reports,

> "I knew a man in Washington—an expert there—who said once, when he leaned over my shoulder (I was working)—that my signature was one of the hardest he knew to imitate. I asked, is it so? And he assured me—yes, its very simplicity protects it. And he himself had a wonderful pen—could imitate pretty near any signature at will, for instance. Had a distinct genius of the sort. And I have often thought of it since." I told W. every bank teller would give him the same assurance. "That makes it more curious still. It must be as the expert said—its very simplicity—just as simplicity, truth, can never be imitated." (*WWWC*, 8:276)

The sense of the impossibility of anyone's imitating his autograph pleases Whitman so much because he feels that it proves both his authenticity and basic morality. That a reproduction (or counterfeit) of it cannot be made allows Whitman to believe in the idea that his own *Leaves*, superintended by himself, express truth simply, sent into the world in what he calls "honest type," a mechanical equivalent of his own cursivity. His alleged irreproducibility underwrites his uniqueness and maintains his esoteric nature, his "aura," a "quality" Whitman called "most real, but wholly indefinable" (*WWWC*, 5:119).

Whitman clearly saw how presence—and signs of presence—had entered the cultural economy and what new demands were being placed on artists in light of that fact. Traubel discloses the following exchange regarding Whitman's signature in a copy of *Leaves* that his publisher David McKay was attempting to sell to a person who doubted it was real:

> McKay yesterday had a customer for the big book. He looked at the signature. "It's not genuine." McKay assured him it was, but the man was not convinced. "Get him to sign his name on some other page, then I'll buy the book." he said. Would W. do it? I asked him this yesterday. He laughed a little: "I don't know whether I want to or not: I want to sell the book: that's a temptation: I'd do anything honest to sell books." He finally said: "Bring the book over." I did so today. He had a good laugh over it. "I wonder

whether I should get a notary to affirm the second signature?" Then: "Tell
Dave we'll do this this time but can't consent to make a practice of it: we are
anxious to sell the books, God knows, but only to those who will accept the
authenticity of the signature as it stands: this fellow must be one of the
skeptical sort: a confirmed semi-petrified business man: one of the doubters
of everybody: one who throws cold water on people—is always expecting to
be swindled, always being ready himself to swindle. It's a hell of a habit to
get into." (*WWWC*, 4:396)

Whitman's ideal reader (and purchaser) is someone who takes on faith the
authenticity of his work and of his presence within the work, someone who
puts trust in character and whose ethical sense can be counted on.

Questions of authenticity and reproducibility also interestingly bear on
the recording apparatus of Traubel himself and his "recital" of Whitman's
conversations in his final years, a part of the continuing story of Whitman's
performativity and of our performative reenactment of Whitman and his
texts. In Traubel's address to the reader in the preface to the first installment
(1906) of the multivolume *With Walt Whitman in Camden*, he informs,

> My story is left as it was originally written. I have made no attempt to im-
> prove it. I have taken nothing off and put nothing on. . . . Here is the record
> as it virginally came from my hands in the quick of the struggle it describes.
> . . . The formal grace of the recital might have been improved. I have pre-
> ferred to respect its integrity. To let it remain untouched by a censorship. To
> let it continue, for good or bad, in its then native atmosphere. I do not want
> to reshape those years. I want them left as they were. I keep them forever
> contemporary. I trust in the spontaneity of their first inspirations. (vii)

If Traubel leaves matters unchanged in his "recital" of Whitman's spoken
word, Whitman worked otherwise; indeed, Whitman's modus operandi is
precisely the reverse of Traubel's, as he finds that the only way to keep his
poems "forever contemporary" is to revise them through time. Traubel's
recorded conversations are described as a "virtual transcript" of his daily
conversations with Walt ("It talks his words"), his recording a valuable
archive even if it is only "virtual," that is, not the exact rendering of speech
that a phonograph would provide (*WWWC*, 1:viii). However, as Traubel's
contemporary Harrison Morris attests, like a phonograph, "Horace has
caught the very accent of Walt's voice. . . . I can detect the phrase and mod-

ulation of Walt's slow hesitating and sonorous speech on every page of Traubel's . . . imperishable files."[57]

The notion of the "virtual" leads us to the ways in which these matters resound around and through Whitman in a digital age. With hypertext, we find ourselves in a condition of infinite reproducibility—one that poses a challenge to current copyright laws. As Kenneth M. Price has remarked, "The complicated textual history of Whitman's poetry makes it ideally suited to hypertext. By 'hypertext' we mean an electronic document characterized by links that allow readers to experience the text in various sequences as they choose to follow different avenues of information via connecting points." He particularly points to "the multiplicity of Whitman materials and his habit of process writing" as conditions that make him suitable for presentation online. The poem as event, with the work not identical to any one graphical or performative realization of it, obtains here. By being able to click through various versions of a single poem—or looking at the changing shape of *Leaves* as a sequence of poems over its six editions—we are involved as readers "in a less univocal process": "Hypertext encourages lively, even aggressive reading because it calls for active participation."[58] In a wired state, we are no longer passive recipients of the word; rather, we can determine what we will read or hear, and when, operating in our own way improvisationally.

Not only is Whitman's performative quality captured best by hypertext; so is his publicity most fully realized, as Whitman is able to reach out to masses of readers, on an international basis, through electronic media. As Price attests: "The Walt Whitman Hypertext Archive has the great advantage of being able to distribute, in digital form, large amounts of material at low cost and thus to make rare Whitman items—once restricted to those able to undertake expensive travel available—to a broad audience." Indeed, Whitman sensed early on the benefit of electrotype and new reproduction technologies to his project of communicating to the American people en masse. His unpublished prose tract "The Eighteenth Presidency!" (1856), which he wrote toward the close of Buchanan's term in office and before the election of Lincoln and which is concerned with greed and the treatment of American workers, encouraged those reading it to "Circulate and reprint this Voice of mine for the working-men's sake. I hereby permit and invite any rich person, anywhere, to stereotype it, or re-produce it in any form, to deluge the cities of The States with it, North, South, East, and West" (*PP*, 1347). Notwithstanding his subsequent embrace of copyright, he recognizes here that it is only through mass reproduction of the text, and the disregard of copyright, that it can be properly publicized, and it is ironic that the tract is not published in Whitman's lifetime. The material text of *Leaves* was read as a sign of his publicity as well, with a reviewer of the 1860 edition noting that it "is electrotyped for the sake of cheapness, the publishers evidently designing to sell it by millions, if possible."[59]

In "Note at End of Complete Poems and Prose," Whitman suggests that it has in fact not been his own "voice" that has generated *Leaves*, but that it stands rather as "an autochthonic record and expression, freely render'd, of and out of these 30 to 35 years [1855–1888]—of the soul and evolution of America" (*PP*, 1364). Again detracting from his own authorial agency, in the 1872 preface to *Leaves*, he explains that his book "already publish'd, is, in its intentions, the song of a great composite *democratic individual*, male or female. And following on and amplifying the same purpose, I suppose I have in my mind to run through the chants of this volume, (if ever completed,) the thread-voice, more or less audible, of an aggregated, inseparable, unprecedented, vast, composite, electric *democratic nationality*" (*PP*, 1028–29). Whitman has Emerson in his mind, too, and feels free to revise him, noting that "Emerson says *manners* form the representative apex and final charm and captivation of humanity: but he might as well have changed the typicality to voice" (*PP*, 1293). Whitman knew well the representative power of the voice, its symbolic motive: For him, its exercise, "more or less audible," performed the republic itself, from "*the still small voice* vibrating" on "Election Day, November, 1884" to the "barbaric yawp" sounding over the rooftops (*PP*, 620).

For so long we have not positioned Whitman as the father of a potent line of spoken word poetry, more typically construing him as the ("pigheaded") father of free verse (as Ezra Pound did) rather than as a poet whose modalities shape those of later (more patently "live") performance poets as diverse as Vachel Lindsay, Langston Hughes, Allen Ginsberg, Anne Waldman, Sonia Sanchez, and twenty-first-century slammers. In fact, though, in the multiple performances of *Leaves* and in his own fashioning of a critical concept of "liveness," Whitman plants himself as forebear of these poets—poets performing for "the common people" (as he insists his audience is in his late poem "L. of G.") (*PP*, 1299) and dedicated to building community on a grand scale both on and off the page.

CHAPTER 2

The Ordeal of Vachel Lindsay, or
The Cultural Politics of the Spoken Word

Who else has, or ever has had, such a voice
As his is, Vachel Lindsay's?

   —AMY LOWELL, FROM *A CRITICAL FABLE*

I would give almost anything to escape forever the reciting and chanting Vachel. . . .
My whole heart is set on escaping my old self (completely as I may, to be human
and frail as we all are).

   —VACHEL LINDSAY, TO HARRIET MONROE

ALTHOUGH VACHEL LINDSAY is not well known today, for a time during
the first half of the twentieth century he was one of the most popular poets in the United States. Harriet Monroe, who printed Lindsay's first poem
in 1913 in her influential magazine *Poetry*, noted of him in 1924: "the obscure aspirant of ten years ago has become probably the best and farthest
known of all our American poets of this vocal decade."[1] Lindsay's reputation came as a result of his success as a poet-performer; as he calculated in
1924, he had recited his poetry to over one million Americans over the
course of twelve years; by the time of his death in 1931 that figure roughly
would be tripled. In light of his spectacular fade-out—his erasure from cultural memory—Cary Nelson has sought to remind us of Lindsay's "doomed
fantasy of a truly public and participatory democratic poetry."[2] If this fantasy was doomed (for Lindsay, in his lifetime), it was as a result of an emergent mass culture whose terms of worth threatened the sanctity of "Poetry," as Lindsay and his peers understood it, and with which it would have
to compete for an increasingly distracted and work-weary public. Indeed,
Lindsay expressed a deep ambivalence about commercial popular entertainment, carefully distinguishing his art as "high," even as he traded on

55

"low" amusements like blackface minstrelsy and their cultural capital in order to get across his civic message, to help vitalize the public sphere. In his
effort to reenfranchise Americans who felt that poetry no longer spoke to
them, he drew on performance modalities that oddly undercut the unity he
sought by virtue of their racial and gender politics. Lindsay's struggle with
the problem and promise of public poetry—and his often hostile con-
frontations with new mass communication and sound-recording technologies—is informed by the modernist moment of which he is a part and the
changing role of art and the artist in it.

Lindsay's attitude toward Whitman and his legacy sheds light on his
sense of the place of performance poetry in America and the cultural construction of it. Recognizing Whitman as the poet who, before him, had
most earnestly sought public acclaim and the mantle of the "people's
poet," Lindsay calls attention to his own history of live performance and
draws a distinction between Whitman and himself on that very score:
"Whitman only *fancied* the crowd. I have *met* them face to face" (*L*, 300).
Further insisting on Whitman's limitations as a public poet, Lindsay
boasted in 1923 to his girlfriend Elizabeth Mann Wills, "Whitman never
saw the America I have seen and loved," going on to claim that "Whitman
in his wildest dreams was only a pretended troubadour. He sat still in
cafes—never such a troubadour for audiences as [William Jennings] Bryan
or a thousand Chautauqua men. He was an infinitely more skillful writer
than any other American. But I can beat him as *troubadour*" (*L*, 297–98). It
is not incidental that the primary purpose of this letter is to court a woman,
and it was Whitman's inability to place a woman at the center of his life
and to mythologize her properly, Lindsay felt, that prevented the country
from fully absorbing him:

> *So many critics*—so many critics have said to me "Be our Walt Whitman." I
> suppose those that sincerely and steadily insist the most on my continu-
> ing to be a poet say this. They pour all America into my lap and beg me to
> sing about it. *I cannot.* And here is a secret:—Well—I always considered
> Whitman as a man and a citizen a genius, but rather crooked and shabby
> old man with a streak of perversion. I can forgive this, but it keeps the
> American people from finding leadership in him. I never mention it out
> loud. But it spoils him for a model for me. I had rather imitate St. Paul a
> thousand miles off. For St. Paul was a true traveller, a true democrat and
> saint. (*L*, 297)

Lindsay's homophobia is pronounced here, as he reads Whitman's adhesiveness in purely sexual terms, telling his beloved that Whitman "will always fail, as the law-giver for America—because he had no Elizabeth. You are my one great advantage over him" (*L*, 298).

In the *New Republic* in 1923, he went public with his view of Whitman's compromised manhood, claiming that that poet had no "real ginger in his life": "Not all the personal tales of Whitman equal the single simple narrative of John Randolph, fresh from hunting, marching into Congress and down the aisle with his hound-dogs in front of him and a dog-whip in his hand."[3] Lindsay was not the first to feel this way. Thomas Wentworth Higginson, in a series of articles from 1881 to 1898, laid out his reasons for believing that Whitman "never seemed . . . a thoroughly wholesome or manly man," calling into question Whitman's service in the Civil War as a nurse and not a soldier.[4] As his performance poetry was intended to signify, Lindsay was every bit a man, and his career tells us a great deal not only about the business of poetry—and poetry recital—in these years, but about the ways in which identity is performed, as he seeks to enact a white working-class manhood on the surface of his body and in the grain of his voice in response to a growing sense of the routine and dullness of urban-industrial culture beginning in the 1890s.[5]

As it turned out, the "vocal decade" of the 1920s (bristling with the noises of a rampant capitalism) brought Lindsay both fame and bitterness, as he grew increasingly disgusted by the commodification of the spoken word and the regulated life of the public poet, railing against his "Barnumised" fate (*L*, 181). He worried that he would not be allowed by his public to perform an evolving identity, to be granted the freedom to shift from one register to another. His growing sense of entrapment as audiences demanded he repeat himself in performance and reissue for them a static self—one lacking sincerity and a sense of genuineness—led to his renunciation of a poetics of utterance in favor of one that was purely inscriptional in nature, and not fan-based. Ultimately, his predicament was that of an artist caught in a circuit of production and consumption that he wanted, but could not afford, to escape.

RACE, GENDER, AND THE PERFORMANCE OF THE PRIMITIVE

The historian E. Anthony Rotundo has observed that in the late nineteenth century men believed that true manhood involved a primal virility; according to him, this "masculine primitive" stressed "the belief that all males—civilized or not—shared in the same primordial instincts for survival," and that "civilized men—more than women—were primitives in many important ways."[6] Lindsay's linkage of powerful manhood to the "primitivism" and "savagery" of dark-skinned races, in particular as depicted on vaudeville stages across America, did not stand alone, nor were his anxieties about manliness unique within the modernist poetic arena.[7]

Lindsay's public poetry was in effect an answer to James Lane Allen's plea of 1897 for "a reassertion of the masculine principle of virility and instinctive action in a literature too much dominated by the feminine principle of refinement and delicacy."[8] His determination to be a popular poet at a time when literary popularity (and mass culture itself) was deemed feminizing led him to a performance style that sought to break that connection by ritualized masculinist displays.[9] By listening closely to the performance-centered texts in what Lindsay referred to as his "system of noises" in the first section of his 1914 book *The Congo and Other Poems* ("Poems intended to be read aloud, or chanted") and other poems that figure his poetics and politics of vocalism, I show how his desire to compete successfully against other entertainment forms shaped his art and how his poetry performs a self that contests the artificiality and effeteness of a highly mechanized life (*L*, 97).[10]

At the age of twenty-six, Lindsay, like Whitman, saw the advantage of self-publication and self-promotion, selling copies of his poems door-to-door for a few cents each on the streets of New York; trading on his live presence, he advertised as follows: "You can see me the author."[11] In the summer of 1906, still twenty-six, Lindsay went on a walking tour of the South (from Florida to Kentucky), handing out his poem "The Tree of Laughing Bells" and performing his verse in return for food and lodging. In 1908, he traveled, again on foot, from New York City to Hiram, Ohio, supporting himself in similar fashion. In 1912, he tramped west, going from Illinois to New Mexico, printing himself *Rhymes To Be Traded for Bread* (May 1912) "expressly as a substitute for money."[12] Evidence of his early interest in the siting of his performance poetry, one of the poems in that pamphlet, "Eden in Winter," comes with the following reading direction: "Supposed to be chanted to some rude instrument at a modern fireplace"; another entails this multimediatic instruction: "A chant to which it is intended a group of children shall dance and improvise pantomime led by their dancing-teacher" (*PVL*, 1:114, 119). In the self-published *Gen-*

eral William Booth Enters into Heaven and Other Poems (November 1913), Lindsay incorporates a section entitled "A Gospel of Beauty," a medley of poems that he recited "more than any others" in his "mendicant preaching tour through the West" that trumpets small-town American values (*PVL*, 1:166).

Lindsay's launch of his poem "The Congo," composed during his 1912 trek, at the Lincoln Day banquet on February 12, 1914, in his hometown of Springfield, Illinois, was a watershed event in his career. He rehearsed "The Congo"—which would become one of his signature pieces—for friends prior to the banquet, and he later said that when he recited it he "unconsciously introduced a new element of chanting, akin to the Gregorian Chant I had heard in the Paulist Fathers' Church" (*PVL*, 3:840). Following the event, Lindsay could not help crowing about his success in a letter to Harriet Monroe: "I have just recited it for the big fat-sides Lincoln Banquet here—audience of 1000 in the Arsenal and boomed it to the very back of the building. . . . Since conquering my fellow-citizens in the Arsenal—I feel very scrappy indeed. You must give me a license to rattle the Cliff-Dwellers' Windows and pound the table *hard*" (*L*, 88). Clearly, he was pleased with his ability to project his voice with such manly vigor, to penetrate the assembly with his torrent of sound, and his sense of the radical departure of his poetry from traditional tinkling lyric is registered in his proposed rattling of the windows of the Cliff Dwellers—an all-male literary club Lindsay joined in 1910 under the sponsorship of Hamlin Garland that (as the name suggests) promoted the principle of savage manliness.

To Monroe, Lindsay identified the sources on which he draws in the poem and specified the performance mode that inspires it:

> The Congo is part sung-part recited-part chanted. . . . Much has gone into it—the Dahomey-dancers at the World's Fair, the story of the Pygmies and the Mountains of the Moon—in Stanley's Darkest Africa—Joseph Conrad's haunting African sketches full of fever and Voodoo and marsh, Mark Twain's assault on King Leopold, and the Race Riots in Springfield Illinois several years ago,—and The Souls of Black Folk, by Burghardt Du Bois, *and* the recent death of a missionary on the Congo known and loved by many of my friends, and all that and all that, very much condensed—into a ragtime epic that takes about seven minutes. It will be far more effective than any speech I can make—I am sure. General Booth finally wears out, as a recitation, but the Congo never wears out. (*L*, 88–89)

"General William Booth Enters into Heaven," a poem composed in 1912 "To be sung to the [Salvation Army] tune of 'The Blood of the Lamb' with indicated instrument," he admits, had begun to wear thin; and although he says that "the Congo," in contrast, "never wears out," he soon would grow tired of the popular demand for that as well (*PVL*, 1:148). Important to note here is the range of texts that Lindsay lists as influences on "The Congo"—colonial fictions, anthropological narratives, a political uprising (the 1908 race riots in Springfield during which two black citizens were lynched), an attraction at a world's fair—all of which signify the extent to which his poem is embedded not just in literary, but in popular, culture.

Of course, the one element that unites these various source texts is race, and Lindsay's evocation of the spirit of blackness in "The Congo" (subtitled "A Study of the Negro Race") depends more on a body of racist commercial performance—one with which his audience would have been quite familiar—than it does, say, on Du Bois's *The Souls of Black Folk*. The West African "Dahomey-dancers" on display at the 1893 Chicago World's Fair (known as the World's Columbian Exposition) on the Midway Plaisance—the mile-long street of theaters, shops, restaurants, and rides adjacent to the White City—was one such performance. Aside from the giant Ferris wheel, the Midway's main attraction was its collection of ethnological villages, which featured natives of various lands, including Ireland, Algeria, Dahomey, Germany, Java, and Egypt. When Lindsay tells Monroe in a letter that "The Congo" "is elaborately syncopated, and imitates Dahomey War-Drums," he again links his poem to that sideshow and, indirectly, to the minstrel show and vaudeville, which incorporated the syncopated, polyrhythmic music of ragtime (*L*, 90).[13]

Lindsay drew a relation between his performance aesthetic and the vocal culture of vaudeville more directly in other explanations of his poetic practice. In her preface to *The Congo* Monroe quotes Lindsay's own introduction to three of his poems (one of them "The Congo") first published in *Poetry* in 1913, where he cites Edward Bliss Reed's claim in *The English Lyric:* "In all Greek lyrics, even in the choral odes, music was the handmaid of verse. . . . The poet himself composed the accompaniment"; he connects that lyric conception to "American vaudeville, where every line may be two-thirds spoken and one-third sung, the entire rendering, musical and elocutionary, depending upon the improvising power and sure instinct of the performer."[14] In a letter to Monroe written while composing "The Congo," Lindsay reiterates his reliance on the types and tones of blackface minstrelsy, a staple of the vaudeville stage; he will include in it, he says, "Every kind of a war-drum ever heard. Then a Minstrel's Heaven—then a glorified camp-meeting. Boomlay Boomlay Boomlay Boom," and adds, "I am doubtful whether this stuff is poetry. But I discover a lot of it in me. One composes it—not by listening to the inner voice and following the gleam— but by pounding the table with a ruler and looking out the window at the Electric signs. Also by going to Vaudeville which I have all my life ab- horred—I at last grasp what those painted folks are up to" (*L*, 81). In these remarks we hear Lindsay struggling against his own (and his culture's) con- cept of "Poetry," going so far as to question some of his work *as* poetry since it does not conform to the ideal of quiet lyric intensity, but rather marches to the beat of a boisterous capitalism under the garish blazon ("Electric signs") of American advertising.

In his introduction to his poems in *Poetry* he was less doubtful, telling readers that he preferred "eloquence" to the notion of poetry as speech "*over*heard"—a notion that descends from John Stuart Mill and that as- sumes a quiet poetic text. To the poet and anthologist Jessie B. Rittenhouse, for ten years secretary of the Poetry Society, Lindsay also confessed his new attitude: "Up until this year [1913] I have looked upon actual vaudeville with loathing. Now I suddenly understand, without altogether approving. Still I am all keyed up on the issue. I see how a great many massive super- structures can be built upon that primitive foundation." His spoken word poetry—what he called "the Higher Vaudeville"—was one of those "mas- sive superstructures" intended to carry out important cultural work (*PVL*, 3:861). Lindsay was keenly aware of the extent to which poetry no longer communicated to ordinary people—how it had become a form of high cul- tural expression by the turn of the twentieth century, notwithstanding the success of James Whitcomb Riley and others—and saw the danger of such a separation; he responded by returning poetry to an idiom that would be accessible to most, even as he tried to lead his audiences to "higher" ground. In a letter to Rittenhouse (January 1914), Lindsay explained that "The American people hate and abhor poetry. I am inventing a sort of rag- time manner that deceives them into thinking they are at a vaudeville show, and yet I try to keep it to a real art." In an earlier letter he related to her his strategic ordering of poems in what would become *General William Booth Enters into Heaven and Other Poems,* with the raucous performance po- ems slated first to draw people in: "I have crowded to the front and chosen for the show-case of this first book, poems that I thought the non-reader of poetry would like." Lindsay worried, though, that "the real lovers of verse will put me down as loud, for this very course of action," and urged Rittenhouse to call attention in her review to "all the delicate early pieces you honestly can"—those pieces not meant to be chanted publicly that were composed before he turned to the business of constructing performance-centered texts.[15]

Lindsay's vigorous corporeal poetics is meant to capture the ear of America, to compete with the high-volume enthusiasms of mass-marketed theatrical entertainment, but he feels dirty in his pursuit of an audience through it. He admitted that his performance poems embody "a physical self and a physical energy that never before did I find an outlet for in literature," and found that "with the classic method and this method [the performance method] I can put my sinful as well as my saintly self into my work, my unredeemed clay and the Mystic Word as well."[16] To characterize the persona behind the high-energy poetry as "sinful" is to call up ragtime, which, rooted in black musical culture (plantation spirituals and work songs), was regarded as "symbolic of the primitive morality and perceptible moral limitations of the negro type."[17] But Lindsay was not always willing to consign poems like "The Congo" to the clay, and confides to Harriet Monroe that his frenzied "vaudeville tunes" in fact are not beyond the pale of the lyrical: "I find particular delight in bawling them into Springfield ears, but I think *you* will find cadences in them and overtones not at first obvious." There is, Lindsay insists, a public surface as well as a more nuanced interior to the performance pieces themselves.

Regarding "The Congo" as essentially a "noise," Lindsay was quick, then, to insist that it had "a silk lining," which is to say it redeemed as "Poetry" the most raucous elements of vaudeville; at the same time, its reinscription (and ritual reenactment) of blackface firmly ties it to the popular discursive field and represents a strategy to perform a melodramatic manliness in gesture and voice (*L,* 90). To the literary critic Louis Untermeyer, Lindsay again itemized the cultural ingredients that make up "The Congo," including some not listed in his letter to Monroe, and made clear in the process the importance to the poem of racist caricature and, paradoxically, his own progressive views on race:

It is equal parts (1) The death of a Missionary on the Congo. (2) a Cannibal War dance. (3) The Springfield Illinois Race Riots (4) The Burnings alive of negroes in the South. (5) The Camp-Meetings of half-Wild Negroes. (6) A

Bert Williams Negro Comedy Co. (7) A Minstrel Show. (8) Joseph Conrad's African sketches. (9) Uncle Tom's Cabin. (10) The Emancipation Proclamation. (11) The Songs of Stephen Collins Foster (12) The Souls of Black Folk by W. E. B. Du Bois. All boiled down and served to a rag time tune. (*L,* 95)

Next to Harriet Beecher Stowe's abolitionist novel and Du Bois's decidedly antiracist study of the lives of African Americans stand popular entertainment forms such as Foster's nostalgic plantation melodies and the black comedy-and-song team of Bert Williams and George Walker, who boosted the fad of the cakewalk, which, like the "coon song," was a forerunner of ragtime. Indeed, the complicated politics of the cakewalk at the turn of the century inform the racial logic of Lindsay's poem and his performance of identity through it. It was a dance said to have originated as early as 1840 with slaves who dressed up in high fashion and mimicked the formal dances of their masters. Their caricatures were picked up by white performers and used in the grand finale of the minstrel shows. Later, after the Civil War, blacks performing in the black-stereotype mold of the white minstrel shows picked up the dance. By the ragtime era, which began in 1896, the cakewalk was being performed by blacks imitating whites who were imitating whites imitating blacks.

This form of multilayered racialized mimicry directly shapes the performance aesthetic of "The Congo" as well as one of its central tropes. As Lindsay explains, "In the second section [of the poem] the Irrepressible High Spirits of the negro—as set forth in a sort of Grand Opera Minstrel Show in a part compensates for and overcomes the Hoodoo ["the ill fate and sinister power of Africa" also termed "Voodoo"] he brings. All the ragtime elements of our minstrelsy and the Cake-Walk, etc are here symbolized" (*L,* 90):

Just then from the doorway, as fat as shotes,   *With overwhelming*
Came the cake-walk princes in their long red coats   *assurance, good*
Canes with a brilliant lacquer shine,   *cheer, and pomp.*
And tall silk hats that were red as wine.
And they pranced with their butterfly partners there,   *With growing*
Coal-black maidens with pearls in their hair,   *speed and*
Knee-skirts trimmed with the jassamine sweet,   *sharply marked*
And bells on their ankles and little black feet.   *dance-rhythm.*
. . . .

The cake-walk royalty then began

To walk for a cake that was tall as a man
To the tune of "Boomlay, boomlay, BOOM,"
While the witch-men laughed, with a sinister air,   *With a touch of*
And sang with the scalawags prancing there:—   *Negro dialect,*
"Walk with care, walk with care,   *and*
Or Mumbo-Jumbo, God of the Congo,   *as rapidly as possible*
And all of the other Gods of the Congo,   *toward the end.*
Mumbo-Jumbo will hoo-doo you.

(*PVL*, 1:176)

The couples in this "Minstrel's Heaven" may appear "black," but in fact
they are either white actors in blackface or black actors in blackface, in either case actors performing "blackness" based on a performance of "whiteness." The final performance cue, or vocal stage direction, in the passage
quoted (*"With a touch of Negro dialect"*) indicates yet another level of impersonation—that of Lindsay, or Lindsay's reader, who, in reciting the
poem, must take on the identity of a black man in the act of reproducing
that man's speech.

As a poet-entertainer imitating racialized manners and speech on stage,
Lindsay was in effect operating as a blackface performer, but without the
burnt cork, and much critical attention was given to the contours of his
"physical self."[18] Randolph Bourne's review of *The Congo* in *New Republic*
(December 5, 1914) insists on the need to see and hear Lindsay himself perform the title piece, notwithstanding the delineation of paralinguistic and
kinesic features on the printed page:

> You must hear Mr. Lindsay recite his own "Congo," his body tense and
> swaying, his hands keeping time like an orchestral leader to his own
> rhythms, his tone changing color in response to the noise and savage im-
> agery of the lines, the riotous picture of the Negro mind set against the
> weird background of the primitive Congo, the "futurist" phrases crashing
> through the scene like a glorious college yell—you must hear this yourself,
> and learn what an arresting, exciting person this new indigenous Illinois
> poet is.[19]

Bourne remarks on the animated nature of Lindsay's performance, and dis-
cerns in his histrionics "the riotous picture of the Negro mind," although ultimately he deems him insincere. Lindsay's physical presence becomes,

then, a site of "blackness," with his "savage" delivery of the lines symboliz-
ing to his audiences "The Basic Savagery" (the title of the first section of the
poem) of the black race. In blackface minstrelsy, Eric Lott has argued, "To
put on the cultural forms of 'blackness' was to engage in a complex affair of
manly mimicry," as white male performers fascinated by black men sought
to reproduce their rhythms.[20] In "The Congo" Lindsay, too, puts on the cultural forms of "blackness," and, in the process, he *and* his tone "chang[e]
color," a transformation that effectively (and ironically) enacts white masculinity by tying his identity to a "Negro" "primitive." Notwithstanding
Bourne's view, the *Springfield Republican* determined that *The Congo* had hit
"a racy, pungent," utterly "authentic" note, as did Edgar Lee Masters, who
praised the text's raucous "melodies" as "sincere, authentic."[21]

The public perception of Lindsay as a cross-racial performer (based on
"The Congo") was summed up by the poet Amy Lowell's description of him
as a "white nigger," a phrase that frequently appeared in press notices before he would appear in a town to give a recital (*L*, 368). The epithet points
back to the minstrel show, where white performers in blackface were described in that way; Lindsay's annoyance with the tag bespeaks his growing
resistance to being categorized as a "dime museum freak," even though it
properly exposes Lindsay's racial contradictions/crossings and accurately
reads his romance with black expressive culture (*L*, 198).[22] In a 1919 letter to
the British writer John Drinkwater, Lindsay encouraged him to dramatize
Uncle Tom's Cabin for the English: "[Y]ou can write the whole thing here in
this town [Springfield], simply by going to Negro church with me every
Sunday. You can get it all in one Sunday morning service, and the only object in going back the next Sunday would be getting it so thoroughly you
not only understand it, but write it down" (*L*, 187–88). His desire to see and
hear African Americans in their "natural" setting is consistent with the experiences of minstrel men, many of whom sought out occasions to observe
African Americans firsthand in an effort to make their mimicry more authentic.[23] Lindsay documented his own interracial contact when he noted,
"All the brotherhood I have for the blacks dates from the Springfield race-
riots of 1908 when, for six months thereafter as a local Y.M.C.A. worker, etc,
I cultivated a people I thought deeply wronged" (*L*, 128–29). Indeed, his
personal relationship with "the Soot-black [Springfield] lawyer" Charles
Gibbs stands behind "The Congo"; referring to Gibbs as "the black African
Chieftain," Lindsay states, "You will find him in the first section of 'The
Congo,' and you may be sure it is pretty well modeled on him, and on hav-

ing known him for many a day, a gigantic Negro warrior disguised as a lawyer in the Bad Lands. He was surely made to prance with a 'coffin-headed shield and a shovel spear'" (L, 188, 349).

In that first section of the poem, Lindsay markets a racialized image of masculinity: "Fat black bucks in a wine-barrel room, / Barrel-house kings, with feet unstable, / Sagged and reeled and pounded on the table." This scene leads onto the narrator's "vision" of a performance ritual in the heart of the Congo:

> Tattooed cannibals danced in files;
> Then I heard the boom of the blood-lust song
> And a thigh-bone beating on a tin-pan gong.
> And "BLOOD" screamed the whistles and the fifes of the warriors,
> "BLOOD" screamed the skull-faced, lean witch-doctors . . .
>
> (PVL, 1:174)

As these images suggest, Lindsay's poetry, like minstrelsy, commodified "blackness" and, in doing so, served up a racist counterfeit—one that audiences would pay to see in the belief that what they were seeing was an authentic display of Negroism. Thus, despite Lindsay's low regard for those who would capitalize on racist depiction (those who "reduce him [the black man] to dialect and monkeyshines know nothing about him"), his own art, by bowing to established entertainment conventions, does just that, as he attempts to impress upon audiences and critics his forceful manhood by releasing his own inner savage (L, 188).

Some prominent African Americans were disheartened for this very reason. To Joel E. Spingarn, chairman of the directors of the NAACP, Lindsay expressed his dismay at the black backlash against his work: "My 'Congo' and 'Booker T. Washington Trilogy' have both been denounced by the Colored people, for reasons that I cannot fathom. So far as I can see they have not taken the trouble to read them through. The third section of the Congo is certainly as hopeful as any human being dare to be in regard to any race" (L, 134). (His own family in Kentucky heard it that way, going so far as to accuse him of expressing in "The Congo" "too Harriet-Beecher-Stowe a point of view") (L, 179). The third section ("The Hope of Their Religion") enacts, Lindsay said, "an idealized Camp-meeting—transferred to the banks of the Congo, along with a prophecy of the redemption of the race through their religious instinct, and the death of Mumbo-Jumbo" (L, 90).

There we see the Congo "transfigured" from a land of voodoo worship to an outpost of Christendom, with "the twelve Apostles" hymning the death of heathen ritual and a company of angels hailing a "Redeemed" "negro nation" (*PVL*, 1:178). In his letter of reply to Lindsay, Spingarn laid out his objection: "You look forward to a colored Utopia separate and different from the hope of the white man; they [African Americans] have only one overwhelming desire; and that is to share in a common civilization in which all distinctions of race are blurred (or forgotten) by common aspirations and common labors."[24] Lindsay's effort also was criticized by Du Bois, who was unsettled by Lindsay's racial mimicry and his separatist vision of black culture; as Lindsay told Spingarn: "The Crisis [the magazine that Du Bois edited] took the trouble to skin me not long ago" (*L*, 135).[25] Lindsay's statement further blurs the color line, highlighting his racial impersonation by imagining himself as a victim of a lynching, in which often skinning would occur, at a time when African Americans in increasing numbers were meeting that fate. Clearly, such criticism stung, not least because he believed that a participatory poetry performance—with whites and blacks in the audience, chanting together—could foster racial harmony.[26]

In another of Lindsay's most popular performance pieces—his self-described "hoot" entitled "The Santa Fe Trail," which appears immediately after the title poem in the first section of *The Congo*—he again negotiates the complex issues of race and gender in his performance of modern American culture (*L*, 95). The act opens with a scene of interracial familiarity:

I asked the old Negro: "What is that bird that sings so well?" He answered: "That is the Rachel-Jane." "Hasn't it another name, lark, or thrush, or the like?" "No. Jus' Rachel-Jane." (*PVL*, 1:179)

Appealing to the "old Negro" as an instinctual being—one in tune with the rhythms of nature—the white speaker defers to his judgment by giving him the last word, but not without giving us a sense of his own superior understanding, and in private remarks about the poem Lindsay reveals that he knows very well that the other name of the Rachel-Jane bird, the technical name, is "Meadow lark" (*L*, 93). The black man's poetical name of "Rachel-Jane" puts up resistance to a mechanical, unpoetical America, just as the bird's trill in the poem is designed to serve as sonic counterpoint to the noise of a hundred cars speeding along "the blistering Kansas plain," westward bound (*PVL*, 1:181).

Beyond its initial rehearsal of racialized minstrel types and tones in the colloquy with "the old Negro," the poem and its sound systems are shaped largely by the performance of gender in popular culture. Lindsay wrote in May 1914 about "The Santa Fe Trail" that it "express[es] my wrath and life-long aversion to the automobile. It stands as a sign, as a symbol of *America,* from the standpoint of those who despise her most and get her superficial aspects in a triple dose. I have considered the voice of the auto at its worst—the most obscene and unclean sound on the face of the earth. (Also very mechanical. Hence the forced rhymes)." He goes on to detail the gendered considerations that affect his process of composition, which included public auditions of the poem before select audiences: "it was *all Hog* horn when I began. Gradually I added the twilight zone—and the sweetness of the horns—in the distance—and the Rachel Jane was the very last afterthought, put in as a sort of final concession to the ladies who shrunk from the rude blasts of my satire, and the mechanical rhyme-repetitions. . . . I have tried—like the lion in Pyramus and Thisbe—to roar so as not to frighten the ladies—still I must roar" (*L*, 98). Worried as he is about the impression that the onslaught of brute sounds in the poem will make on the finer sensibilities of women, Lindsay tells Monroe of other experiences performing the piece that have made clear to him the need to make certain sonic alterations: "I read the lady the Santa Fe Trail and was properly chastened and will make it a bit less like an unmitigated noise before I forward it to you. It is a Kallyope yell with a few flute notes at present. It needs a few more flute-notes from the Rachel-Jane bird (Meadow lark) to mellow the middle. Then you shall have it." In the same letter he again mentions the grating effect of the "noise-poem" on his girlfriend: "I am awfully anxious to send you the Santa Fe Trail but prudence dictates I should read it aloud at least a week longer to weave in this Rachel-Jane tune just right. . . . Sara [Teasdale] was all commendation—but I could just see the harshness of the auto-horns jarred her. I must put in a bird and surprise her." A few days later he is able to report that "Sara likes the Santa Fe Trail now that I have put a little bird in it to sort of soften it down and give it tone" (*L*, 93–94, 95).

In the poem on the page, we are directed to hear the "rude blasts" in the manly "roar"ing "voice" of car horns, which are juxtaposed to—and, as Lindsay would have it, leavened by—the mild song of the bird, as in the following passage:

Listen to the iron-horns, ripping, racking.   *To be given*
Listen to the quack-horns, slack and clacking.   *very harshly,*
Way down the road, trilling like a toad,   *with a*
Here comes the *dice*-horn, here comes the *vice*-horn, *snapping*
Here comes the *snarl*-horn, *brawl*-horn, *lewd*-horn, *explosiveness.*
Followed by the prude-horn, bleak and squeaking:—
(Some of them from Kansas, some of them from Kansas.)
Here comes the *hod*-horn, *plod*-horn, *sod*-horn,
Nevermore to *roam*-horn, *loam*-horn, *home*-horn.
(Some of them from Kansas, some of them from Kansas.)

        Far away the Rachel-Jane   *To be read or*
        Not defeated by the horns   *sung, well-nigh*
        Sings amid a hedge of thorns:—   *in a whisper.*
        "Love and life,
        Eternal youth—
        Sweet, sweet, sweet, sweet,
        Dew and glory,
        Love and truth,
        Sweet, sweet, sweet, sweet."

                    (*PVL*, 1:181)

Here the person performing the poem is instructed marginally to increase the volume and plosiveness in impersonation of the horns and temper the tone when acting out the birdsong. The careful scoring of the vocalization of acoustic features in the body of the poem, as in "The Congo," makes writable prosodic levels of pitch, tempo, and intensity. In "The Congo" we encounter capitalization to denote increases in volume in such lines as "Boomlay, boomlay, boomlay, / BOOM" and "THEN I SAW THE CONGO, CREEPING THROUGH THE BLACK, / CUTTING THROUGH THE JUNGLE WITH A GOLDEN TRACK"; in the final fade-out, to be uttered in *"a penetrating, terrified whisper,"* ellipses slow delivery down: "Mumbo . . . Jumbo . . . will . . . hoo-doo . . . you." In "Santa Fe Trail" the performer must possess great vocal range, shifting from *"a snapping explosiveness"* to *"a whisper"*; at another point the performer is called on to recite *"Louder and louder, faster and faster"* in the capitalized section beginning with the line, "WHILE SMOKE-BLACK FREIGHTS ON THE DOUBLE-TRACKED RAILROAD" (*PVL*, 1:175, 178, 181).

Lindsay's decision to dilute the raucous vocalism of the poem is instructed by his image of an ideal female spectator/auditor—an image that he shared with the managers of vaudeville. M. Alison Kibler points out that "Vaudeville's fare, according to much of the advertising, appealed to women's special aesthetic sensibility." Lindsay's sense of his polite ("charming") female audience, who must be protected from "ugly," "obscene," "unclean," "rude" noises, corresponds to that of the vaudeville managers, who "coded loud interruptions such as stamping feet and guying performers as masculine."[27] That those managers believed female patrons were "particularly impressionable and fearful" is apparent from their weekly reports: "The Great Lafayette's sketch had 'quite a sensational finish which was startling enough to have a lot of women run up the aisle, out of their seats.' Harry Jordan noted in 1913 that the comedy team of Cressy and Dayne created 'continuous and uproarious [laughter] and several times, women were threatened with hysteria.'"[28] This supposed tendency toward overexcitement brought out "managers' paternal anxieties," just as it does Lindsay's: Sara does not tell him that she is agitated by the noises in the poem; rather, Lindsay says that he "could just see the harshness of the auto-horns jarred her." If "'ladies' appeared to be the censors of vaudeville acts," with managers "invok[ing] women's tastes as an indication of an act's acceptability," that same figure of the female censor determines the content of Lindsay's poem, as we see him auditioning it for women in search of their stamp of approval. His performance of "The Santa Fe Trail"—both on and off the page—rearticulates stereotyped notions about gender commodified in U.S. culture (most visibly on the vaudeville stage), as he seeks to assert his masculine authority and control as a poet in and of the public sphere.[29]

However, even as Lindsay courted and acceded to women's opinion as he composed "The Santa Fe Trail," he was deeply disturbed by the feminization of American culture, disparaging the groups of women for whom he recited and perforce continues to recite. To Harriet Moody he remarks: "Of course ladies in parlors thought it all very pretty for me to recite 'The Santa Fe Trail,' now it was all behind me. But of course henceforth I was to recite such a poem as a parlor ornament" (*L*, 351). To Mary Austin, an ardent feminist and researcher into American Indian life, he testifies: "With a very few exceptions I have never spoken willingly for a Woman's Club or a Chautauqua. I have spoken, since I was a beggar, almost exclusively for the English Departments of various schools and Universities, and then, generally because I received no money from my publisher, and had to keep the wolf from the door. But I have seldom been poor enough to speak for Woman's Clubs" (*L*, 369–70). On December 29, 1925, the *New York Times* in a column titled "Poet Drops Club Women" noted that Lindsay instead "Prefers Housewives": "I prefer hostesses who do their own work and who also read." He rails at the husbands of club women, who, if present, "are the kind of business men who find their chief nourishment in the full page advertisements of office supplies. Their only ideal is to keep their wives like these supplied with tea, poets and servants, while they themselves, as good business men, keep on attending peppy business men's banquets."[30] Performance in the effete setting of the parlor stood as a sign for Lindsay of artistic failure, of the failure of America to take his poetry seriously, and is shaped by his own sharp gender and class politics.

As opposed to Yeats's and Pound's vatic presence, Lindsay belted out his poetry in an effort to verify his own passionate manhood, to portray himself as a muscular male artist, one in touch with the masses, and he seems to have been successful at making such an impression. Sir Walter Raleigh, who attended Lindsay's reading at Oxford, called Lindsay "the most virile poet, representing the most virile nation," the critic Conrad Aiken referred to the "broad and rugged rhythms" of "The Firemen's Ball" and "The Santa-Fe Trail," and Amy Lowell remarked on the "virile" rhythm of "The Kallyope Yell."[31] A review of *General William Booth* in the *New York Times* (February 1914) similarly refers to Lindsay's verse "as ringing and virile," and thereby empowered to "awaken an indifferent public" in "a practical, commercialized age." As an audience member recalled of one of his recitals in the Ivy League:

> The nice boys from the ivory towers of the best schools and the Gothic dormitories of Yale tittered at first. But as he began to swing the persuasive rhythms of General William Booth Enters into Heaven and The Congo, and as the rich imagery lifted the homely language into poetry, they warmed, and soon were chanting with him. Yet to them it was only a show—America, a rather vulgar America speaking, but not literature as they had been taught to regard literature.[32]

The gendered description here—the "nice boys" "tittered," a sign of their effeteness and effeminacy—throws into relief the swinging, chanting, vulgar, masculine Lindsay, who comes to stand for populist America itself. At a recital at Harvard, Carl Carmer, a student there at the time, reported that "Tennyson was a pale wraith within us as Lindsay's bold accents beat the living daylights out of our polite concepts of poetry!"[33] Once again Lindsay's live poetry performance is imagined as performing a working-class manhood, with his show of force compelling nothing less than a reconsideration of generic categories.

TEXTING THE "VOICE OF THE DEMOCRACY"

Although Lindsay did not value very highly the making of money, and condemned the capitalist ethos of the eastern United States as against what he viewed as the spiritually rich Midwest, he hoped to be able to live off his poetry proceeds, and to that end exhorted Harriet Monroe in May 1914 to "fix up your introduction [to *The Congo*] so that the reader will be craftily and unsuspectingly led to desire to hear me *recite* these verses, but even *more* prompted to try to recite them himself. It looks to me like my only chance at an income." Lindsay's ambivalence is pointed here, as he wants to secure a future reciting his verse for the money it will bring in, but at the same time insist that his book stands on its own (and so is worth buying) as a script for the dramatic reader; he goes on to urge Monroe: "*But* please make the point that many reciters over the country are reciting or chanting my pieces, who have never seen me—stirred to do so by the directions on the margins" (*L*, 96).

Such directions, which Lindsay referred to as "side-line coaching," are financially motivated, and his desire to make money was particularly acute when he wrote to Monroe, because he wanted to marry Sara Teasdale but was unsure of his means of support. While Lindsay could and did make money performing live, he knew that he feasibly could reach only so many people in that way, and, without an income from the sale of books, he feared that his vocational aspirations would be dashed. Such rhetorical questions as "But where will the intonation of Lindsay's poem be found except in his own voice?" (asked by the poet Edgar Lee Masters) suggest what Lindsay was up against as he sought to construct a popular audience for his printed word.[34] Carl Van Doren similarly remarked, "To appreciate them [Lindsay's poetic feats] it is necessary to have heard him read his own verse."[35] In response, Lindsay cannily advertised the entwinement of print and oral text:

My publisher (Macmillan's) want [sic] me to come back to New York about October and launch my book by reciting from it to audiences well picked in New York for the amount of talking they will do, and commenting which will lead the newspapers to comment on my poems as vocal things, chants. That is going to be my whole publicity policy, so people will ask me to get up and chant them, also attempt to chant them for themselves. (*L*, 102)

His scoring of the voice for readers in his performance-centered texts allows them to perform for themselves the poems (as one critic exhorted, "Read him aloud, and hear how his words roll with the solemnity of a great prayer or snap, crackle, wink and dance with all the humorous rhythms of a piece of 'rag-time'"), even as it makes those same readers feel to some extent the deficiencies of script and so drums up business for his recitals.[36]

Lindsay imagined his performance-centered texts as a necessary measure in a mass-mediated society. In *A Letter about My Four Programmes for Committees in Correspondence* (1916), a publicity tract sent out to sponsors before his arrival in town, Lindsay notes, "The devices of marginal directions, the naming of the tune, printing with dots, dashes and capitals, etc., are . . . a concession to the tired business man, just as books printed by embossed points are a concession to the blind" (*PVL*, 3:848). As with Braille, his cues are meant as an aid to the impaired reader, in this case a reader disabled by materialism. Vaudeville, too, was staged for those already enervated by their participation in the cultural economy, and was billed in like fashion as a form that "appeals to the businessman, tired and worn, who drops in for half an hour on his way home, to the person who has an hour or two before a train goes, or before a business appointment, to the woman who is wearying of shopping."[37] Some critics lamented Lindsay's concessions, saying, as Louis Untermeyer did, that Lindsay "frequently cheapened himself and caricatured his own gift by pandering to the vaudeville instinct, putting a noisy 'punch' into everything, regardless of taste, artistry, or a sense of proportion."[38] In a similar vein, Conrad Aiken, who noted the "delightful, unrestrained vaudeville vigor and humor" and "ragtime rhythms" of his performance poetry, instructed Lindsay to "suppress the good-natured buffoon . . . and remember that it is the poet's office not merely to entertain, but also, on a higher plane, to delight with beauty and to amaze with understanding."[39] Of course, Lindsay was intending to do just that, but the lyrical overtones that he told Harriet Monroe were to be found even in his noisier performance poems often went undetected. As the *New York Times* pronounced of "The Santa-Fe Trail," it sounded like "advertising," an assessment that follows from poetry turned commodity in search of an audience.[40]

Lindsay's construction of a mass audience through oral poetic performance rests on a politics of primitivism central to modernist literary doctrine and directly related to his communitarian ideal. At a March 1914 dinner sponsored by *Poetry* in honor of Yeats, Lindsay recited to thunderous applause, and Yeats responded enthusiastically, observing that in American vaudeville (the half-sung, half-spoken delivery of such acts as Tambo and Bones dialogues) and Lindsay's performance pieces the "primitive singing of poetry" still survived.[41] In her preface to *The Congo* Monroe similarly focused on the primitivist strain running through Lindsay's public poetry; drawing on F. T. Marinetti's article "Futurism and the Theatre," where "he urges the revolutionary value of 'American eccentrics,' citing the fundamental primitive quality of their vaudeville art," she remarks on "Mr. Lindsay's plea for a closer relation between the poet and his audience, for a return to the healthier open-air conditions, and immediate personal contacts, in the art of the Greeks and of primitive nations," and observes that "Such conditions and contacts may still be found, if the world only knew it, in the wonderful song-dances of the Hopis and others of our aboriginal tribes. They may be found, also, in a measure, in the quick response between artist and audience in modern vaudeville."[42]

According to T. S. Eliot, this "return to primitive sympathies between artist and audience" structures the cultural form of the British music-hall as well: "The working man who went to the music-hall . . . and joined in the chorus was himself performing part of the act. . . . [H]e was engaged in that collaboration of the audience with the artist which is necessary in all art and most obviously in dramatic art."[43] Participation in such a ritual, Eliot believed, generates the communal solidarity he admired in tribal societies, for ritual allows members of the tribe to "partake in a common nature from which other men are excluded."[44] Of course, racist and sexist elements exist as the troubling side of this othering, as they do in Lindsay's work. Although Eliot averred that the poet "would like to be something of a popular entertainer," David Chinitz reminds us that Eliot's eventual renunciation of poetry (in favor of drama) substantiates his view that that status is impossible if one is to retain distinction as an artist: "A genuine reconciliation with popular culture cannot take place on poetry's terms, for nothing one might do with poetry in contemporary Western society seems likely to make it a truly public or popular art. A poeticized (or 'refined') music hall is a much likelier prospect, particularly if a music-hall audience can be brought along with it."[45] Lindsay attempted just such a reconciliation, reimagining poetry as a popular art through presence as he worked to solidify a sense of community at a time of seismic disturbances in American cultural life.[46]

Lindsay's notion of presence—of the personality of the poet—dissents from Eliot's "Impersonal theory of poetry"—a theory set forth in his essay "Tradition and the Individual Talent" (1919).[47] Believing that "The progress of an artist is a continual self-sacrifice, a continual extinction of personality," Eliot insists on the need "To divert interest from the poet to the poetry," concluding that "Poetry is not a turning loose of emotion, but an escape from emotion; it is not the expression of personality, but an escape from personality."[48] Reactions to Lindsay's powerful presence as a poet-performer verify an alternative posture: " 'As Vachel Lindsay came forward on a stage,' one critic was to write, 'the force of his personality brought an immediate sense of expectancy in his audience.' Another spoke of his 'electric presence,' of how he 'set the throng on fire.' "[49] Not surprisingly, after hearing Lindsay recite in London in 1920, Eliot said that he was "appalled" and dismissed him as "impossible."[50] Although Eliot, like Lindsay, believed in the fortifying effects of popular culture ("Fine art is the *refinement*, not the antithesis, of popular art"), he was not one of those who found Lindsay's poetic performance (either in print or on stage) credible, apparently deeming his "higher vaudeville" aesthetic not nearly high enough.[51] Eliot's remark, "The interest of a performer is almost certain to be centered in himself. . . . The performer is interested not in form but in opportunities for virtuosity or in the communication of his 'personality,' " points to his low opinion of a poet like Lindsay, who, he feels, stakes his reputation on theatrical displays of subjectivity as opposed to the intellectual rigors of "form."[52]

Although Ezra Pound was enamored of the troubadour tradition and performed his poetry live on numerous occasions, he did not find anything to praise in Lindsay's public poetry either. When he heard Lindsay perform he is said to have exclaimed "Oh gawd!!!" in horrified disgust; ridiculing Lindsay's craftsmanship, Pound claimed that "one can write it by the hour as fast as one scribbles."[53] In the *Little Review* Pound published a parody of Lindsay's poem "General William Booth Enters into Heaven" "written (he said) in precisely four minutes and thirty one seconds," a description that mocks Lindsay's notation of the time it takes to vocalize (not to compose) one of his poems:

> Whoop-golly-ip-Zopp, bop BIP!!
> I'm Mr. Lindsay with the new sheep-dip,
> I'm a loud-voiced yeller, I'm a prancing preacher,
> Gawd's in his heaven! I'm the real High Reacher.[54]

These lines with their wild acoustic effects and description of Lindsay as storefront evangel and salesman are meant to signify that poet's remove from the precincts of poetic solemnity.

Other modernist poets weighed in on Lindsay as well. Marianne Moore's review of Lindsay's *Collected Poems* in *The Dial* (November 1923) expresses what Eliot does not spell out, as she finds fault with Lindsay for a "lack of aesthetic rigor," specifically in reference to his performance aesthetic and the relative sophistication of his audience: "In stage directions, the most expert craftsman such as Shaw and Yeats barely escape pedantry and one feels that however necessary to Mr. Lindsay's conception of the spoken word particular information may be, when he asks us 'to keep as lightfooted as possible,' to read 'orotund fashion,' 'with heavy buzzing bass,' et cetera, one can but feel, unfairly or not, that he is subordinating a poorly endowed audience to wit which he proposes to furnish."[55] Wallace Stevens grimaced at the news of Lindsay's public appearances, and expressed particular distaste at the idea of his signing his name in books for sale at recitals: "Lindsay comes [to Hartford, CT] next week with other early songsters. Autograph copies of his poems are to be sold in the lobby of the High School. My word!"[56] In a letter in which he refused to read at the Museum of Modern Art in 1943, Stevens made known his repugnance at the spoken word: "I am not a troubadour and I think the public reading of poetry is something particularly ghastly."[57] He also bristled at a statement that found its way into the designer's note of the 1937 edition of his book *The Man with the Blue Guitar and Other Poems* that read, "In some of the lines appear unusual blank spaces *** By this experimental device the author wishes to indicate a desirable pause or emphasis suggested by the sense"; as Stevens objected, "This is pure nonsense. I never said any such thing and have a horror of poetry pretending to be contemporaneous because of typographical queerness."[58] The "queerness" of Lindsay's performance-centered texts—his attempts to indicate prosodic levels of pitch and tempo—struck Stevens as a trendy supplement in violation of poetic decorum.

Lindsay's early emphasis on a poetics of sound—his relentless attention to the listening ear—further distances him from mainstream modernists, in particular the prophets of imagism and their highbrow conception of poetry and culture. In his introduction to *General William Booth*, he writes, "Poetry has too long been manufactured and read in the study . . . the enmity between the poet and the populace has its origin in *print;* whereby poetry has lost its 'springiness'; has become a thing too much of the eye."[59] In *The Congo* Lindsay declares that the performance poetry in the first section of the book is intended to "restore poetry to its proper place—the audience-chamber, and take it out of the library, the closet. In the library it has become, so far as the people are concerned, almost a lost art, and perhaps it can be restored to the people only through a renewal of its appeal to the ear."[60] Elsewhere, he indicted the imagist camp as an "aesthetic aristocracy" "singing on an island to one another while the people perish"; as he is quick to point out, "this is precisely not the point of view of the Kallyope."[61]

Like the car horns in "The Santa Fe Trail," the calliope, a keyboard instrument similar to an organ that was a fixture of circuses and fairs, stands for a garish American industrialism, "a symbol," Lindsay believed, "of many things—among them are street-car advertisements, bill boards, automobile horns, electric signs, megaphones, phonographs, motion pictures, automobile horns, uplift magazines, girl-and-music shows, brass bands, yellow journals, and the like. By these the powers of attention of the tired business man, highly concentrated in office hours, are frayed into a thousand pieces once the roller-top desk is closed" (*PVL*, 3:861). In "The Kallyope Yell," Lindsay transforms himself into the calliope, and his muscular melody serves as a figure for a scrappy participatory American democracy:[62]

> I am the Kallyope, Kallyope, Kallyope,
> Tooting hope, tooting hope, tooting hope, tooting hope;
> Shaking window-pane and door
> With a crashing cosmic tune,
> With the war-cry of the spheres,
> Rhythm of the roar of noon,
> Rhythm of Niagara's roar,
> Voicing planet, star and moon,
> SHRIEKING of the better years.

Prophet-singers will arise,
Prophets coming after me,
Sing my song in softer guise
With more delicate surprise;
I am but the Pioneer
Voice of the Democracy;
I am the gutter dream,
I am the golden dream,
Singing science, singing steam.

(*PVL*, 1:249–50)

The "Pioneer / Voice of the Democracy" finds it must be loud and harsh to be heard above the commercial clang of the public sphere, but predicts that a quieter tune is to come, once Americans grow out of their materialist phase and begin to appreciate their finer, spiritual natures.[63]

Lindsay modeled his calliope on America's boisterous democratic political heroes. He was particularly enthralled by the populist politician William Jennings Bryan, telling Carl Sandburg that "Bryan is really the American poet, till we can take the Chautauqua platform, and sing to as many" (*L*, 142). (Lindsay's positive view of Chautauqua in January 1917 is far different from what it would become.) Bryan's oratorical skills were the key to his political career and also his primary source of income from 1896 on. Lindsay would boast in 1923 that he had surpassed Bryan (much as he felt he had Whitman) both in his geographical coverage and his vocal effects: "I have almost out-travelled and out-shouted Bryan in the last seven years" (*L*, 280). Lindsay's chant-poem "Bryan Bryan Bryan Bryan" addresses him as "The one American poet who could sing outdoors," "That Homer Bryan, who sang from the West," and pointedly figures his voice in hypermasculinist terms, "Gigantic troubadour, speaking like a siege gun, / Splashing Plymouth Rock with his boulders from the West" (*PVL*, 1:343–49). Elsewhere, Lindsay claims that he has "as much to say to the American people as Hoover or [Charles Evans] Hughes or Bryan, and in as loud a *voice*."[64] In "When Bryan Speaks," a poem composed in the nation's capital in 1915, Lindsay imagines the politician's live voice bringing capitalist profiteers to their knees: "When Bryan speaks, the wigwam shakes. / The corporation magnate quakes." The power of his spoken word is capable of effecting a new order, one in which the people own collectively the nation's wealth: "the sky is ours, / The wheat, the forests, and the flowers /

And who is here to say us nay?" That Bryan made common cause with the Socialist Party is signified by his resounding vocal presence: "His is the strange composite voice / Of many million singing souls / Who make world-brotherhood their choice" (*PVL*, 1:284). When Bryan speaks, then, he does not speak alone. The poem appeared in the section of *The Chinese Nightingale and Other Poems* (1917) entitled "America Watching The War, August, 1914, to April, 1917"; Bryan, like Lindsay, was opposed to U.S. involvement in World War I. The trope of public utterance presented in the poem rings with that antimilitarist message. In another poem in the same section of the book, "To Jane Addams at the Hague," Lindsay imagines the force of a solitary voice in the peace movement, in a woman's stereotypically more delicate strains: "Lady of Light speak, though you speak alone, / Though your voice may seem as a dove's in this howling flood, / It is heard tonight by every senate and throne" (*PVL*, 1:285).

Lindsay also looked to the political arena for precedents for his oral performance poetics. In "Preface to Bob Taylor's Birthday," a "Rhymed Oration" for the governor of Tennessee ("the greatest state Governor America has ever had") that Lindsay recited at the Harvard commencement (as the Phi Beta Kappa poem) in 1922, and, as Lindsay notes, "of all my productions, the one least intended for cold print," he hails the fiddle-playing populist politician, telling his readers to "amend it [the poem] as they read it," to treat it as a text upon which to improvise, as Taylor famously improvised on the stump (*PVL*, 2:502). Further, Lindsay exhorts, the poem, to perform its civic duty, is "to be read to a big crowd, out of doors, presumably July 1, Bob Taylor's birthday. If it is read while you sit down, in the house, it means nothing"; he conceives of Taylor as "the livest and greatest new prophet in America, an unconscious prophet, far closer to the future than Whitman, because actually elected to office again and again. Whitman was a thwarted Tammany brave" (*PVL*, 2:504).[65] In "Babylon, Babylon, Babylon the Great," Lindsay again highlights the politics of extemporaneity, stating that "Lincoln at Cooper Union, improvised and chanted, / Threw away his speech, and told tales out of school," as he brazenly defended the right of the federal government to regulate slavery in the new territories (*PVL*, 2:500). The speech, "nowhere written down," nonetheless "burned every gate of the famous old town," and the poem directs the populist artist Carl Sandburg, to whom the poem is inscribed, to follow Lincoln's example: "Tear up your set speeches, improvise once more" (*PVL*, 2:501).[66]

MASS MEDIA AND THE WAGES OF THE POPULAR

Not long after Lindsay burst onto the recital scene, and notwithstanding his triumphs there, he grew to despise it, struggling to define himself as an artist under the pressure of consumer culture and the celebrity he had become. As early as December 1914 he announced the start of a new phase of his career, forecasting his future in "a certain decorative, pictorial type of verse," an inscriptional aesthetic that stands in stark contrast to his orally conceived poetry (L, 116). His body, he says, no longer can withstand the demands of performance, and in November 1913 he fumes, "I have recited the General ["General William Booth Enters into Heaven"] till my jaws ache—4444 times. The silly things think it is the only good poem I ever wrote, simply because it *forces* attention" (L, 81). Ten years later, however, Lindsay is still on the platform to keep out of debt and even more disgusted with his commodification: "Though people call me a 'poet' they have not the least notion that an imagination burnt out by too much reiteration is worse than physical sickness. People howl for me to recite Booth and the Congo till I am ready to vomit. And they threaten me if I refuse, till I am ready to swear myself crazy. . . . The whole world is in a conspiracy to sell for a high price my stalest fancies and kill off all my new ones" (L, 267–68). In 1931 to Hamlin Garland he reports that he has "almost had fist-fights to keep from being mobbed into reciting poems like The Congo and General Booth." Lindsay goes on to thank Garland for praising his recent poem-drawings as opposed to the performance pieces: "You have saved me from being 'Congoed' into permanent fury" (L, 457). Rejecting the label "vaude-ville man," Lindsay argues that his reputation—"The whole jazzy notion of my work"—"is as hard to endure as contempt, and has nothing whatever to do with my ambitions and aspirations" (L, 169, 260).

On national tour (from early March through June 1920 Lindsay made the first of three such tours), he refused to be handled by Pond's Lecture Bureau, which had managed his public appearances up to that time and promoted him as America's "jazz poet"; instead, Lindsay signed up with an agent in Texas, A. Joseph Armstrong, a professor of English at Baylor University, to whom he confessed: "Your greatest use to me as a sponsor is to kill off the *Jazz* and *advertising* quality that the professional bureau insists in putting into their introduction of a literary figure" (L, 228). Resisting his own commodification as a poet-entertainer, he worked through Armstrong and others to secure select audiences, preferring "the Colleges and High

Schools, and Negro Schools": "I assure you the longer I live the more I dislike an audience that makes a curiosity out of me, and a committee that makes me talk about myself and listens and listens and listens for queer things" (*L*, 181). Lindsay felt that ideally each member of his audience should have to pass an exam on his books, thus proving their seriousness, to gain entrance.[67] Lindsay also wanted to restrict his recitals to the South and West "for the simple reason that the people out there tell me so much about themselves and their states on the second day, and I feel myself growing with the country"; with the East, a region that Lindsay felt was ruled by commercial interests, he says he is "entirely through . . . *as a public person*" (*L*, 205).

In retreat, then, Lindsay adopted and promulgated a new aesthetic—or, as he framed it, a renewed one ("close to the hieroglyphic I knew in Springfield before 1912")—imagining himself (as of 1923) at a distance from the "kallyope" of American commercial culture, with which poetry recitation was implicated: "I am a million miles away from the Pullman car, the glittering hotel lobby, the loud lecture platform, the howling newsboys, the automobiles, the magazines" (*PVL*, 3:973, 968).[68] He realized that the hectic nature of life on the road was part and parcel of the business of poetry recital, a business that did not allow for improvisation: "I have been looking out standardized windows of 'The Flat-Wheeled Pullman Car.' I have been living in standardized hotels, have been eating jazzed meals as impersonal as patent breakfast-food."

Rebelling against "professional standardization," Lindsay performed a new poetic self, staunchly resisting his own mass-marketing: "I refuse to be put into uniform paraffin packages for the trade, like Uneeda Biscuit" (*PVL*, 3:958). (As the copy of one Uneeda Biscuit ad read: "From the greatest metropolis to the humblest hamlet the demand has grown in volume until everybody, everywhere, knows Uneeda Biscuit.")[69] In his 1928 poem "Twenty Years Ago," he proclaims, "My works are unstandardized, and not Peruna-advertised," and from now on, he insists, he will be nobody's freak:

I choose to be an etcher studying James M. Whistler.
You say I am a rhymer, but who am I?
You silly big-timer, to do a turn for you?
Your Tom Thumb in the side show to make talk?
I tell you, Lord Chesterfield, I'm no man's baby wonder.

(*PVL*, 2:724–25, 726)

Lindsay wanted "to be something besides a noise," not continue to perform as "a conventionalized 'reciter' of my own verses" (*PVL*, 3:957–58). He was desperate not to play the "buffoon," not to be seen as "a queer one or a curiosity," and, for all his admiration of Bryan, not to be turned into "a kind of Bryan sensation" (*L*, 199, 180).

The idea of the performativity of identity is perhaps nowhere better expressed by Lindsay than in his letters to friends laying out his plight. He wrote to Harriet Monroe saying that "a certain public self is forced upon me by my friends—the Vachel I was to them many years ago; and I would as soon wear a plaster cast all over, or mediaeval armor. . . . I would give almost anything to escape forever the reciting and chanting Vachel. . . . My whole heart is set on escaping my old self (completely as I may, to be human and frail as we all are)" (*L*, 213). (He is like the rock star pressured by market forces to repeat his standard hits; he has entered the economy of repetition.) Feeling himself "to be the slave of past performances or habits," he asserts his desire to put forth his "genuine *public self* to my little public, and keep from being the parrot and ape of yesterday," an act, ironically, that will require "putting money I make as a reciter into zinc-etchings" of his new picture-poems to appease the "ferocious economizers" at his publisher Macmillan, or as he jokes on one occasion "Macmillion" (*L*, 213, 205–6, 100). But it is not just to finance his pictorial art that he continues on the poetry reading circuit; he also confronts the high cost of living: "But just financially—I cannot afford to quit [reciting] *entirely,* so I recite from hand-to-mouth, as one may say. My books only bring me five hundred dollars a year, at best—that is—this last year, and up to that time one to two hundred dollars a year. So I must recite a bit now and then to keep out of debt" (*L*, 222). For Lindsay, the performance of poetry and its commodification—the insatiable demand for him to reissue over and over a static persona—while it led to his enormous, if momentary, cultural power, also sealed his doom.

During the 1920s and 1930s Lindsay lashed out increasingly at effects of mass commercialization and mediatization, particularly as registered by the radio and jazz. In "A Curse for the Saxophone" (1924) he yearns for a more refined acoustic, linking jazz to violence and sin:

When Cain killed Abel to end a perfect day,
He founded a city, called the City of Cain,
And he ordered the saxophones to play.

But give me a city where they play the silver flute,
Where they play a silver flute, at the dawn of the day,
Where the xylophone and saxophone and radio are mute,
And they play the Irish Harp at the end of the day.

(*PVL*, 2:577)

Later in the poem, another assassin, John Wilkes Booth, is heard picking "up a saxophone, grunting and rasping, / The red-hot horn in his hot hands clasping, / And he played a typical radio jazz"; as the speaker declares: "Our nerves all razzed, and our thoughts all jazzed, / Booth and his saxophone started the war!" (*PVL*, 2:578). Clearly, Lindsay wants to disassociate himself from this vulgar noise machine. In a note at the end of the poem, he states that the piece "was dictated by me with Stoddard King at the typewriter," thereby establishing himself as an oral poet who is not the instrument of his own mediation (*PVL*, 2:578). In his 1930 lyric "The Jazz Age," which, we are told, is "To be read and chanted, quite aloud, by an open hearth-fire, with the radio turned off. Reading time: 4 minutes 3 seconds," Lindsay bids a final farewell to the Jazz Age and nostalgically returns home, to a simpler place where the live spoken word prevails: there, he insists, we "will not be shattered by noise," including the "radio squalls" (*PVL*, 2:771, 774).

Lindsay consistently valorizes the live over the mediatized, decrying the separation of body and voice through the magnification of sound. In his book *Every Soul Is a Circus* (1929), Lindsay announces his stern opposition to a range of technologies, denouncing "orchestra, saxophone, megaphone, radio, talking movie, telephone, or other mechanical intruder" as "all a part of the mechanical weight against which poetry and the spoken word has to struggle" (*PVL*, 3:986). For Lindsay, these items tamper with the auratic purity and humane quality of the authentic unenhanced voice, and he sees himself as leading a battle against the amplified forces of consumer capitalism, including the popular phonograph record, which, he says, "has, at present, a mechanical hollowness to which we pray we may never become reconciled. . . . I have recently beheld, from many distances, the Nebraska State Capitol building erected in a transfigured sky-scraper style. We have no voice reproduction machinery which reaches that beauty." To the idea of "setting poetry to music," he groans, "It is jambing one more butterfly down the funnel of our machine-made civilization"; artists, he insists, must "renounce . . . any such mechanical thing which bullies them and moves them toward our overwhelming mechanical Molochs, with the air of someone taking someone to an electric chair."[70]

In spite of Lindsay's feelings about the baseness of audio recording, he sought out the opportunity to magnetize his voice. R. D. Darrell in "Phonographic Insurance on American Art" (April 1931), a newspaper item that Lindsay clipped, states the importance of preserving a voice as rich and indispensable as Lindsay's. Echoing others, Darrell finds of Lindsay's poems that, "Fine as they are to the eye, they are only shells of themselves until they are *sounded*, and Mr. Lindsay's is the only voice that can squeeze out the full richness of their musical juices":

> Fortunately Mr. Lindsay has been able to reach what is probably the largest audience any modern poet had directly addressed. But he cannot recite for ever to new hordes of students as they come on: and the precise vocal tune, which can never be recorded by musical notation on paper, will inevitably be lost unless there is enough common sense alive in the land to take out insurance on some of the finest things in American art. Phonograph records of every poem in this book, exactly as Mr. Lindsay chants it, ought to be made, and be made at once.[71]

Professor Cabell Greet at Columbia University had put Lindsay before the microphone in January 1931; the product of the session was a batch of forty double-sided records embodying some thirty poems. Greet is quoted in Lindsay's obituary in the *New York Times* (December 6, 1931) as saying, "The auditions were made at the request of Mr. Lindsay and include many of his more famous poems, such as 'The Congo,' 'General William Booth Enters Heaven' and 'The Chinese Nightingale.' This is the first time that I know of that records of a poet's voice will be kept for posterity after his death."[72] It would seem that Lindsay's desire to have his voice preserved was an attempt on his part to secure a future for himself and for his poetry, to try to convey something of his vocal presence for posterity, no matter the playback quality.[73] Better a mechanical voice than no voice at all.

It is instructive to set Lindsay next to Edna St. Vincent Millay, perhaps the only person who rivaled him for popularity in the poetry recital world and someone who pioneered poetic use of the "mechanical Moloch" of the radio in order to reach large audiences. On Christmas Day, 1932, Millay began the first of a series of Sunday-night readings of her poems over the air on a nationwide hookup. Some of the thousands of people who heard Millay's voice that night (and every Sunday night for eight weeks running after that) "told her that her voice was as lovely as her poetry": "It's simply intoxicating. Don't, don't ever change, and become stiff or formal or eloquent. . . . You sound so real, so natural, so—so very much alive." (Ironically, in light of her audience's sense of her naturalness, she said that she felt "at times exquisitely unreal.") At the end of that series of radio broadcasts, which Millay described as "exhausting hard work," even she was taken with her voice when she heard it played back to her, remarking, "Quite lovely, isn't it?" Edmund Wilson wrote to her to tell her how much her recordings of her poetry meant to him, and at her friends the Untermeyers in 1913 she moved her hostess almost to tears with her live reading. Louis Untermeyer proclaimed Millay "artless": "There was no other voice like hers in America. It was the sound of the ax on fresh wood."[74]

But if her embrace of the radio sets her apart from Lindsay, her artful performance of gender does not. In recital, she wore elaborate gauzy dresses and scarves, performing "femininity" as Lindsay was performing "masculinity" on stages across America. John Crowe Ransom's condescending characterization of Millay as "rarely and barely very intellectual," as "the best of the poets who are 'popular,' and loved by Circles and Leagues of young ladies," reflects his misogyny and speaks to the fate of the public poet or "poetess" in America.[75] Lindsay actually mentions Millay and her style of vocalization in an unpublished piece titled "Beauty of Word in the United States": "There will be a tiny pantheon built for the poets by the Chicago World's Fair 1933. There bards of all nations will be invited to give their songs, each in his native tongue, his own poems. Let Ruth St. Denis dance in that delicate, sound-proof room, with her softest footfall to the softest voiced whisperers of this United States. People who read as Edna St. Vincent Millay reads."[76] As this statement suggests, he was attracted to her stereotyped "feminine" orality, one at a distance from his own loud "masculine" soundings, which he no longer credited.

During a 1923 reading tour, Millay felt demeaned by the public performances she was giving much as Lindsay did, and, like Lindsay, she too went so far as to wish she could disappear as a star poet: "I hope I shall never write a poem again that more than five people will like."[77] Overcome by her celebrity, she insisted, "I should *never* have consented to read my poems in public. It makes them sound so blatant. I feel like a prostitute."[78] Despite the fact that Lindsay shared with Millay her sentiment about the cheapening effect of recital, he continued to harp on the revivifying effects of a genuine public poetry. In his 1928 poem "Every Soul Is a Circus," which looks ahead to the Chicago World's Fair of 1933, he exhorts his poetic peers to participate fully in American democratic culture—a culture epitomized by P. T. Barnum's circus attractions on parade:

My brothers of the poet-trade,
Leave your ivory towers, and stand
On the porch, and watch this ardent band
And praise, with me,
This Masquerade.

(*PVL*, 2:669)

The speaker's imperative to "Leave your ivory towers" presages beat poet Lawrence Ferlinghetti's populist plea to poets almost fifty years later to "come down," mix with the people, and craft a social poetry. Taking another swipe at jazz ("Oh Radio, Oh Saxophone, Oh Slide Trombone, Oh Horns that moan"), Lindsay goes on in the poem to pronounce the circus and its unmediatized sounds ("Ten thousand years before your jazz he [the lion] roared a deeper rage") as far more pure and genuine (*PVL*, 2:673). "Every Soul Is a Circus" ends with the following performance note:

This poem is not to be set to musical notation. It is not to be identified with any form of musical composition or orchestra. It is to be read with a bardic and troubadour chanting according to the spelling of the words, the manner of Welsh preaching and praying to this day. Let the whispered passages be whispered. Let the reader select certain refrains to be chanted antiphonally with the audience. Let the poem feel at home at an Eisteddfod. (*PVL*, 2:675)

Here Lindsay makes clear that the poem is not to be subjected to mechanical reproduction, imagining it as an occasion to enact "communitas," a shared intimacy that comes from being connected locally with others. This romantic direction to reader-performers is in line with the poet's politics of "the new localism," the belief that *We should make our own home and neighborhood the most democratic, the most beautiful and the holiest in the world.* It is on such a scale, Lindsay felt, that the promise of America would be proven.

Like Mark Twain before him, Lindsay was forced to reconcile his artistic integrity with his desire to be popular. Indeed, Lindsay refers to the literary critic Van Wyck Brooks's Freudian study *The Ordeal of Mark Twain* (1920) in a letter, and rebuts the charge Brooks (one of "our psychoanalyzers") makes there that Twain "was a pessimist and a cynic from the very start" (*L*, 225): He seems to see how the demands of being a public performer turned his mood in that direction. Unlike Twain, Lindsay did not bow in the end to the pressures of American market capitalism, and his suicide in 1932 is in part a result of his refusal of and by those business interests. The agon he underwent stands as a lesson and challenge to all those "brother-poets of the trade"—and sister-poets—to come.[79]

CHAPTER 3

"The Black Man Speaks": Langston Hughes, the New Negro, and the Sounds of Citizenship

Put perpetual motion in his arms,
Fill him full of the dynamite of thy power,
Anoint him all over with the oil of thy salvation,
And set his tongue on fire.

    —JAMES WELDON JOHNSON, FROM "LISTEN, LORD—A PRAYER"

I swear to the Lord
I still can't see
Why Democracy means
Everybody but me.

    —LANGSTON HUGHES, FROM "THE BLACK MAN SPEAKS"

PERHAPS SURPRISINGLY, in light of the sometimes racist imperson-ations/ventriloquizings of earlier white poets, black spoken-word artists coming of age in the 1920s looked back to both Whitman and Lindsay as models for their performance of race and nation and theorizing of the rela-tion between speech and text. Hughes, for one, visited Whitman's Cam-den, New Jersey, home in 1927, and explained on that occasion that his own verse was shaped by Whitman's public poetics: "poetry should be di-rect, comprehensible, and the epitome of simplicity."[1] In 1945, Hughes wrote "The Ceaseless Rings of Walt Whitman," an introduction to an an-thology of Whitman's poetry for young readers that emphasizes his spirit of inclusiveness and public-mindedness in a Cold War climate: "In this atomic age of ours, when the ceaseless rings are multiplied a millionfold, the Whitman spiral is upward and outward toward a freer, better life for all, not narrowing downward toward death and destruction. Singing the great-ness of the individual, Whitman also sings the greatness of unity, coopera-tion, and understanding."[2] Stemming from his work on that introduction,

Hughes prepared another anthology of poems by Whitman, this one centered on the subjects of blacks and Native Americans to be titled "Walt Whitman's Darker Brothers"; although he never found a publisher for it, he strongly felt where Whitman's sympathies lay, and in one of his columns for the *Chicago Defender* he defended Whitman from the charge, made by Lorenzo Dow Turner of Roosevelt College in Chicago, of his being "pro-slavery and anti-Negro" (*LLH,* 2:225).

In addition to Whitman, Lindsay meant much to Hughes, on both a personal and professional level. In 1924 Hughes was working as a busboy at the Wardman Park Hotel in Washington, DC, when Lindsay came there to give a reading; Hughes describes the scene in his autobiography *The Big Sea* (1940):

> That afternoon I wrote out three poems, "Jazzonia," "Negro Dancers," and "The Weary Blues," on some pieces of paper and put them in the pocket of my white bus boy's coat. In the evening when Mr. Lindsay came down to dinner, quickly I laid them beside his plate and went away, afraid to say anything to so famous a poet, except to tell him I liked his poems and that these were poems of mine. I looked back once and saw Mr. Lindsay reading the poems, as I picked up a tray of dirty dishes from a side table and started for the dumb-waiter.
>
> The next morning on the way to work, as usual I bought a paper—and there I read that Vachel Lindsay had discovered a Negro bus boy poet! At the hotel the reporters were already waiting for me. They interviewed me. And they took my picture, holding up a tray of dirty dishes in the middle of the dining room. The picture, copyrighted by Underwood and Underwood, appeared in lots of newspapers throughout the country. It was my first publicity break.[3]

As Hughes's biographer Arnold Rampersad rightly points out, Lindsay did not "discover" Hughes, since Hughes already had won a prize for his poetry; nevertheless, Hughes did not miss the opportunity to capitalize on a famous poet's generosity, allowing himself in effect to be rediscovered by Lindsay for the publicity it would bring. That publicity, it was hoped, would translate into popularity and an income on which to live, but Lindsay, who once had been where Hughes was, warned him in 1925 to buck the tide: "Do not let any lionizers stampede you. Hide and write and study and think. I know what factions do. Beware of them. I know what flatterers do. Beware of them. I know what lionizers do. Beware of them" (L, 364). Later, after Lindsay's death, Hughes would defend him, too, against charges of racism, stating that "personally, I regard him as having been a great poet" (LLH, 13).

The African American poet Sterling Brown also responded to Lindsay's example, but with far more ambivalence: on the one hand, he hailed Lindsay's rhythmic effects (the "marvelous ragtime fling" of "The Congo," for instance), but found, on the other hand, that his poetic performances, while formally adept, were at heart racist, his portrayal of blacks in "The Congo" superficial and condescending.[4] In Brown's verse parody of "The Congo" entitled "The New Congo," subheaded "With no apologies to Vachel Lindsay," he exposes the racist attitudes on which he believes that poem rests:

> Then I saw the Uncle Tom, creeping through the black
> Cutting through the bigwoods with his trousers slack
> With hinges on his knees, and with putty up his back.[5]

The replacement of the "heathen" Congo with Uncle Tom, a stock minstrel figure, points up Brown's view of Lindsay's racist conception of the transfiguring force of white culture; rather than hailing Lindsay's delineation of black character as authentic folk expression, Brown pronounces his effort "phony."[6] Here again the matter of authenticity looms large, in this case in the performance of poetry and ethnic and national affiliation by New Negro poets who have not always been authorized to speak, and who begin to be regarded as racial "spokesmen." For Brown, Whitman was another matter, and he is clearly under his spell when he attests that "the Negro must write so that whatsoever touches his book touches a man," a reissue of that earlier poet's powerful fiction of presence.[7]

James Weldon Johnson, the author of "Lift Every Voice and Sing" (often referred to as the Negro National Anthem), has little to say about Lindsay, but does cite his reading of Leaves of Grass in 1900 as a turning point in his artistic career. Explaining that he was "engulfed and submerged by the book," Johnson attributes to it his having "got a sudden realization of the artificiality of conventionalized Negro dialect poetry," a kind of poetry he had been writing under the influence of his friend, Paul Laurence Dunbar, whom he first met after hearing him read a poem at the World's Columbian Exposition in 1893. As Johnson came to see, Dunbar cannot break the racist mold of dialect poetry that he inherits, blaming it on the fact that Dunbar "wrote mainly for the delectation of an audience that was an outside group," namely whites.[8]

Although a negative example in some ways, it is also the case that Dunbar provided these New Negro poets with a crucial positive model of the cultural work of poetry recital. As Lorenzo Thomas has observed, "Because he was a talented humorist, Dunbar's recitals were above all entertaining; but his was clearly always entertainment with a message. . . . His message, made explicit in his journalistic pieces, was a celebration of African American kinship and strong, moral families and communities."[9] His effort to uplift the race predicts Hughes's, just as critical response to Hughes's on- and off-page performances smacks of that directed at Dunbar's. Reviewers claimed Dunbar's dialect poetry as the "real" Dunbar, its authenticity secured by the fact that "no one but a real negro" could write as he does. His essentialized presence was felt as well in his oral performance of his verse; as Max Bennett Thrasher wrote in the *New York Evening Post:* "No one can read his [Dunbar's] own production as well as he can, and being a good singer as well as a reciter, he frequently gives entertainments all by himself."[10] By attending to the performance, or embodiment, of versions of "blackness" in the work of New Negro poets and the tropes of utterance and audition that constitute it, we can begin to hear how such performance accrues radical political meaning.

THE SERMONIC STRAIN AND THE COLOR LINE

The best-known oratorical figure in African American culture in the 1920s and 1930s certainly was the preacher, and the sermonic poetry composed by black artists between the wars testifies to the pervasiveness of his influence. For both preacher and poet, the question of transcription and textual performance was unavoidable: how effective can the printed page be in transmitting the spirit infusing a live oratorical event? In *Black Preaching* (1970) Henry H. Mitchell speculates that "Perhaps one reason many of the finest Black preachers avoid publication is that they have seen the transcripts and sensed the loss of so much that is vital when the Word that is *preached* is reduced to words to be *read,* and they judged their own work not suitable for publication." Mitchell is writing to future black theological students and to whites properly "oriented to Black religious culture," and further notes that sermons "in the Black tradition, were preached and *heard*, not written to be read. Much of their real impact, therefore, is lost, unless one knows how they would have sounded and, in his mind, turns up the volume as he reads."[11] He does not provide recital cues along with his transcriptions of sermons to aid the uninitiated in their vocalization, since he sees himself as addressing an audience (white and black) that already is accustomed to the paralinguistic features of sermonic performance through direct experience.

In *Say Amen, Brother!* (1951), William H. Pipes records on the page specimens of "Old-Time Negro Preaching" from Macon County, Georgia, and, while he admits that recordings of the sermons in print "are unable to reproduce all" aspects of the performance and its atmosphere, he believes that they can "go a long way toward a true presentation of these characteristics"; unlike Mitchell, Pipes works to create a context through bracketed descriptions of the proxemics of the speaker and the dialogic relationship between speaker and audience: "[Chuckles.]"; "['No, he ain't,' from the audience.]"; "['No, no,' from the audience.]."[12] Noting the "freedom of expression" that reigns in the black church, Pipes observes: "The Black worshipper does not merely acknowledge the Word delivered by the preacher; he talks back!"[13] (The Reverend C. L. Franklin, father of Aretha Franklin, addresses squarely this pattern of call-and-response in black sermonics: " 'I hope I can get somebody to pray with me to-night,' he began, warming them up, 'because you know, I'm a *Negro* preacher, and I like to talk to people and have people talk *back* to me.' ")[14] Pipes also recognizes the unstable nature of the sermonic text—the improvisational quality of pulpit performance ("*nothing* is certain or fixed")—and the way in which tone in preaching "signal[s] a kind of affirmation of Black identity which in turn begets a real religious experience," that is, the way it is able to authenticate racially the performance and the performer.[15] Finally, he points up "the virile phenomenon" that is "Black folk-preaching," thereby highlighting the politics of gender embedded in such performance, a politics that is alive for Whitman and Lindsay as well.[16]

The transcription of black sermonic performance bears on the charged issue of racial representation in America at this time, both in popular and poetic culture. One white recorder of such performance—Dr. Edward Clarkson Leverett (Ned) Adams—sought to provide a sense of its dialogism through his performance-centered texts. In *Congaree Sketches* (1927), which contains "Scenes from Negro Life in the Swamps of Congaree," Adams in-

corporates the call-and-response pattern of the black sermon into his transcription of that event. In "Fragment of a Negro Sermon" the preacher's
words are punctuated at intervals by the voices of the congregation:

Our Brother is dead,
He rests from de labor
An' he sleeps,—

(Shrill voice of sister)   He sleeps, Oh, he sleeps!

Wey de tall pines grow,

(Another voice)   On the banks of a river.

On the banks of a river.

(Several voices)   On the banks of a river.

In the same ethnographic rendering we find the stage directions, *"Voices
chanting throughout congregation"* and *"Shrill voice of Sister and taken up by
congregation chanting and swaying."*[17] Upon reading Adams, Sterling Brown
could tell that he had special access to the private world of African Americans, one denied most whites: "It is clear that he has overheard, or been allowed to hear, a great deal. And that is why his work is so superior to local
color" (100).[18] James Weldon Johnson (then executive secretary of the
NAACP) also sensed Adams's sympathies—his distance from racist caricature—calling the introduction to *Congaree Sketches* "one of the finest ap-
proaches by the written word to interracial understanding and good will
ever made." In 1931 Adams attended a poetry reading by Langston Hughes
in Columbia, South Carolina, and invited the poet to his farm lodge outside of town afterward.[19]

Zora Neale Hurston also embeds marks of orality in her renderings of
black preacherly performance. One sermon that Hurston heard in Florida
on May 3, 1929, entitled "The Wounds of Jesus," a sermon that dramatically represents Christ's crucifixion and that she puts in the mouth of the
preacher John Pearson in her novel *Jonah's Gourd Vine* (1934), was assessed
by a *New York Times* reviewer of the book as "too good, too brilliantly
splashed with poetic imagery to be product of any one Negro preacher."[20]

That sermonic poem (with mild dialect—"de"; "dat"—and occasional clipped word endings) includes such expressions as "ha!" at the ends of some lines and attempts to transcribe the actual sound of the speaker in drawn-out language such as "Aa-aah!" "Oh-h-hhh!" and "I can see-eee-ee."[21] (As Hurston explains elsewhere, "The 'hah' [or 'ha!'] is a breathing device, done rhythmically to punctuate the lines. The congregation wants to hear the preacher breathing or 'straining'"; evidence of such "straining," she argues, is a hallmark of black sermonic art.)[22] On May 8, 1934, Hurston wrote to Johnson expressing her disappointment at the white *Times* critic's ignorance:

> He means well, I guess, but I never saw such a lack of information about us. It just seems that he is unwilling to believe that a Negro preacher could have so much poetry in him. When you and I (who seem to be the only ones even among Negroes who recognize the barbaric poetry in their sermons) know that there are hundreds of preachers who are equalling that sermon weekly. He does not know that merely being a good man is not enough to hold a Negro preacher in an important charge. He must also be an artist. He must be both a poet and an actor of a very high order, and then he must have the voice and figure. He does not realize or is unwilling to admit that the light that shone from GOD'S TROMBONES was handed to you, as was the sermon to me in Jonah's Gourd Vine.

She goes on in the letter to urge Johnson to write an article about "Negro preachers that would explain their hold upon their people truthfully," and expresses again her sense that they "are the first artists, the ones intelligible to the masses." In another letter (to Lewis Gannett) a few days later, Hurston insists that "great poems are breathed out every Sunday in our numerous churches," but that the "Niggerati," that is, the "Negro literati," do not recognize the sermon as art: "Only James Weldon Johnson and I give it praise. . . . [T]he truth is, the greatest poets among us are in our pulpits and the greatest poetry has come out of them. It is merely not set down. It passes from mouth to mouth as in the days of Homer."[23]

Of the genesis of his book of "sermon-poems," *God's Trombones* (1927), Johnson recalls listening to a famous black evangelist in a church in Kansas City one Sunday night, in a performance that fired his imagination: although the preacher began with "a formal sermon from a formal text," sounding "flat" and with "the congregation . . . apathetic and dozing," he then shifted register "and began intoning the rambling Negro sermon that begins with the creation of the world, touches various high spots in the trials and tribulations of the Hebrew children, and ends with the Judgment Day":

> There was an instantaneous change in the preacher and in the congregation. He was free, at ease, and the complete master of himself and his hearers. The congregation responded to him as a willow to the winds. He strode the pulpit up and down, and brought into play the full gamut of a voice that excited my envy. He intoned, he moaned, he pleaded—he blared, he crashed, he thundered. A woman sprang to her feet, uttered a piercing scream, threw her handbag to the pulpit, striking the preacher full in the chest, whirled round several times, and fainted. The congregation reached a state of ecstasy. I was fascinated by this exhibition; moreover, something primordial in me was stirred. Before the preacher finished, I took a slip of paper from my pocket and somewhat surreptitiously jotted down some ideas for my first poem ["The Creation"].

In *God's Trombones,* Johnson works to represent the "tone and timbre" of "the old-time Negro preacher's voice," but also "to take the primitive stuff of the old-time Negro sermon and, through art-governed expression, make it into poetry."[24] In other words, he seeks to transform folk material into a "higher" art, much as Lindsay labored to clarify the coarser elements of the popular stage into verse he called "the Higher Vaudeville."

Breaking with Lindsay, though, Johnson does not present the reader with a script but rather with a transcript, a record of a performance event, and a minimally coded one at that, flowing from his stated belief that there is "no way of recreating the atmosphere—the fervor of the congregation, the amens and hallelujahs, the undertone of singing which was often a soft accompaniment to parts of the sermon; nor the personality of the preacher—his physical magnetism, his gestures and gesticulations, his changes of tempo, his pauses for effect, and, more than all, his tones of voice." As Johnson feels, kinesics (gestures and movements) and other paralinguistic features are not really representable in print: One must have heard a performance like it before fully to hear the poem on the page, applying that firsthand aural experience to the scripted utterance. In the preface to *God's Trombones,* he notes that in the first poem, "Listen, Lord—A Prayer," he has "not attempted to set down" "the chorus of responses which give it [the preliminary prayer] an antiphonal quality," figuring that such dialogism cannot be captured adequately in the medium of print (*GT*, 10–11). Johnson advises that three poems in the book—"Listen, Lord," "The Crucifixion," and "The Judgment Day"—"would better be intoned than read," but then goes on to say that "the intoning practiced by the old-time preacher is a thing next to impossible to describe; it must be heard, and it is extremely difficult to imitate even when heard" (*GT*, 10). Here is how "Listen, Lord" is articulated in print:

> We come this morning—
> Like empty pitchers to a full fountain,
> With no merits of our own.
> O Lord—open up a window of heaven,
> And lean out far over the battlements of glory,
> And listen this morning.

What has been referred to as Johnson's "phonographism" is on full display here: just as he sensed that ragtime music embodies a "telling inarticulacy," that its rhythms "can't be put on . . . paper," so he believed that sermonic transcription is unable to dissolve the racialized difference between writing and voice.[25] In this invocation, God is called on to give ear to the words of his people, but the full contextual performance of that chant is open only to the initiated.

Occasions for such hearings by most white Americans were rare, and Johnson is able to cite only one recent theatrical staging that such an outsider-reader might draw on: "The finest, and perhaps the only demonstration ever given to a New York public, was the intoning of the dream in Ridgely Torrence's Rider of Dreams by Opal Cooper of the Negro Players at the Madison Square Theatre in 1917." Johnson gives a general sense of what intoning entails in his preface to *God's Trombones* ("a matter of crescendo and diminuendo in the intensity—a rising and falling between plain speaking and wild chanting"), but again refuses to cue the reader in the text of the poem itself or in its margins ("Oh-h-hhh!"s and "No-oooo-ooo-oo-o!"s are not in favor here), as he insists that a racially authenticated ear be brought to the text, that is, the listening ear of the insider (*GT*, 10). While Johnson does attempt to score the voice on the page to some extent through his prosodic arrangement ("The tempos of the preacher I have endeavored to indicate by the line arrangement of the poems, and a certain sort of pause that is marked by a quick intaking and an audible expulsion of the breath I have indicated by dashes"), and gives a general indication of how to hear the preacher's characteristic "syncopation of speech" ("The rhythmical stress of this syncopation is partly obtained by a marked silent fraction of a beat; frequently this silent fraction is filled in by a hand clap"), he decides that the deciphering of paralanguage ("the crowding in of many syllables or the lengthening out of a few") ultimately "must be left to the reader's ear" (*GT,* 10–11).

What Johnson says about his eschewal of dialect in these poems ("The old-time Negro preachers, though they actually used dialect in their ordinary intercourse, stepped out from its narrow confines when they preached") bears on his reluctance to construct performance-centered texts: "the colored poet in the United States . . . needs to find a form that will express the racial spirit by symbols from within rather than by symbols from without—such as the mere mutilation of English spelling and pronunciation" (*GT,* 8). As he believed, symbols to denote recitation style in his poetry in essence would mutilate it, making it appear "queer," as some regarded Lindsay's scripted verse; they also would cater to the outsider, deracinating the printed word in the process. Although Eric J. Sundquist argues that authority and authenticity attach to Hurston's folk dialectal performance more than to Johnson's more "formal" poetry (as a sign of her ambivalence, Hurston herself charged Johnson with "passing for colored" in his life and art, thus impeaching his racial integrity), to agree is to miss the highly stylized effort on Johnson's part to reveal the performativity and multiformity of race, his disavowal of an essentialized notion of black speech.[26]

Some critics expressed frustration at the lack of oral cues in *God's Trombones,* and their racially tinged interpretations hinge on their sense of how successful Johnson's text is as script. In 1963 Jean Wagner, a white scholar, responded to the sermon-poems with ambivalence, finding fault with the fact that all are in the form of monologue rather than dialogue between preacher and congregation: "Here the presence of the latter [dialogue] is not even suggested, as it might have been by appropriate monologue technique—for example, by using the repeated question, as Irwin Russell and Page and Gordon [all dialect writers] had done. Nor is the monologue able to reproduce the oratorical gestures, always so important for the Negro preacher, who is equally actor and orator"; he also finds that Johnson has shown an "excessive zeal in idealizing and refining—or, in other words, for having thought it necessary to impose too much respectability on essentially popular material whose crudity is one of its charms, as it is also a voucher for its authenticity. His sermons are still folklore, perhaps, but stylized folklore."[27] Wagner calls into question the racial authenticity of Johnson's poems, claiming that the poems themselves are in effect passing, "garbed in the distinction and respectability of whiteness," and, thus, "at odds with that total coming to awareness marked by the Negro Renaissance." The white poet Joseph Moncure March also criticized *God's Trombones* for not indicating in the poems how they are to be performed. In "Is Negro Exhorting High Art, Too?" (1927), he states that the importance of Johnson's sermonic poems "is chiefly one of recordance, and their relation to Afro-American as such is dubious," with the absence of dialect and paralinguistic cues rendering them, to his mind, incomplete; as he finds, there is "too much lacking, too great a gap to be filled in by imagination," and so too little "of the emotional side . . . seeps through."[28]

Not everyone shared this view. Joseph Auslander hailed Johnson's sermonic poems as "native, necessary, valid," "Racial at the root."[29] Sterling Brown noted of *God's Trombones* that "material which is usually made ludicrous, is here invested with dignity, power and beauty"; he especially was pleased (as was Alain Locke, who included "The Creation" in his landmark 1925 anthology *The New Negro*) by Johnson's refusal to bow to racist literary convention: "Convinced that dialect smacks too much of the minstrel stage, Johnson attempts to give truth to folk idioms rather than mere misspellings."[30] (As Johnson felt, dialect was "an instrument with but two complete stops, pathos and humor," and preachers did not preach in dialect anyway, but rather "were all saturated with the sublime phraseology of the Hebrew prophets and steeped in the idioms of King James English.") Brown compared Johnson's achievement favorably to Lindsay's poems in the voices of black preachers, namely "Simon Legree" and "John Brown," judging that Lindsay "preceded James Weldon Johnson's *God's Trombones* without equalling them: the short rhymed lines are not so near the mark as Johnson's chanting free verse."[31] Also unlike Johnson's, Lindsay's sermon-poems are performance-centered: in the case of "John Brown," Lindsay interpolates the line "*What did you see in Palestine?*" at regular junctures, with a headnote advising that the poem is "To be sung by a leader and chorus, the leader singing the body of the poem, while the chorus interrupts with the question"; "Simon Legree" is "To be read in your own variety of negro dialect" and includes an italicized line at the end of most stanzas that appears intended to designate its choral nature as well as its emphatic delivery (*PVL*, 1:318, 320). Lindsay's texts throb with recital cues that confer power on the (white) reader arguably at the expense of the authenticity and racial veracity of the material.

In reader responses to Johnson's printed text, the question of audience necessarily arises: Who is authorized to hear these sermons as printed and who is left in the acoustical dark? In his essay "The Dilemma of the Negro Artist" (1928) Johnson addresses the problem of the "double audience" (blacks on the one hand, and whites on the other) for which black authors perforce must write, looking toward the day when black and white audiences would be combined, "fuse[d] into one interested and approving audience."[32] In her discussion of Johnson's song lyrics, Joan Rubin frames the problem as being one of "how to sustain the competing claims of Americanness and ethnicity, how to appeal to white audiences without betraying one's own people in the act of 'passing,'" and that is precisely the (color) line that Johnson is toeing throughout *God's Trombones.*[33]

Johnson composed "The Creation," the first sermon-poem in the book after the preliminary prayer, in 1918 and published it two years later bearing the subtitle "A Negro Sermon" in *The Freeman.* He reports in his autobiography that he chose for the poem "a loose rhythmic instead of a strict metric form, because it was the first only that could accommodate itself to the movement, the abandon, the changes of tempo, and the characteristic syncopations of the primitive material."[34] In the beginning (of the poem) is the spoken word, alone and resonant in an originating universe:

> Then God smiled,
> And the light broke,
> And the darkness rolled up on one side,
> And the light stood shining on the other,
> And God said, "That's good!"

> (*GT,* 17)

The preacher here is the single stage presence, adopting a voice of "orotundity," as Johnson instructs in the preface of *God's Trombones* should be used when reciting "The Creation"; such a voice, characterized by strength, fullness, and clearness—the utterance that issues from a rounded mouth—at times even ventriloquizes God ("And God said . . ."), sounding sonorously out of a racialized "Darkness,"[35] that same primordialism that the Kansas City preacher activated in Johnson.

In the only known recording of Johnson reading the poem (at Columbia University in 1935), we sense his plangency and orotundity. He sounds as a trombone, "the instrument," Johnson remarks, "possessing above all others the power to express the wide and varied range of emotions encompassed by the human voice": the voice is deep and oracular as it plays up and down the chromatic scale. His intoned lines sometimes pitch up at the end, sometimes down into a quiet colloquialism ("And God said: That's good!"). He lengthens some words for dramatic effect ("roooolled"; "ablaaaazing") and heightens and diminishes intensity and tempo in order to give us a humanized picture of a black God at the moment of Creation, "Like a mammy bending over her baby." Carl Van Vechten marveled at Johnson's intoning of these sermons, and notes the many times that he had occasion to hear Johnson in recital, including in Johnson's apartment, his own apartment, and many other people's houses.[36] The image of the black figure in the black-and-white drawing by Aaron Douglas facing the poem on the page accentuates the radically racialized performance of identity (of *self*-creation) that the poem simultaneously stages.

For Johnson, the figurative motive of vocal performance was as strong as it was for Whitman and Lindsay. In "Listen, Lord," Johnson first presents the twin tropes of orality and aurality, as the prayer leader (sometimes it would be a woman, Johnson tells us in the preface) calls on God to inspirit the preacher ("this man of God"), to "Pin his ear to the wisdom-post, / And make his words sledge hammers of truth"; as the leader exhorts,

> Put perpetual motion in his arms,
> Fill him full of the dynamite of thy power,
> Anoint him all over with the oil of thy salvation,
> And set his tongue on fire.

(GT, 14)

In this invocation the speaker understands the full range of resources—linguistic, paralinguistic, kinesic—that must be instilled in order for the preacherly performance to succeed. In the penultimate poem "Let My People Go," Johnson again metaphorizes the potency of the performed word. There the preacher relates that Moses, before the burning bush, "heard the voice, / But he saw no man." This disembodied voice takes a variety of turns, sounding as a "still, small voice" before swelling to "a voice of thunder" (*GT,* 45, 46). God's oratorical voice is mimicked by the black preacher, whose voice modulates, we are told, "from a sepulchral whisper into a crashing thunder clap" (*GT,* 5). When in the poem Moses confesses, "I'm slow of tongue," and God replies, "I will be thy mouth and I will be thy tongue," we hear rehearsed for us an originary ventriloquism, with divinity speaking through the medium of Moses (*GT,* 46, 47). Of course, the intermediary position that Moses occupies ("Thus saith . . .") is not unlike that of the reciter of the poem, who is vocally mediating the "old-time Negro preachers," who in turn (at times) are mimicking the voice of God. This sort of mimicry is not an instance of vocal deception, nor does it resemble the cross-racialized mimicry that underwrites blackface minstrelsy; rather, it allegorizes the channeling of an authentic black subjectivity.

Langston Hughes would take his own crack at the form of the sermon-poem some fifteen years later. His parodic "Sunday Morning Prophecy" (1942), which carries as a headnote the contextualizing statement, "An old Negro minister concludes his sermon in his loudest voice, having previously pointed out the sins of this world," begins in medias res (". . . and now") and entails a variety of exclamatory statements in imitation of the preacherly voice: "Oh-ooo-oo-o!"; "Lord-d-d-d-ah"; "No-oooo-ooo-oo-o!" (*CPLH,* 242). At the close of the poem, the minister shepherds his parishioners into the church, revealing his interest in more than just the state of their souls: "be saved—/ And give freely / In the collection basket." Hughes's scoring verifies his artistic interest in encoding on the page qualities of oralness, even as it works to convey through the radical deformity of language something of the moral and spiritual deformity of this cultural practitioner. Hughes's sly angle on the genre testifies to his nuanced performance of "blackness" and the fraught politics of textuality, orality, and aurality—a politics symbolized neatly by Hughes's short story character Simple's command to his audience "Listen fluently now!" before he is about to recite a poem he has written about Martin Luther King, Jr.[37]

RECITATIONS OF RACE AND NATION

Hughes was ever seeking to sharpen and extend his publicity through live performance. After the publication of his first book, *The Weary Blues,* in 1925, Hughes read on January 15, 1926, at the Playhouse in Washington,

DC, to a mixed-race audience, with an admission fee of one dollar, and complained in a letter the next day that, although he had chosen "a Seventh Street bluesman, funky and unfettered, to howl during the intermission," Alain Locke "sneaked in" a more sedate musician in deference to "all the respectable black folks and whites who would come" to the show (qtd. *LLH*, 1:123). (Some cite this event as the first ever to combine poetry and jazz.) Hughes kept up a brisk schedule and on January 31, 1926, gave a reading near Columbia University, where, afterward, he "signed books until his wrist ached." Requests for appearances piled up, and so did Hughes's concerns about becoming a regular performer. It was not long before he grew weary of the demands of public recital. Just before heading off to attend college at Lincoln University in the winter of 1926, he wrote Carl Van Vechten, alluding to his many fans who would recite his poetry to him when they met him, "You see, I'm going into seclusion, weary of the world, like Pearl White when she retired to her convent. And I hope nobody there reads poetry" (qtd. *LLH*, 1:124). After entering into a contract with a patron, Charlotte Mason, in 1928, he is relieved that he will be able to be more selective about where he recites: "I no longer read my poetry to ladies clubs, Y.W.C.A., and the leading literary societies in places like Columbus—as I did for two winters." By this time, as his biographer Arnold Rampersad reports, "He had begun to hate his own poetry and being exhibited to schoolchildren as a model or 'like a prize dog'" (*LLH*, 1:158). Lindsay's early words of warning no doubt rang in his ears.

Hughes soon would have a change of heart, however, newly determined to take his poetry on the road—into the Deep South and ultimately to the Midwest, Texas, and California—to reach an untapped audience of average black Americans.[38] He had his encouragers. Mary McLeod Bethune, founder of a school for black women, told Hughes, "You must go all over the South with your poems. People need poetry."[39] She was echoing Zora Neale Hurston, who had told him (in a letter dated November 22, 1928) "to make a loafing tour of the South like the blind Homer, singing your songs. . . . You are the poet of the people and your subjects are crazy about you. Why not?" (qtd. *LLH*, 1:212–13). On August 5, 1931, Hughes wrote to the black writer Walter White, informing him, "I'd like to make a reading tour of the whole South in order to build up a sustaining Negro audience for my work and that of other Negro writers and artists. I want to create an interest in racial expression through books, and do what I can to encourage young literary talent among our people." He would need a car to get around, he says, so as to avoid the segregated railroad, and imagined the enormous benefits of a concerted effort to dig in native soil: "I feel that a consecutive tour of the South would do a great deal to link the younger writers with the black public they must have, if their work is to be racially sound" (qtd. *LLH,* 1:214). Hughes's mission, then, is to authenticate himself and his message through direct contact with the black masses—to create a "racially sound" and sounding poetry—in an effort to forge a viable black public sphere.

In performance Hughes knew how to pitch himself to white audiences as well, and his crossover appeal is key to his artistic success. Seeking financial backing for his southern tour, he performed his poetry in 1931 before a convention of YMCA officials in New York, and, as Rampersad records, "Apparently his performance was flawless; charming and unthreatening, yet powerful. Hughes seemed to one white official 'a rare personality. His sheer simplicity captivates one.' Even white Southerners in the audience seemed to like him" (*LLH,* 1:214). Once on tour (he set out in late 1931), Hughes continued to captivate, developing a rapport with his audiences, despite dire predictions: "Lots of New Yorkers tried to tell me that I would have no audiences in the South, or understanding" (qtd. *LLH,* 1:214). Such was not the case: A triumphant Hughes wrote in March 1932, after his tour had ended, "I have met the South. . . . I've never had a finer response anywhere, or met more beautiful people," and thus he stood convinced that "poetry can mean something to uneducated people" (qtd. *LLH,* 233–34). He focused on black schools and colleges, and often got as much as one hundred dollars for an appearance, but his performances frequently drew whites and blacks, and so stood in stark contrast to the segregated conditions that stamped Lindsay's recital at the Wardman Park Hotel, from which Hughes remembers being barred ("I wanted very much to hear him read his poems, but I knew they did not admit colored people to the auditorium").[40]

In a chapter of the second installment of his autobiography *I Wonder as I Wander* (1956) entitled "Making Poetry Pay," a heading that does not hide the economic motive behind his performance ventures, Hughes explains the nature of his poetic program, recalling, "By midwinter [of 1932] I had worked out a 'public routine' of reading my poetry that almost never failed to provoke, after each poem, some sort of audible audience response—laughter, applause, a grunt, a groan, a sigh, or an 'Amen!'"[41] Hughes tells how he would orchestrate the attention of his audience through the careful ordering of his poems (much like Lindsay), with the more humorous material toward the front: "I wanted them to laugh a lot early in the program, so that later in the evening they would not laugh when I read poems like 'Porter.'" If he saw that his audience was becoming "restless—as audiences sometimes will, no matter what a speaker is saying—or if I looked down from the platform and noticed someone about to go to sleep, I would pull out my ace in the hole, a poem called 'Cross.'" In addition, Hughes would modulate his tone of voice when reading to keep his hearers interested and alert and to enhance dramatically the content of individual lines: Some parts of "Cross," Hughes notes, are to be read "in a loud voice," others "in a more subdued tone," and still others "in a low, sad, thoughtful tragic vein"; at the end of the poem, "I would let my voice trail off into a lonely silence. Then I would stand quite still for a long time, because I knew I had the complete attention of my listeners again." Often at the end of an evening's program "after a resume of the racial situation in our country, with an optimistic listing of past achievements on the part of Negroes, and future possibilities," he would recite "I, Too, Sing America."[42] His design was meant to instill hope and to remind African Americans of the gains that they had made. A review of a November 7, 1931, reading at Hampton Institute, where Hughes was observed "swaying the emotions of his large audience, now into hilarious guffaws, then into a death-like silence," attests to his performative mastery (qtd. *LLH*, 1:223).

In his recital of his poetry across America, Hughes was seeking to educate and entertain, and in the process he also was performing "blackness," with the timbre of his voice in recital serving as an index of his intentions. Carter Wesley in the *Houston Informer* noted of Hughes's oral style: "He read his poems with precise and elegant diction—even those written in the blues stanza form: His purpose was not to impersonate the unlettered, but to elevate their idiom to a plane where its poetic qualities would be recognized"; refusing a stage accent, Hughes effectively distanced himself from the minstrel tradition and its racist caricatures.[43] It was not "impersonation," then, that lay at the heart of his aesthetic, but rather "personation": the presentation of a racially genuine person who could be seen and heard as both black and literate, a figure worthy of full enfranchisement. A reviewer for the *Nashville Banner* (January 30, 1932) succinctly points up the racial dynamics of Hughes's vocalism, as well as its political overtones: "He does not speak for the Negro. He speaks as a Negro" (qtd. *LLH*, 1:226). The sense here is that Hughes embodies "blackness" on and off the page and thus serves as a self-authenticating racialized presence.

Hughes is cited on the back flap of the *Langston Hughes Reader* (1958) as "the unchallenged spokesman of the American Negro," a title that charges Hughes with the duty of politically representing all African Americans. Through his advocacy, though, Hughes, like Johnson, who recognized "the fixing effects" of dialect in minstrelsy, deliberately tried to unfix racial identity in his stagings of the spoken word, as he sought to allow blacks to speak for themselves. If in minstrelsy dialect served to "remind white consciousness that black men and women are *mis-speakers* bereft of humanity," Johnson and Hughes, in their different ways, sought to illustrate the African American citizen's essential humanity as speakers whose utterances authenticated them racially and simultaneously proved their Americanness in an evolving, contentious democracy.

One set of poems particularly important in Hughes's performance of race in the context of the struggle for full American citizenship are the performance-centered texts of *The Negro Mother and Other Dramatic Recitations* (1931)—texts that are scripted so that ordinary African Americans could activate them through voice and gesture and thereby enact their cultural identities through them. Hughes wrote Prentiss Taylor (October 13, 1931), who with Hughes started Golden Stair Press with the financial aid of Carl Van Vechten, that for some time he had believed that "the modern Negro Art Movement" was "largely over the heads, and out of reach, of the masses of the Negro people"; he had noticed in recent black poetry "a distinct lack of rhymed poems dramatizing current racial interests in simple, understandable verse, pleasing to the ear, and suitable for reading aloud, or for recitation in school, churches, lodges, etc.," and so had written a group of "unpretentious" poems to fit that bill (qtd. *LLH,* 1:221). Hughes decided to distribute *The Negro Mother* himself on his southern tour. An ad for the twenty-five-cent booklet of "ballads" that appeared in his book *Scottsboro Limited* (1932) describes the poems as "passionately lyrical representations of widely known and well-beloved Negro characters delineated in a broadly popular manner not associated with Negro poetry since the death of Paul Lawrence [*sic*] Dunbar . . . suitable for recitation by amateurs in schools, churches, and clubs." Notably, though, unlike Dunbar's, Hughes's "Negro characters" would not be speaking in dialect. *The Negro Mother* went through seven printings and sold about 1,700 copies; in Birmingham in February 1932, copies "sold like reefers on 131st Street," Hughes joked to Van Vechten.[44]

While Hughes performed live on a regular basis, he also wanted certain

of his poems, particularly those of *The Negro Mother*, to function successfully as scripts for others to perform theatrically in the public sphere. As
preface to one of these pieces, "The Colored Soldier," Hughes explains that
it is "A dramatic recitation to be done in the half-dark by a young brown
fellow who has a vision of his brother killed in France while fighting for the
United States of America. Martial music on a piano, or by an orchestra, may
accompany the recitation—echoing softly, 'Over There,' 'There's a Rose
That Grows in No-Man's Land,' 'Joan of Arc,' and various other war-time
melodies" (*CPLH,* 147). The marginal directions running down the left-
hand side of the page of the dramatic monologue, reminiscent of Lindsay's
layout, score the voice and the contours of the body in delivery:

Calmly	My brother died in France—but I came back.
telling	We were just two colored boys, brown and black,
the story.	Who joined up to fight for the U.S.A.
Proudly	When the Nation called us that mighty day.
and	We were sent to training camp, then overseas—
expectantly	And me and my brother were happy as you please
with	Thinking we were fighting for Democracy's true reign
head up,	And that our dark blood would wipe away the stain
shoulders	Of prejudice, and hate, and the false color line—
back,	And give us the rights that are yours and mine.
and eyes	They told us America would know no black or white:
shining.	So we marched to the front, happy to fight.

(*CPLH,* 147)

This expectant speech gives way to bitter disillusionment, as the dead
brother appears in a dream asserting his naive belief that Jim Crow must be
dead and buried: "Didn't our government tell us things would be fine /
When we got through fighting, Over There, and dying?" The surviving soldier (in the body of the reader on stage) "becomes suddenly fierce and an-
gry," as the marginal cues tell us, exclaiming:

It's a lie! It's a lie! Every word they said.
And it's better a thousand times you're in France dead.
For here in the South there's no votes and no right.
And I'm still just a "nigger" in America tonight.

In this passage the proud air of the opening shatters, as the speaker acknowledges his second-class citizenship, with the hypocrisies of the dominant white culture unambiguously exposed. The performance of citizenship by the black man on stage, against the ironic backdrop of martial melodies, insists that the fight for freedom, at least for African Americans, is far from over.

The sentimental title poem, "The Negro Mother," rehearses the history of Africans in America—"a story of the long dark way / That I had to climb, that I had to know / In order that the race might live and grow"—captured, shipped across the Atlantic, and set to work in the fields of the plantation under the master's whip ("Three hundred years in the deepest South"). This figure performs for a younger generation whom she calls on to fulfill her dreams, to climb the stair to a more just future: "I was the seed of the coming Free," she pronounces. In its original publication the poem includes the following stage directions: "A poem to be done by a woman in the bandana and apron of the Old South—but with great dignity and strength and beauty in her face as she speaks. The music of the spirituals may be played by a piano or an orchestra as the aged mother talks to her modern sons and daughters."[45] This characterization lets the audience know that even in the shadows of slavery, the mammy figure does not surrender her proud sense of self. The spirituals tuned to her speech deny allegations of that music's ideology of surrender, and point up instead its theme of heroic endurance, reminding the matriarch's progeny of their connection to her generation. The woman is a ghost, a disembodied form who speaks from the grave, but she is given substance by the physical presence of the person performing; her embodiment before the audience is a sign of the resilience of the black body, its refusal to be laid to rest. Indeed, she gestures deictically in the poem to the fact of her racial identity, "Look at my face—dark as the night— / Yet shining like the sun with love's true light," with her paradoxical body (dark and yet light) staged as a site of political resistance. In Prentiss Taylor's decoration of the poem, the woman holds her left hand high in the air, seemingly pointing to the stair depicted behind her up which she "Impel[s]" "my dark children." However, we also are impelled to see in that picture a reverse, or negative, image of the Statue of Liberty (whose torch is held high in her *right* hand), an image that signifies a competing claim, the as-yet-unguaranteed freedom of African Americans.[46]

Other poems in the book *The Negro Mother* similarly rely on musical accompaniment to get their points across and to subtend their emotional effects. "Broke," we are told under the poem's title, stages "A complaint to be given by a dejected looking fellow shuffling along in an old suit and a battered hat, to the tune of a slow-drag stomp or a weary blues"; "The Black Clown" is "A dramatic monologue to be spoken by a pure-blooded Negro in the white suit and hat of a clown, to the music of a piano, or an orchestra," and has running down the left margin reading directions under the heading "The Mood." "The Big-Timer," a "moral poem to be rendered by a man in a straw hat with a bright band, a diamond ring, a cigarette holder, and a cane, to the music of piano or orchestra," also contains cues running vertical left. The poems achieve irony through syncopation, and express the complicated transit of the feelings of the speaker—one minute gay, the next dejected, sometimes laughing to keep from crying, as Hughes terms the emotional logic of the blues. In "The Black Clown," for instance, the title figure shuttles from "humorous defiance" to "loud joy" to "sudden sadness" to a feeling of "humiliation and helplessness"; finally transformed, the actor takes off his costume, unveiling *"the clothes of a modern man," and "proclaims himself"* "a man!"[47] The music accompanying his speech fluctuates as wildly, underwriting the man's mood at any given moment: he begins against "A gay and low-down blues," and then we hear coming in at various junctures "Melancholy jazz," a spiritual, "gay martial music," and a "mournful tom-tom," among other strains. The speaker's proud performance of identity—the literal casting off of black stereotype and bodily investiture of manhood ("Manhood's true right")—constitutes his "Cry to the world"—and is choreographed by his change of posture through the poem: early on, *"Back bent as / in the fields. The slow step. / The bowed head";* at the end, *"standing / forth, straight / and strong."* He refuses through a figurative kinesics to be crushed down any longer.

In the final poem of *The Negro Mother,* "Dark Youth of the U.S.A.," Hughes throws light on the performance of nationality in a monologue about the importance of education to the realization of African American freedom, with the protagonist "a Negro boy, bright, clean, and neatly dressed, carrying his books to school." Taylor illustrates this poem with a drawing of a black child standing in front of a map of America with a row of stars and stripes at top, and in the poem itself the boy insists on his patriotism, "American am I, none can deny," setting himself the "mission" of "Lifting my race to its rightful place." At the end of the performance, the boy imagines himself in the company of whites, moving into the future together with them:

> So I climb toward tomorrow, out of past sorrow,
> Treading the modern way
> With the White and the Black whom nothing holds back—
> The American Youth of today.

On the page, Taylor depicts a white youth and a black youth holding hands, parting a curtain with their free hands to let the audience in on their performance of racial cooperation and understanding. Such a graphic embodied interracialism points up not only the performed (or constructed) nature of subjectivity but the essence of what Hughes was trying to achieve on tour and in the very production of the book *The Negro Mother:* "Since Prentiss Taylor was white, a Southerner from Virginia, and I, colored, I thought maybe such a book, evidence in itself of interracial collaboration and good will, might help democracy a little in the South where it seemed so hard for people to be friends across the color line."[48]

Hughes's attention to the popularized spoken word and its racial effects also shapes his later book *Shakespeare in Harlem* (1942), which, he notes, contains "Blues, ballads and reels to be read aloud, crooned, shouted, recited, and sung. Some with gestures, some not—as you like. None with a far-away voice."[49] Here he leaves much up to the individual performer ("as you like"), with little in the way of cueing vocalization in the poems themselves, but he does insist that none of the pieces be read in an orotund or vatic manner ("a far-away voice"); rather, they are to be read with verve. Alfred Kreymbourg's review (April 1942) of the book stresses its popular entertainment value, tracing it to blackface minstrelsy: "The intimate relation with the old music halls is a happy reminder of such mastersingers of vaudeville as Bert Williams and Eddie Leonard. For here is no highbrow verse, no heavy thinking, and nothing low-born either"; it is "social and sociable."[50] Indeed, everything about the book was designed for mass consumption, down to the selection of its typeface: the headings of the book are set in Vogue Extra-Bold, a font that the publisher explains is "designed in our time with the aim to express the utmost simplicity."[51] The bold type used in the headings and in the bodies of the poems raises the words off the page, creating an illusion of amplitude. And it is in *Shakespeare in Harlem* that we begin to see Hughes expressively scoring words on the page as a key to oral performance, as in "Hey-Hey Blues," where we hear the whoop "Yee-ee-e-who-ooo-oo-o!"

More than one reviewer noted the racial authenticity of Hughes's performance on the page, convinced, on the evidence of *Shakespeare in Harlem*, that Hughes is "an honest poet," that "No white man imitating the Negro spirit could approach the spirit of this book," but precisely what one heard depended on one's racial perspective.[52] One critic paid tribute to Hughes's "sympathetic ear and a voice which is faithful echo to this special section of his people," that is, his gift for black voice transcription: he is judged to be "speaking for Harlem in recognizable accents."[53] However, the black critic and playwright Owen Dodson in *Phylon* was troubled by the voice that he heard in the poems, which called to his mind racist vaudeville acts (along the lines of Bert Williams): "We see and hear a cartoon doing a black-face, white-lip number, trying terribly to please the populace." Dodson ends his review by noting, "After hearing some of these poems read aloud a fellow who hadn't heard of Mr. Hughes said: 'that Langston Hughes must be a cracker.' Lord have mercy!"[54] The idea that the voice behind the poems could be heard as that of an uneducated racist southern white man cuts to the complexities of racial performance and vocalization in a direct way, as it highlights the vocal ambiguities that obtain on the printed page and the contest over authenticity that can rage there.

Hughes's *Ask Your Mama: 12 Moods for Jazz,* which he began composing at the 1960 Newport Jazz Festival and first read publicly at the Market Place Gallery in Harlem on February 6, 1961, raises some of these same issues. When it was published in 1961 readers were split over what they heard and how well the poems performed on the page. Paul Engle of the *Chicago Tribune* warned that "Hughes has written these poems essentially for reading to music. They must be wholly alive and diverting that way. On the page, they are less so."[55] Dudley Fitts understood the poems primarily as oral messages, but noted the success of the score, with its expressive use of typography and other devices: the poems, he noted, "are non-literary—oral, vocal, compositions to be spoken, or shouted, to the accompaniment of drum and flute and bass. For that matter, they speak from the page, the verses being set in capitals throughout; and there is a running gloss of dynamic signs and indications for the proper instrument to use at the moment." Charting its lineage, he adds that *Ask Your Mama* "goes back to Vachel Lindsay and his *Congo;* and I suppose it is fair to say that this is stunt poetry, a night-club turn. The fury of indignation and the wild comedy, however, are very far from Lindsay."[56] For sure, the poem ought to be heard as a clever rebuttal to Lindsay, as it ridicules the refusal of whites to try to understand blacks, with ignorant questions met with the retort, "Ask your mama," in the tradition of "the dozens."

The book itself is framed as a record album, and Hughes mocks the uninitiated in his audience with "LINER NOTES: For the Poetically Unhep," where he spells out the meaning of certain figures in the poem, usually with a dose of irony. Such a format calls attention to Hughes's straddling of the line between the sonic and the visual, his insistence on the performativity of the book itself. One reviewer criticized the format, noting that, though "original," it is "an awkward size for handling": the "modernistic painting" on the cover along with the "salmon-colored" paper and the "blue and brown printing" make for "an attention-getting volume to compensate for the lack of literary merit in the contents." Another regarded the typography of the book positively and read it analogically: "The contrast of dessicated pink [page color] and the crisp blue and brown ink comments on the method of the poems: the juxtaposition of the unlikely to produce a syncopated view of the paradoxes of our racial times."[57] At the back of the book, in the colophon, we encounter a full description (in blue ink) of the typeface used: an Egyptian slab serif font ("Ionic No. 5"). The typestyle originated early in the nineteenth century and, because it was bold and easy to read, proved ideal for advertising posters, made possible through wider availability of printing technology. Ionic was introduced in 1925, designed for newspaper typesetting. Hughes trades on these associations, further establishing his poems as "timely," as standing fully within the public sphere and therefore constituting a vital part of the public record.

In keeping with its miked debut on stage in Harlem, the mediatized voice operates as a crucial motif in *Ask Your Mama* and entails in it a distinct cultural politics. In the section titled "Blues in Stereo," Hughes remarks on new sound-recording technologies with respect to the African American community:

IN A TOWN NAMED AFTER STANLEY	
NIGHT EACH NIGHT COMES NIGHTLY	*African*
AND THE MUSIC OF OLD MUSIC'S	*drum-*
BORROWED FOR THE HORNS	*beats*
THAT DON'T KNOW HOW TO PLAY	*over*

ON LPs THAT WONDER   *blues*
HOW THEY EVER GOT THAT WAY.   *that*
                                                       gradually
    WHAT TIME IS IT, MAMA?   *mount*
    WHAT TIME IS IT NOW?   *in*
    MAKES NO DIFFERENCE TO ME—   *intensity*
    BUT I'M ASKING ANYHOW.   *to*
    WHAT TIME IS IT, MAMA?   *end*
    WHAT TIME NOW?   *in*
                                                       climax.

DOWN THE LONG HARD ROW THAT I BEEN HOEING   TACIT
I THOUGHT I HEARD THE HORN OF PLENTY BLOWING.
BUT I GOT TO GET A NEW ANTENNA, LORD—
MY TV KEEPS ON SNOWING.

Here the recorded phonographic voice and the televisual image suffer interference; the audience cannot be sure of the message and so cannot be mobilized through these technologies. As Hughes humorously demonstrates, with the advance of corporate capitalism such mediatization is potentially deauthenticating and can serve as a hegemonic instrument.

Notwithstanding his concern over the mishearings that can arise through technological transmission, Hughes recorded his poems, both with and without musical accompaniment. In a 1951 article "Ten Ways To Use Poetry in Teaching," he noted that one way was through "Recordings of Poets Reading Their Own Poems," and itemized resources as follows: "The late James Weldon Johnson recorded his God's Trombones. Vachel Lindsay's The Congo is available, as well as the readings of Carl Sandburg and other distinguished American poets. I have made an album of some of my poems. And the Library of Congress has recorded many living American poets."[58] Hughes's first commercial recording was in 1945 on the Asch label, and included four ten-inch discs under the title *The Poems of Langston Hughes*. Folkways Records released Hughes's *The Dream Keeper and Other Poems* in 1955. In the spring of 1958 Hughes read with a jazz band and continued to do so with frequency throughout that year and into the next. Liner notes to his album *The Weary Blues and Other Poems Read by Langston Hughes* (recorded at Verve Records in New York in March 1958 with two bands—one led by Red Allen and the other by Charles Mingus—and arranged by Leonard Feather) call attention to earlier experiments in the form, citing Lindsay and the beats.[59] In 1959 *Langston Hughes Reads and Talks About His Poetry* (Spoken Arts) appeared. He also read and was taped at the Library of Congress on May 1, 1959, and just prior to his death in 1967 he recorded a selection of his poems for Caedmon. Of the 1958 poetry-and-jazz session, Hughes explained to jazz critic Nat Hentoff his theory of the dialogic relationship between the two arts: "The music should not only be a background to the poetry, but should comment on it. I tell the musicians . . . to improvise as much as they care to around what I read. Whatever they bring of themselves to the poetry is welcome to me. I merely suggest the mood of each piece as a general orientation. Then I listen to what they say in their playing, and that affects my own rhythms when I read. We listen to each other."[60] Hughes brought a similar improvisational sense to *Langston Hughes Reads and Talks About His Poetry:* as the title suggests, he not only reads his work but discusses extempore his life and art between recitations, rapping informally about being black in America in direct, simple speech in a way that predicts the slightly later Black Arts poets.

As with Hughes's live performances, these recordings are not theatrical, although when he wanted to he could heighten his expressive effects, as in his recital of "Bad Man" on the 1995 Folkways CD *The Voice of Langston Hughes,* a reissue of material from some 1950s Folkways recordings, where Meta DuEwa Jones finds he brings a heavy vibrato to the pronunciation of the repeated word "bad" in the poem and an overall "brassy timbre," which helps him portray the swaggering nature of the black title character.[61] Hughes's then is not a deracinated voice, but it is a voice that does not fully absorb "the idiom, cadence, and tones of folk speech," as Sterling Brown's voice is said to do on his Folkways recording *The Poetry of Sterling Brown* (1995). It is Hughes's idea of America and Americanness that drives his performance aesthetic, one that allows his spoken words, like Brown's, to "resonate with dignity and truth" as he proclaims himself and his race.[62]

NEW SONGS: RESOUNDING THE RADICAL LEFT

If the poems of *The Negro Mother* are intended to be performed solo (by black men, women, or children) and speak to civic inclusiveness, other performance poems composed by Hughes around the same time stage a concert of voices conjoined in an effort to effect—and symbolically represent—the solidarity required to produce partisan political change. In "Chant for

Tom Mooney," Hughes, a committed leftist when the poem was first published (as "For Tom Mooney") in the socialist *New Masses* in September
1932, protests the incarceration of that San Francisco area labor leader, who
was arrested in 1916 in connection with a bombing and sentenced to die on
the basis of perjured testimony. (Hughes visited Mooney in prison in 1932
while on a reading tour.) The poem begins with a striking image of the political efficacy of the spoken word:

> Tom Mooney!
> A man with the title of governor has spoken:
> And you do not go free.
> A man with the title of governor has spoken:
> And the steel bars surround you,
> And the prison walls wrap you about,
> > And you do not go free.
>
> > > > (*CPLH*, 164)

The finality of the sentence—delivered not by a judge but by an elected
official—rings clear, as the speech act of the governor makes things happen, sealing Mooney's fate. However, there is a countervailing voice heard
in lines immediately after these, as the workers speak the labor leader's
name:

> And the sound vibrates in waves
> > From Africa to China,
> > India to Germany,
> > Russia to the Argentine,
> > Shaking the bars,
> > Shaking the walls,
> > Shaking the earth
> Until the whole world falls into the hands of
> The workers.

Hughes wrote the poem as a "mass chant" to be read through a megaphone
at a political rally, and on May 8, 1932, he read it at such an event: as
Hughes recalled, "every one yelled beautifully at the proper moments."[63]
The mediatized voice of the poet calls forth the unmediatized crescendo of
the laboring masses, and that ritualized dialogic enactment is imagined ra-

diating out Jericho fashion in performance of a new socialist world order.

In the 1930s Hughes's socialist aspirations and ideals frequently are figured in terms of voice and its illocutionary effects. Hughes's "Chant for May Day," "To be read by a Workman with, for background, the rhythmic waves of rising and re-rising Mass Voices, multiplying like the roar of the sea," immediately follows "Chant for Tom Mooney" in *A New Song* (1938), a pamphlet published by the International Workers Order "in the desire to make available literature which would otherwise be out of the reach of wage earners" (*CPLH*, 209).[64] The holiday of May Day is associated with the commemoration of the social and economic achievements of the labor movement, and the poem begins in a single voice (that of the "Worker") before swelling to as many as one hundred in its articulation of a political message of interracial proletarianism ("White workers"; "Black workers"; "Yellow workers"):

20 VOICES	Arise,
40 VOICES	Grow strong,
60 VOICES	Take power,
80 VOICES	Till the forces of the earth are yours
100 VOICES	From this hour.

(*CPLH*, 209)

The accretion of voices in the rhythmic chant of the poem represents the growing political heft of the labor movement, and synecdochically the bodies of the workers themselves that some day, it is imagined, will be numerous enough to "Take power."

At the beginning of the pamphlet's title poem, "A New Song," Hughes first tropes black vocality as ideology: "I speak in the name of the black millions / Awakening to action. / Let all others keep silent a moment" (*CPLH*, 170).[65] A later lyric, one that stands at the entrance to *Jim Crow's Last Stand* (1943), further foregrounds, through its title, "The Black Man Speaks," the politics of orality:

I swear to the Lord
I still can't see
Why Democracy means
Everybody but me.

(*CPLH*, 288)

This is the whole poem, and in it Hughes succinctly figures political representation—and the full exercise of citizenship—as utterance (voice as vote). The title—with its racial markings and use of the definite article—suggests that the person talking is a type, a black Everyman, speaking for a disenfranchised group of citizens who are, as the poem goes to print, fighting for freedom alongside whites in Europe. That Hughes should position these poems at the fronts of books signifies that he is also performing authorship through them, seeking to authenticate his own poetic voice (himself a black man speaking) as he spotlights social and racial injustice (as "A New Song" goes: "I have this word to bring, / This thing to say, / This song to sing").

Hughes's performance-centered poem "August 19th . . ." also features vocalism—and the cultural politics of vocalism—prominently in both form and theme. When the poem first appeared in the leftist *Daily Worker* in June 1938, the following note appeared with it: "Read this poem aloud, and think of young Clarence Norris pacing his lonely cell in the death house of Alabama, doomed to die on August 18. When used for public performances, on the last two verses punctuate the poem with a single drumbeat after each line. . . . During the final stanza, let the beat go faster, and faster following the line, until at the end the drum goes on alone, unceasing, like the beating of a heart" (*CPLH*, 647). Clarence Norris was one of the Scottsboro defendants who was sentenced to death, and the poem reflects gravely on matters of minority citizenship—what exactly the meaning of America to a young black man in such a predicament could be ("What flag will fly for me / When I die? / What flag of red and white and blue, / Half-mast, against the sky?"). At intervals throughout the poem flashes the brief declarative sentence in boldface (presumably a cue to the reader to speak the words in a loud voice, with a sense of foreboding): "**August 19th is the date.**" The repetition of the line intensifies in the middle of the poem and then again at the close, where we are told to read at a faster pace:

AUGUST 19th IS THE DATE.
Will you let me die?
 AUGUST 19th IS THE DATE.
AUGUST 19th IS THE DATE.
AUGUST 19th . . . AUGUST 19th . . .
AUGUST 19th . . . AUGUST 19th . . .
AUGUST 19th . . .

                                                              (*CPLH*, 206)

The punctuating drumbeat after each iteration of the looming date of exe-cution is meant to represent the finality of sentence, the power of that sen-tence to close time off. The ellipsis at the end (and within the title of the poem), along with the insistent drumbeat, conversely is meant to illustrate the unrelenting march of time, a fate that cannot be forestalled. Hughes structures the poem as a public performance piece—presumably to be read to protest the Scottsboro situation—in order to give his audience a means by which to enact their civic identity. Norris's questioning voice inter-leaved in the poem challenges us to intervene on his behalf, to speak for him and others like him who do not have a voice.

Hughes, like Whitman before him, was actively engaged in revising pre-viously published poetry to meet changing cultural conditions, further proof of his commitments to publicity and performativity. Although he sometimes promoted an image of himself as a spontaneous composer, re-marking that "there are seldom many changes in my poems, once they're down," in fact his poems frequently went through multiple versions after first publication, whether in book or magazine, in an effort to remain *au courant*.[66] Of course, one charge leveled at the public poet is that of topical-ity—a cheap writing to contemporary events that will not stand the test of time. Hughes happily pledged himself to such timeliness, realizing that in order for his poems to make a difference in the world they would have to tackle immediate concerns, be "documentary, journalistic, topical."[67] One way to do this was to keep them on the page in a constant state of change.

While I agree with Karen Ford's claim that not enough attention has been paid to Hughes's revisions, I disagree with what she calls his "record of capitulation and compromise in publishing," which I read rather as a record of public performativity, a record that stages ambivalence. As Ford finds, "Throughout his career Hughes did indeed follow his moral and aes-thetic instincts in his writing. However, when he *marketed* that writing, he made many concessions to audience, using the poems and reusing them, packaging and repackaging them, promoting and sometimes suppressing them"; what she refers to, rather cynically, as Hughes's "marketing tech-niques" should be read instead as his earnest attempts to remain a viable force on the American political and cultural landscape. While it may be, as Faith Berry argues, that, for his *Selected Poems* and the *Langston Hughes Reader,* Hughes "selected not his best poems, but those he thought would go over best with the public," excluding his more politically controversial verse, such a decision does not brand him a sellout. And when Ford says that "Hughes obviously acquiesced to the conservative tastes of the 1950s," because he refused to subscribe wholesale to the creed of an emergent black nationalism, we should not necessarily read that as a failure, but rather regard his ironic questioning as an honest attempt to come to terms with that emergent ideology and its rhetoric.[68]

Ford is particularly displeased with alterations Hughes makes to "Christ in Alabama," concluding that in the 1967 version of the poem in *The Panther and the Lash* the poet "tidies up the typography and punctuation, editing out the ironies created by the italics and capitalizations. . . . The revised version is repackaged in subtle ways to reflect the certitude of the 1960s; its single typeface embodies the uniformity of the black nationalist vision and obscures the significantly more ambiguous representation of racism conveyed in the original version." Citing it as an example of his "commodified poetry," she notes his desire "to convert old poetry into a new cultural currency" and contends that in *The Panther and the Lash* Hughes dehistoricizes his poetry: while "the poems reprinted from earlier volumes seem belated, nostalgic, and out of step with the times of *The Panther and the Lash*," "Too many of the new poems," she finds, "are tentative, even unfinished, if we take a string of question marks to indicate a failure of vision. They seem to want to participate in the moment, yet they lack commitment and confidence." Of one of these new poems, she concludes: "In its emphasis on black victimization, its distrust of militancy, and its retreat at the end into a riddle, 'Black Panther' carries no political force." This is at best a dubious charge: After all, simply because a poem does not stridently pronounce a position does not mean that it does not wield a politics. Poems that are "deeply suspicious of the political developments they herald" do not perforce betray a movement or cause; indeed, they are ironic and probing in the same way that the original version of "Christ in Alabama" is, the version that Ford claims to prefer for these very reasons.[69]

"Refugee in America," which is published for the first time in 1943, is retitled in *The Panther and the Lash* "Words Like Freedom." Although Ford laments that in the revised poem "there is no trace of the original speaker of the poem—the refugee in post–World War II America," and that, therefore, it is somehow not true to itself, it is so only if one invests too much in the concept of an original and does not recognize the spontaneous poetics at play.[70] Indeed, the changeableness, or topicality, of *The Panther and the Lash* ("Poems of Our Time," as the subtitle announces) spoke through its very font, with capitalized titles in bold alluding to the look of headlines of the day.[71]

Many of the nominal changes that Hughes makes to his poems are meant to keep pace with the times, to meet new cultural conditions in America. For example, in "Negro," first published in 1922, the line "They lynch me now in Texas" appears in all printings up until the 1959 *Selected Poems,* at which point the line becomes "They lynch me still in Mississippi" in response to a string of lynchings in Mississippi in 1955, most notably that of Emmett Till, that dominated the news. The earlier versions of the poem reflect instead a 1919 lynching in Texas that was lodged in the public mind, an event that by 1959 had faded from memory and been trumped by more recent horrors. Likewise, tailoring occurs between "Freedom [2]," published in *Jim Crow's Last Stand* (1943) , and "Freedom [3]," published posthumously in *Crisis* (February 1968): The phrase "burning books" becomes "burning churches" in recognition of the rash of church arsons in the 1960s; "Nehru," no longer in the news (he had spent time in prison between 1921 and 1946), is edited out; and the phrase "lynching a Negro" becomes "killing a man," sign of the fact that lynchings of black men were on the wane in the South by 1968. The end of the poem is altered as well, although in both versions "Freedom" has the last laugh: in "Freedom [2]" that allegorical figure exclaims, *"You'll never kill me!";* in "Freedom [3]" we hear, *"No— / Not so! / No!"* The crucial difference here is in the final retort "No!" where the speaker's voice reenters (the word is not in italics) to stand in league with Freedom and serve as its protector.

Other of Hughes's revised poems seek to respond to new rhetorical urgencies. For instance, Hughes's poem "Militant," originally titled "Pride" in the magazine *Opportunity* (December 1930), concluded in that printing as follows:

Your spit is in my face.
And so my fist is clenched—
Too weak I know

But longing to be strong
To strike your face.

The final lines in the revised version (in *The Panther and the Lash*) read somewhat differently:

Your spit is in my face,
And so my fist is clenched

Today—
To strike your face.

With just a slight tweaking, this poem written almost forty years before its appearance in *The Panther and the Lash* is made consonant with the spirit of the Black Power movement: lashing out in the name of justice is no longer a mere "longing," but an immediate capacity. In another revisionary gesture, Hughes updates a poem in line with new concerns about national feeling, reporting that "To help us all remember what America is, and how its future belongs to us all, recently [c. 1958] I added two new lines to an old poem of mine—the last two lines to help us remember to walk together." Reprinted in the *Langston Hughes Reader* with the two added lines, the poem reads as follows:

We march!
Americans together,
We march!72

This 1958 version insists on the common purpose needed to move ahead, a purpose that Hughes calls attention to at the dawn of the civil rights movement. In *Crisis* (August 1924) the poem ended with the first "We march!" which is omitted from the version published in *The Weary Blues* (1926) but then restored in *The Dream Keeper* (1932). (The poem appears under the title "Youth" in *The Dream Keeper*.) In *Crisis* the poem functions as a call to African Americans only; later, it sounds as a Whitmanesque herald to all Americans, regardless of race, expressing the need for a united effort in the battle against racism at the same time that leaders of the civil rights movement were making just such interracial appeals.

Hughes's "A New Song" also changes endings in a politically charged way in the space of just a few years. In 1933 (in *Opportunity* and in *Crisis*), the finale reads:

Take care!
    Black world
    Against the wall,
    Open your eyes—

The long white snake of greed has struck to kill!

Be wary and
Be wise!

(CPLH, 643)

In this original version, the poem accentuates matters of race, with the
"Black world" in jeopardy from the "long white snake" of hegemony. In
1938, in the pamphlet *A New Song*, it takes on a socialist cast:

Revolt! Arise!

> The Black
> And White World
> Shall be one!
> The Worker's World!

The past is done!

Here it is of the essence to downplay racial strife and promote international
brotherhood. In fact, such was the express purpose behind the publication
of Hughes's *A New Song* by the Industrial Workers of the World (the Wob-
blies), an international labor union, as the leftist writer Michael Gold
confirms in his introduction to the book: "The Negroes are enslaved, but so
are the white workers, and the two are brothers in suffering and struggle."[73]

Gold is not blind to racial inequalities, though, and cites Lindsay's
championing of Hughes as he remarks on the racist conditions that kept
Hughes from attending Lindsay's reading at the Wardman Park Hotel.
Gold's recognition of Lindsay as a populist poet chimes with his view of
Hughes, as he calls Lindsay a "Y.M.C.A. Mayakovsky, who put the populist
theories of Bryan, Altgeld, Tom Johnson into thrilling song. . . . Before
women's clubs, Chambers of Commerce, universities, all the social gather-
ings of the middle class, he chanted poetry, American poetry, his own and
that of the contemporaries he believed most American." (Of course, as I
have noted, Lindsay's willingness to submit to women's clubs and other
bourgeois sites ebbed after his initial performance successes.) Gold goes on
to invoke Whitman as a public poet in his final sentence: "If the International Workers Order with its 140,000 members can create a great people's
audience for poetry here, it will have contributed mightily to the rise of
that democratic culture of which Walt Whitman prayed and dreamed."[74]

Other poems composed during Hughes's socialist period come in for re-modeling as well. His four-line poem "Justice" (first published in 1923) stands as a protest against the unsecured rights of African Americans under the law:

That Justice is a blind goddess
Is a thing to which we black are wise.
Her bandage hides two festering sores
That once perhaps were eyes.

While the poem was not written in response to the Scottsboro trial, which began in 1931, it was included by Hughes in his book *Scottsboro Limited* (1932), where the word "black" took on even more weight, since the trial shed a glaring light on racial inequality. However, when the poem was reprinted in 1938 in *A New Song*, the word "black" becomes "poor," a change that again signifies Hughes's understanding that interracial solidarity is crucial to the success of the labor movement. Robert Shulman finds that the poem "loses some of its disturbing, subversive power when it is re-moved from the context of the animating passions and particulars of the Scottsboro case," that "Justice" as it appears in *A New Song* as part of the se-quence "Let America Be America Again" (the 1938, not the usually anthol-ogized version) "gives us a significantly different poem than the one in *Scottsboro Limited*." He goes on to argue that the fact of the two versions "raises the general issues of textual reliability . . . and textual change (from "black" to "poor") and the particular issue of why or to what effect Hughes made the change, and is correct to see that the differences emanate "from the dynamics of the shifting relations of race and class in 1930s left politics generally and the Popular Front in particular" as Hughes understood them. Ultimately, Shulman wonders, "How fixed is the meaning of the poem? How do we deal with the different historical contexts, 1923, 1931, 1938? And what role does the interpreter play?"[75] The answer, I believe, is that the meaning of the poem is not fixed, as it is meant to assume new meanings with each new performance.

In a panel on "The Poet and the Public" at the Library of Congress in 1962, Hughes, we are told by his biographer, "declared flatly that he wrote with the public in mind and yet had enjoyed a long career, even if it meant being constantly a 'performer and reading in a loud voice'" (*LLH*, 2:357). A self-proclaimed "social poet," he was intent on reaching the masses with his art from the outset, and, in 1947, a couple of weeks after his arrival in Atlanta to teach at Atlanta University, the degree of his success can be measured by the *Daily World's* crowning him "the troubadour, the people's poet, the bard of the streets" (qtd. *LLH*, 2:128).[76] However, he sometimes felt the wear and tear of a rigorous recital schedule, growing sick of the road, and wrote to Arna Bontemps after his "world premier" performance of *Ask Your Mama* that "I've turned down about 20 lectures for the rest of this season . . . and am taking NONE at all for next season—which I vowed before but this time I MEAN it. Just the art of writing from here on in."[77] Such was not to be the case. In 1962 in performance at the Library of Congress, he again recited *Ask Your Mama*, this time dropping several lines, including "THE PAPERS / THAT HAVE NO NEWS THAT DAY OF MOSCOW," in light of the Cuban missile crisis. His improvisation testifies to his determination to prove his publicity (*LLH*, 2:357).

In a speech in Chicago in January 1957, Hughes expressed his desire that the state of race relations in the United States be dealt with humorously: "with black tongue in white cheek—or vice versa." His image of a biracial orality stands for the democratic America he seeks to sing into existence—an America whose racial ironies must be measured by a sly tonality. On *Langston Hughes Reads and Talks About His Poetry* Hughes wonders aloud whether "I'm a folk poet, myself a folk person," concluding, "Maybe I am," and in his construction of a vocal poetry on stage and off he is able to call into being a liberal democratic social sphere that resists the politics of the dominant culture and places him with the people. By way of "recognizable accents," he locates in the twin conditions of orality and aurality opportunities for political action, and so sets the table for future generations of black performance poets.

CHAPTER 4

Beat Acoustics, Presence, and Resistance

The poetry which has been making itself heard here of late is what should be called street poetry. For it amounts to getting the poet out of the inner esthetic sanctum where he has too long been contemplating his complicated navel. It amounts to getting poetry back into the street where it once was, out of the classroom, out of the speech department, and—in fact—off the printed page.

—LAWRENCE FERLINGHETTI

For me, reading aloud brings the words off the page. My voice is the key instrument in this act. The voice is the character or characters—all the personae and deities.

—ANNE WALDMAN

THE POETS OF THE BEAT GENERATION had their ears to the ground, too, keenly aware of the history of public performance poetry unrolling toward them, a history in both black and white. In an early draft of his poem "America" (the same title as the poem of Whitman's on wax cylinder), Ginsberg unabashedly announces his paternity: "I Allen Ginsberg Bard out of New Jersey take up the laurel tree cudgel from Whitman."[1] Other poets have invoked Whitman as ancestor as well, perhaps most famously Ezra Pound, who in "A Pact" hails him as his "pigheaded father," but whereas Pound imagines his resistance to Whitman, and ultimate accommodation, in terms of the free verse line, Ginsberg frames Whitman as an oral public poet ("Bard") and reads him as part of a counterpublic sphere (with his "gay gang" at Pfaff's beer hall in New York's Bowery district) that ties into his own sexual politics. Ginsberg finds especially prescient Whitman's lyric "Poets To Come," what he calls "a little poem or song to his fellow poets that would be born after him, that, like myself, will sit in a recording studio reading his words aloud to be heard by ears through some kind of movie/television/theater."[2] With the mediatization of the spoken word, Ginsberg is able to disseminate Whitman's poems to mass audiences about which Whitman could only dream. Like Ginsberg, for whom Whitman is "so enormous-voiced," beat poet Gary Snyder understood Whitman principally as a social agent, finding his audibility to be a bonding agent in intimate live settings: "I love to read 'em [Whitman's poems] aloud, to a small audience. He's a good *communal* poet in that way."[3]

Ginsberg also traces his poetics of performance through Lindsay. In "Improvisation in Beijing," he recounts that from early childhood Lindsay was in the air: "I write poetry, because my father reciting Shelley English poet & Vachel Lindsay American poet out loud gave example—big wind inspiration breath."[4] In 1958, fellow poet Gregory Corso gave Ginsberg a copy of Lindsay's *Collected Poems* to cheer him up after he found out that another friend, Neal Cassady, was headed to jail.[5] In a footnote to his tape-recorded poem "Wichita Vortex Sutra," Ginsberg glosses his own gloss of Bryan ("William Jennings Bryan sang / Thou shalt not crucify mankind upon a cross of Gold") with a passage from Lindsay's chant-poem "Bryan, Bryan, Bryan, Bryan" (*CP*, 397, 776). Ginsberg also notes the achievement of "The Congo," which, though "corny" as anthropology, he judges to be "one of the most interesting poems written in America," a poem that is "completely on rhythmically," citing Lindsay as "an early Allen Ginsberg of American poetry," an artist who made "attempts at a social poetry."[6] Years after Lindsay's death, Ginsberg paid his respects in an elegy ("To Lindsay") that recognizes the struggle as a public poet he underwent: In the poem "the radio blares its jazz" to a "heartbroken" man in the act of killing himself, already reduced to a "shade" as he does so (*CP*, 183). In his 1949 essay "On Spoken Poetry," the San Francisco poet Jack Spicer, a contemporary of Ginsberg, also reflects on the lesson of Lindsay, noting that "Thirty years ago Vachel Lindsay saw that poetry must connect itself to vaudeville if it was to regain its voice. (Shakespeare, Webster, and Marlowe had discovered this three centuries before him.) Our problem today is to make this connection, to regain our voices. . . . We must become singers, become entertainers."[7]

In *the populist manifestos* (1981), Lawrence Ferlinghetti harks back to the spoken word artists who paved the way to the beats, focusing on the distance between the "pure" voice (i.e., the perceived truth-bearing quality of the unfiltered, auratic poetic voice) and the mechanical "speech of man" in "electronic existence":

Eighty or ninety years ago
when all the machines began to hum
almost (as it seemed) in unison
Whitman was still singing
the song of himself
the song of our self

In the poem he names Whitman as "a holdover" along with Sandburg
("singing his poems"), Lindsay ("drumming his chants"), Hughes, Ginsberg ("chanting his mantras / singing Blake"), and Kerouac—all poets who
insist in their various ways on liveness. Apart from these bards, the poem
finds that "the speech of most was caught up / in the linotype's hot slug /
and now in the so cold type of IBM / (movable type that doesn't move)."
Ferlinghetti's expression of the inability of type to sufficiently "move" an
audience (he delights in the pun) matches some of Whitman's statements,
although both implement strategies to encode in the text the qualities of
its oralness. His substitution of Ginsberg for "the Word" of God (St. John
1:1) later in the poem ("and in the beginning was Ginsberg / who almost
singlehandedly / took poetry in a new direction") pays tribute to that poet's
originary insistence on a "spontaneous bop prosody," one that is heard as
"picking up on Whitman's mimetic / 'casual spontaneous utterance.' "[8]

In the first poem in *the populist manifestos*, "Populist Manifesto," an
early version of which was broadcast by the author on KPFA/FM (Berkeley)
in April 1975 and which he first performed in front of a live audience on
Walt Whitman Day at Rutgers University–Camden on April 23, 1975, Ferlinghetti exhorts poets to descend from their Ivory Towers and perform for
the people: "Clear your throat and speak up." In the poem, he goes on to
say that poets should "Stop mumbling and speak out / with a new wide-
open poetry / with a new commonsensual 'public surface,'" communicating clearly and directly to the people by "utter[ing] 'the word en-masse'"
(echo of Whitman's "the word Democratic, the word *En-masse*" from
"One's Self I Sing").[9] In his later *Americus: Book I* (2004), Ferlinghetti hails
Whitman as the nation's "greatest soul speaker / with his barbaric 'yawp' /
sounding for the first time / free from the past / the voice of the people of
America," and in this way tethers his populist consciousness to his strident
vocalism.

Gary Snyder shares Ferlinghetti's allegiance to a populist poetics: "There
has to be a public aesthetic that understands and appreciates accessibility

and the subtleties that are within that, rather than this Anglo-American hangover from New Criticism days that wants ambiguity and tension and irony and complexity."[10] In "Poetry, Community, and Climax" Snyder further remarks on the need of poets to "build an audience . . . by going on the road and using your voice and your body to put the poems out there; . . . to speak to the conditions of your own times," noting that the revision and adaptation of poems on the basis of audience "feedback" confirms that "there is a communal aspect to the evolution of the art."[11] This call for a renewed public poetry "amounts to getting the poet out of the inner esthetic sanctum where he has too long been contemplating his complicated navel. It amounts to getting poetry back into the street where it once was, out of the classroom, out of the speech department, and—in fact—off the printed page"; as Ferlinghetti laments, "The printed word has made poetry so silent," and, thus, he urges artists to create "spoken poetry, poetry conceived as oral messages," claiming, with a sly allusion to Pound's exhortation to "make it new," that such an oral poetry 'makes it' aloud." He ends his manifesto by bidding "Whitman's wild children" to "Awake and walk in the open air," with the goal nothing less than "the *resocialization* of poetry."[12]

In the mid-1950s, in an effort to reclaim the lost "voice" of poetry, readings at colleges and universities began to grow in number and appeal. Against the staid and stultifying academic poetry recital (Ferlinghetti refigures the first line of Ginsberg's "Howl" as "We have seen the best minds of our generation / destroyed by boredom at poetry readings" in "Populist Manifesto"), however, beat performance would be freewheeling, improvisatory, and dialogic; as Snyder attests, the poetry event would function as "a kind of communion," where "the poet articulates the semi-known for the tribe": "Something happens with a poem when it's experienced in the company of others different from what happens with the same poem experienced in private. . . . it's communal, it's community spirit, it's convivial."[13] The poet David Meltzer sounds a similar note with respect to the forging of communitarian space in performance: "In the Fifties a poetry reading was a cultural event, a gathering of people in increasing numbers ready to receive the word of poets. There was a celebratory and devotional aspect to these readings. Nonsectarian yet charged with expectation of transformation."[14] Such ritualized theater held out promise by performing for audiences a new identity politics, by staging both a powerful presence and resistance: as Rexroth recalls, "What happened in San Francisco first and spread from there across the world was public poetry, the return of a tribal, preliterate relationship between poet and audience."[15] At the same time, the recorded word had the beats "reaching and preaching to more people in less time than either Gutenberg or Edison dreamed of," and their canny use of sound reproduction technologies helped fuel their formation of an insurgent subaltern counterpublic sphere.[16]

"BODY RHYTHM": SITING THE SEXED AND RACED BODY

A reading staged at the Six Gallery in San Francisco on October 13, 1955 (one hundred years after the first *Leaves of Grass*), emceed by Kenneth Rexroth and featuring performances by six beat poets, including Allen Ginsberg, who read for the first time his unpublished poem "Howl," was a watershed event that effectively challenged the dominant culture and its ideologies. In retrospect, Ginsberg and Corso described the live (and unrecorded) event this way: "In the fall of 1955 a group of six unknown poets in San Francisco, in a moment of drunken enthusiasm, decided to defy the system of academic poetry, official reviews, New York publishing machinery, national sobriety and generally accepted standards to good taste, by giving a free reading of their poetry in a run down secondrate experimental art gallery in the Negro section of San Francisco." Taking care to mark the distance between the reading and mainstream culture, they remembered of the participants, "They got drunk, the audience got drunk, all that was missing was the orgy. This was no ordinary poetry reading. Indeed, it resembled anything but a poetry reading." Corso described Ginsberg's reading of "Howl" that night as a "brilliant shock": "The reading was delivered by the poet, rather surprised at his own power, drunk on the platform, becoming increasingly sober as he read, driving forward with a strange ecstatic intensity, delivering a spiritual confession to an astounded audience—ending in tears." At the edge of the platform sat Kerouac, "back to the poets, eyes closed, nodding at good lines, swigging a bottle of California red wine—at times shouting encouragement or responding with spontaneous images—jazz style—to the long zig-zag rhythms chanted in *Howl*."[17] Clearly, this was a far cry from the institutionalized academic poetry reading. And, like Whitman's "barbaric yawp," Ginsberg's "howl" sounded as a cry in the wilderness, precisely the kind of high-octane "shouted verse" that Richard Eberhart, in his review of the beat scene in the *New York Times*

Book Review in 1956, noted as having made poetry over into "a tangible social force, moving and unifying its audience."[18]

What impressed many in the audience at the Six Gallery that October night was the "insurgent" political power of the spoken word and the body behind it, its resistance to the official life of the nation; indeed, it was greeted hungrily as an antidote to what Ferlinghetti calls the "death of the spirit" occasioned by "our technocratic civilization," its "machines and macho nationalisms."[19] In his recollection of the reading, one participant, the poet Michael McClure, remarked on the overwhelming feeling of oppression as a result of the ideology that created the Cold War and Korean War, all the "inhumanity and the coldness," and the consequent resolve: "There were certain of us (whether we were fearful or brave) who could not help speaking out—we had to speak. We knew we were poets and we had to speak out as poets. We saw that the art of poetry was essentially dead—killed by war, by academies, by neglect, by lack of love, and by disinterest. We knew we could bring it back to life." Here he links spoken word poetry to the refusal of marginalized subjects to be silenced by the dominant culture and its political machinery. Of Ginsberg's vocalization of "Howl" in particular, McClure observes: "In all of our memories no one had been so outspoken in poetry before—we had gone beyond the point of no return. None of us wanted to go back to the gray, chill, militaristic silence, to the intellective void—to the land without poetry—to the spiritual drabness. We wanted to make it new and we wanted to invent it and the process of it as we went into it. We wanted voice and we wanted vision." Ginsberg's somatic performance, his defeat of silence, "left us standing in wonder, or cheering and wondering, but knowing at the deepest level that a barrier had been broken, that a human voice and body had been hurled against the harsh wall of America and its supporting armies and navies and academies and institutions and ownership systems and power-support bases." As breakthrough "epic vocal bard," Ginsberg enacts, through his humane vocal presence, a strenuous resistance to the inhumane military-industrial complex.[20]

As Shepherd Bliss, an enlisted man in the U.S. Army, recorded of another reading staged by Ginsberg years later, the poet's performance of identity showed a way to be in the world that was at odds with all that he had learned in the military, whose associated sites are where masculinities are constructed, reproduced, and deployed perhaps most directly:

Then one day a wandering, bearded poet arrived in Lawrence [Kansas]. I recall a large room, probably a gym, lots of excitement. And he read: harmonium and all, waving of arms, chanting. I had never experienced anything like this during twenty years in the military mind and the military body. Something shook loose, inside. That shaking continued, through the efforts of Martin Luther King, Jr., and others. Poetry and preaching. Gay and Black, other ways of being, radically other. Finally, after all that shaking, something broke.

Counterposing Ginsberg's bodily movement on stage ("fluid, spontaneous, bobbing up and down and around, moving in more than one direction at the same time, poetically inspired") to the "rigid, directed body moving constantly forward, sharp changes, militarily trained," Bliss sees clearly the gendered political ramifications. For Bliss, though, the military is not a wall of silence, as it is for McClure, but of hypermasculine noise: "The ears absorb sound. So, too, do the pores, through the skin. Sound affects motion: stifling it or encouraging it. Sounds of basic training: 'Kill! Kill! Kill!' 'What does it take to be a man? A rifle, sir?' Aggressive sounds, internalized, externalized through fight. . . . Male sounds, loud and powerful." To this chant, he juxtaposes Ginsberg's "softer" timbre, one capable of "opening up new passages": "More musical, less assaultive. Such sound surrounds rather than penetrates, creating comfort rather than anxiety. And it has the power to cause the armor to drop away." In the end, Bliss embraces Ginsberg's alternative "vision of what it means to be a man, a vision which seeks to incorporate aspects more often associated with women," and resigns his commission as a U.S. Army officer, becoming a peace activist under the banner of those more mellow sounds. "Filled with" Ginsberg's "chants and incantations," he is arrested at the 1968 National Democratic Convention in Chicago and laments the lack of communitas in the world that, ironically, he experienced to a degree in the army ("I wish there were more channels for the intimate connection among men which the military affords"). Ginsberg's perceived gender-bending orality is imagined as holding the power to transform Bliss from a man "as straight as could be—red, white, and blue" to one his esteemed military ancestor would decry as "some kind of commie-faggot."[21]

Ginsberg's spontaneity in performance points us back to the 1955 reading at the Six Gallery, to a performance that was not the final word, as subsequent renditions of "Howl"—both on the page and off—improvised on that text in light of changing cultural circumstances. Indeed, the debut performance of the poem itself departed from the previously printed version: "He was reading from the book [*Howl*], which had just come out, but he changed words, improvised freely."[22] Joyce Johnson (at one time girlfriend of Jack Kerouac) noted the "ritual" nature of Ginsberg's first reading of the full version of "Howl" at Berkeley's Town Hall Theater in March 1956 ("Each indictment of Moloch sets off boos and hisses"), calling it a "reenactment" of the earlier Six Gallery reading, with "The same poets, the audience arriving knowing what to expect, and thus part of the performance themselves."[23] On the 1956 recording of this recital of the poem, Ginsberg ad libs, for instance, interjecting the epithet "Holy Gregory" (in honor of Gregory Corso) in his footnote litany.[24] Upon rehearing the tone and tenor of this performance, Ginsberg himself notes, "I still hadn't broken out of the classical Dylan Thomas monotone, maybe appropriate for an ecstatic, mechanical revelation where the divine machine revs up over and over until it takes off."[25] In pulling together tapes for the CD *Holy Soul Jelly Roll* (1994), producer Hal Wilner recognized the "magical quality" of the voice of unvarying pitch on the reel-to-reel Town Hall recording, noting that "Though Allen had not yet perfected his breath approach to reading the poem, listening to the tape transported me, and the excitement of what it must have been like hearing 'Howl' at that time came through."[26] What Wilner finds is that the auratic quality of the event is captured in the graininess of the unremastered voice; as Ginsberg observes, though "coarse," the 1956 taping conveyed the energy of the poem better than subsequent efforts: "I tried recording 'Howl' under better mechanical conditions in studio," he wrote, "but the spirit wasn't in me by then. I'm not in control."[27] Ultimately, he finds, the "spirit" fades as repetition sets in, with mechanical reproduction clouding over handicraft, stripping the voice of its humane force; his endorsement of an old (first) recording with poor production values indicates his anxiety about repetition and mediatization—and the homogenizing effects of both—in a condition of late capitalism.

A few years later, at the 1959 *Big Table* reading in Chicago (a fund-raiser for *Big Table* magazine), which also was recorded (and later released by Fantasy Records), yet another "Howl" is heard. George Bowering's review of the poem ("How I Hear 'Howl'"), which, he says, is based on the Fantasy recording of that reading, notes paradoxically that "A clear sight into Howl . . . needs only listening ear": "the poet begins Part II with a suddenly deliberate pace, after the high flight that ended Part I. By the time the fifteenth and last line of Part II is reached, there is an exciting tension in the voice, great emotion of pain & defiance. Moloch he confronts, maybe a moment before his own brains are to be slurpt down."[28] The poet-performer Paul Blackburn also appreciates Ginsberg's Fantasy recording ("the poem is given its natural weight") and judges him to be "a good reader of his own poems. There is no one with the same build and length of line, emotional pressure and directness." Blackburn goes on to say of the *Big Table* reading that it is "completely direct, sincere, convincing, has a range that is, at least, completely human, with perfect definition and attention." Success is measured by the degree to which the poet's voice is able to move an audience, to sound raw and vulnerable, to produce a sincerity effect.

The vocal impression of vulnerability relates directly to the construction of the specter of a vulnerable Jewish body at this time in history, in the wake of the Holocaust, and Ginsberg appears mindful of that image, even as he takes control of it, using it as a tool of self-expression.[29] At the same time, he poses a challenge to Norman Mailer's association of the deracinated, cerebral Jew with a degraded femininity in his 1957 essay "The White Negro." Bliss, for one, recognizes Ginsberg's performances as embodying femininity, but far from a degraded sort, as well as a new age masculinity. Others saw that Ginsberg's Jewishness was very much on display in his enactments of "Howl," that his was no deracinated or strictly cerebral performance. Of the 1961 Fantasy recording of the poem, Leland S. Meyerzove in the Hillel-published *Burning Bush* notes that Ginsberg's "oral delivery . . . is that of a man quietly seeking the moment of truth. He is not a made man spilling out words without thought of soul, but is listing the total number of blows against the ghetto of the mind where man has walled himself in. But as he reads 'Footnote to Howl' in that same excellent recording, one may picture Ginsberg as an old religious Ghetto Jew, one who is in union with his God, moaning in the synagogue, rocking back and forth, crying out for the holiness that is in each of us."[30] A reviewer of the LP *Kaddish* (a 1966 Atlantic Records release recorded in front of a live audience at the Jewish university Brandeis in 1964) reads race into the performance as well, noting that "every now and then . . . faint Yiddish inflections, a carry-over from the poet's Russian-Jewish background," peppered the Jewish mourning prayer that Ginsberg composed for his mother. The same auditor remarks that Ginsberg's recorded voice is "vulnerable," and not in any way "calculated," that it is authentic and true.[31]

If on many occasions Ginsberg's voice was heard as charged with a racinated pain and sorrow, at other times he could sound uproariously funny. Luc Sante recalls an expurgated early recording of Ginsberg's performance of *Howl*, a recording made in San Francisco soon after the Six Gallery reading, observing that "The blue laws of the era required Allen to cut out the bad words, and he complied by substituting 'censored' for them, as in 'who let themselves be censored in the censored by saintly motorcyclists, and screamed with joy.' The effect was hilarious and somehow subversive, as if the word 'censored' contained more variegated shades of sin than all of the original words put together." This same LP recording—*San Francisco Poets* (1958)—was not pleasing to Paul Blackburn's ears:

> On it [the LP], Ginsberg reads the *Howl, Part I* (taped at some west coast reading?). The poem, even the first section by itself, has both seriousness and weight. Not here. You'd think he'd written the most yuk-yuk poem of the decade. The audience laughs at all the am-bareass-ing parts which destroys the mood, worse, he clowns and plays it to them ("who let themselves be *censored* in the *censored* by saintly motorcyclists"), yes, that too, the text printed in *Evergreen* (earlier version?), and Allen half-drunk besides. Difference between drunken directness (the shattered reading of the Footnote to Howl on the Fantasy disc) and drunken playing for cheap laughs, no wonder he quit reading. Goddamn the Audience.

Blackburn feels that Ginsberg has done a great disservice to his poem, hamming it up in front of a live audience, off whom he feeds; in particular, he cites Ginsberg's utterance of the word "censored" as substitute for the excised portions of the 1957 *Evergreen Review* reprinting of "Howl" ("who let themselves be . . . . . . in the . . . by saintly motorcyclists, and screamed with joy"; "with a vision of ultimate c . . . and come eluding the last gyzym of consciousness") as an example of his oral debasement of a "serious" poem.[32]

Ginsberg's performances of "Howl" are intensely dialogic, as Blackburn hears, and, notwithstanding Blackburn's sense of letdown, Bakhtin's theorizing of the culture of medieval and Renaissance carnival can help make sense of (and legitimize) Ginsberg's often riotous performances and their subversive effects. In *Rabelais and His World* (1965/1968), Bakhtin argues that "carnival celebrated temporary liberation from the prevailing truth and from the established order; it marked the suspension of all hierarchical rank, privileges, norms, and prohibitions." Carnival allowed for "an escape from the usual official way of life," constituting "the people's second life, organized on the basis of laughter." The carnival sense of the world usually involves mockery of all serious, "closed" attitudes about the world, and it also celebrates discrowning, that is, spectacles of inversion that expose the unstable and temporary nature of any hierarchy. In carnival laughter Bakhtin detects an eternally "unofficial," "second truth about the world"— a truth that rejects the existence of all Truth. Carnival laughter, he argues, overcomes all oppressive social norms: "The principle of laughter destroys . . . all pretense of an extratemporal meaning and value of necessity. It frees human consciousness, thought, and imagination for new potentialities." Bakhtin counterposes the people's "second life" to their first, "official life," which celebrates "the triumph of a truth already established" and runs on intimidation, threats, and prohibitions, and claims unfinalizability as the only supreme value: "Everything completed, fixed, or defined is declared to be dogmatic and repressive; only the destruction of all extant or conceivable norms is considered to have value."[33] The unfixed, improvisatory poetry of the beats lives up to this principle.

Marjorie Perloff has remarked on the centrality of such laughter as it pertains to Ginsberg's recitals, noting that "the controversy over the value of Ginsberg's prophetic mode generally tends to bypass the role of the comic, the absurd in his poetry":

To read "Howl" as a serious indictment of American culture, a culture that denies the possibility of spiritual illumination, is to ignore the poet's self-deprecatory humor, his ability to laugh at himself and at his friends. When, in a 1976 reading of the poem at the Naropa Institute in Boulder, Colorado, Ginsberg came to the line

who reappeared on the West Coast investigating the FBI in
beards and shorts with big pacifist eyes sexy in their
dark skin passing out incomprehensible leaflets

the audience laughed delightedly, no doubt at the non sequitur of referring to "the big pacifist eyes" as "sexy," as well as to the open question of what those "incomprehensible leaflets" did, in fact, contain.[34]

The ambivalent laughter that Ginsberg generates ("the poet's self-deprecatory humor, his ability to laugh at himself and at his friends") is in line with Bakhtin's notion of the ambivalent, utopian character of carnival laughter, which is neither negative nor unidirectional: "It is also directed at those who laugh. The people do not exclude themselves from the wholeness of the world. They, too, are incomplete, they also die and are revived and renewed."[35]

In *Time* magazine in 1981, William A. Henry III identifies a major shift in Ginsberg's performance poetics upon hearing him read "Howl" as part of a celebration of the twenty-fifth anniversary of its publication, and he holds his humor against him, clearly meaning to contain the political subversiveness of the poem in his reporting about it. Henry's essay begins on a note of contempt, as he paints the audience as "exhausted" by their earlier political activism, coopted, pale shadows of themselves: "All around are flannel shirts, funny hats, sleeping children, the emblems of safe bourgeois funk. Not many in the crowd notice, let alone cheer, the arrival of one honored guest, Radical and Felon Abbie Hoffman." He goes on to picture the poet himself as fundamentally "changed":

> The puckish little figure, this professorial imp with the loony grin, does not sound angry. He is not wailing about the wickedness of his time. He is mocking the past—mocking the angry radicals, mocking the dreamers, mocking the quest for visions. The audience is laughing with him. They are howling, but in pleasure rather than anger, as he thrusts an arm up for each of the jokes. They hear satire, not nobly expended pain. . . . Some perhaps do not understand the poem. . . . Others, perhaps, are reflecting on their own older-but-wiser bemusement about antiwar and anti-Establishment excesses of the 1960s, a decade later than the poem.

Finding that "Ginsberg's humor is intentional," that "his contemplative, rounded voice has tightened into singsong waggery," and that he "is chatting, singing, wearing a necktie and making his howl a thigh-slapping hoot," Henry effectively drains the poem in performance of any politically resistive power; acknowledging that the audience laughter is self-directed, he nonetheless fails to see that such ambivalent laughter could signify something other than the collapse of the poem to mean what it once did, namely to catalyze political and social change.[36]

Different people heard different things when Ginsberg vocalized "Howl," with the "mixed, uncertain tone" of the poem sensed as "among its slipperiest distinctions."[37] When Ginsberg read aloud, his intonation was not consistently the same, with the condition of unfinalizability that Bakhtin defines as a condition of carnival obtaining here as well; indeed, there is a way to hear certain of Ginsberg's performances of that poem that recognizes not a diminishment of political power but a revision of the terms on which political power rests and an opening up of the poem to a sexual politics, as Ginsberg's adoption of a camp tonality wryly parries U.S. hegemony. As David Bergman notes, "Camp shares many of the qualities of its now academically far more respectable condition, what Mikhail Bakhtin has dubbed, 'the carnivalesque,'" with the two sharing "many of the same cultural positions," despite their differences.[38] Jack Brabuscio associates camp specifically with a "gay sensibility," claiming it as a "a means of asserting one's identity, as well as a form of justification in a society which denies one's essential validity." Through Ginsberg's sometimes campy performance of the poem, he shines a light on his own divergence from a normative sexuality, his so-called "singsong waggery" a vocal sign of his repudiation of compulsory hierarchies.

Paul Berman, when he heard Ginsberg perform his poem-song "Capitol Air" at a protest meeting for Polish Solidarity in early 1982, observed that "When he got to the line, 'I don't like Castro insulting members of my sex,' he held up a limp wrist to show which sex he meant. The effect was charming and funny, since the direness of his bill of political particulars contrasted with the hamming, the silly-sounding rhymes, and the deadpan melody. The audience of sober leftists cheered and laughed appreciatively."[39] He further finds that in the poem on the page what is missing is a fruitful "tension between text and subtext," that "In performance he is able to conjure some of his youthful whimsy and innocence, and pose the contrast." Performing a queer identity in recital, Ginsberg's performance of "Capitol Air" is of a piece with certain stagings and restagings of his signature poem "Howl," through which he seeks to construct a vital subaltern counterpublic sphere and enact what he calls his "multiple identity."[40]

Ginsberg's poem "America" also mounts a trenchant political critique through camp performativity. Pitted against what he calls "McCarthyite demagogic nationalist harsh conformism," the poem, and his comic performance of it, make a deep impression; as Michael McClure recalled after hearing Ginsberg perform it in the 1950s in the Bay Area: "It was both beautiful and hilarious—as if the spirit of the silent comedians had stepped into socially aware words." Ginsberg reflected on the performance history of "America" in his liner notes to *Holy Soul Jelly Roll*, which includes a recording of a 1956 performance of the poem, commenting in particular on its ludic aspect:

> I didn't think "America" was much of a poem, nor did Kerouac. It's one-liners in different voices, sardonic schizophrenic, the tone influenced by Tzara's dada manifestos. I didn't read in 1956 with the same quickness I do now to get subtle changes of temper. After a few lines the audience began laughing, particularly on "Go fuck yourself with your atom bomb," which was unusual, so to speak, to be saying in a poem in that decade. This first reading sounds like a stand-up comedy routine, and the audience response frames a cultural profile of the mid '50s. I'm a little ashamed of milking the gags when I hear this debut, except that I'd read my main work that night, the first complete "Howl" as well as "Sunflower Sutra," and this was dessert.[41]

Here Ginsberg admits that he was playing to the crowd, presenting himself as what one audience member later would refer to as a "clown clowning around."[42] That he imagines his performance that night as "like a stand-up comedy routine" hints that he may have Lenny Bruce on his mind, a stand-up comedian who in the early 1960s would be arrested for uttering obscenities in his act. After a Library of Congress reading of the poem, Ginsberg insisted that it was not anti-American, but, of course, it is anti-Americanist; with his "queer shoulder to the wheel" at the end of the poem, he exposes the intersection of performances of sexuality and of nationality/nationalisms.

Ginsberg's public readings of "Howl" similarly propose an alternative America, a new sense of nationality. Anne Waldman has stated that "Hearing Ginsberg read it live was an event in eternity," but it was not a poem that he consented to read all that often, "not wanting to make the poem stale through overuse. But if he were reading in a state of the union in which he had not read before (i.e., Utah), he would include 'Howl' to commemorate the occasion. He eventually read 'Howl' in all fifty states and countless countries."[43] Ginsberg's selective siting of the poem suggests his desire to reconstitute the country (to re-create it politically) through the spoken word, in effect ratifying the poem—and with it his vision of America—in each of the fifty states in a ritual reenactment of the conceit of a spoken origin of the United States.

In his essay "Notes Written on Finally Recording *Howl*," a version of which was included as liner note to the 1959 recording *"Howl" and Other Poems,* Ginsberg concedes both the limitations of recording and the co-nundrum of live poetry performance (it is telling that he had written his el-egy for Lindsay just a year before): "All these poems are recorded now as best I can, though with sacred love, imperfect to an angelic trumpet in mind. I have quit reading in front of live audiences for a while. I began in obscurity to communicate a live poetry, it's become more a trap and duty than the spontaneous ball it was first."[44] Any lack of polish of his voice on vinyl he turns into a sign of his sincerity and spirituality. In 1966, Ginsberg remarked that he had read *Kaddish* only three times in front of an audience: "I was afraid that reading it over and over, except where there was spiritual reason, would put the scene into the realm of performance, an act, rather than a spontaneous poetic event, happening, in time."[45] His desire not to succumb to mechanical repetition—to put on a show that is somehow pre-scripted—expresses his commitment to a poetics of immediacy, natural-ness, and auratic presence. But if he desired occasional sabbaticals from live performance, they did not last long, as Ginsberg was one of the most prolific poet-performers of the twentieth century. He was always looking for a new place to perform, even plotting a stint on MTV's *Unplugged* series on his deathbed.

As with Lindsay, Ginsberg's voice in recital of his poem was read by some as indispensable to a full experience of it. In Corso's review of *Howl,* he asserts that the title poem is "essentially a poem to be read aloud, but only by the Howler . . . any other Howler would screw it up, thus for those who are unable to hear Ginsberg read his 'Howl' [they] will have to settle for its visuality. And visuality it has, that is, if you're hip enough to visual-ize it. If you're a drag go read [Richard] Wilbur or something."[46] Striking here is the rhetoric of hip, which, Norman Mailer tells us in "The White Negro," precludes imitation or study: "what makes Hip a special language is that it cannot really be taught—if one shares none of the experiences of elation and exhaustion which it is equipped to describe, then it seems merely arch or vulgar or irritating." In another essay, "Hipster and Beatnik" (1957), which he called a "footnote to 'The White Negro,'" Mailer counter-poses the language of the hipster to that of the beatnik, but goes on to ob-serve, "If there are hipsters and beatniks, there are also hipniks and beat-sters like Ginsberg and Kerouac."[47] Ginsberg is seen as occupying a space in-between, part cerebral beatnik (as Mailer maintains, the beatnik is "often Jewish") and part hipster, uninhibited as he enjoys the pleasures of the body in the moment of its performance (Ginsberg's first reading of "Howl" is not unintentionally in "the Negro section of San Francisco").

As Corso insists, if one cannot hear Ginsberg read the poem, that person must fall back on the visual field of the poem on the page, bringing to it his own hipness, which may allow him to hear what is going on: "the way the poem's laid out on the page is a paradigm for the breathing rhythm," a prosodic lesson that Corso tells us Ginsberg learned "more from Kerouac than Olson," the latter of whom issued directives for line arrangement according to breath in his widely influential manifesto "Projective Verse" (1950).[48] Ginsberg expresses his belief that the page is meant to score the performance of the reader ("The breath of the poet ideally is reproduced by the breathing of the reader") through techniques of lineation and marks of punctuation ("typewriter is holy"), but also acknowledges the limits of the page, noting that the poet cannot score pitch, even if he can score time.[49]

Something of the presence associated with live performance also is communicated through the original print form of the poem. "Howl" was published on May 16, 1956, in San Francisco in an impression of twenty-five mimeographed copies, typed by the poet Robert Creeley and run off on a mimeograph machine by Martha Rexroth, wife of the poet Kenneth Rexroth. This instantiation of the poem—with its poor production values— calls attention to its distance from the main currents of the cultural economy. In liner notes to a recording he made of William Blake's poems to music, Ginsberg admired that poet's closeness to the artifact: Blake "engraved his own picture plates, hand colored, and of *Songs of Innocence and Experience* (1789–1794) printed only a couple dozen copies. Thus every word, every picture, and every print of the book he made in his life bore the impress of his own intelligent body; there was no robot mechanical repetition in any copy."[50] Although others are involved in the production and reproduction of the typescript of "Howl," the relative directness of mimeograph—its unincorporated quality—preserves something of the personality of the artist behind it. Notably, too, the first edition of his second book, *Siesta in Xbalba* (1956), in mimeograph form, was produced by Ginsberg himself on board a merchant ship off the coast of Alaska, with only fifty-two copies produced for free distribution to friends.

With the coming of new technologies—in particular the widespread use of the tape recorder beginning in the 1950s—new forms of dictation emerged, and Ginsberg was quick to put them to poetic use. The title poem

of *The Fall of America,* a book dedicated to Whitman and bearing an epigraph from *Democratic Vistas,* was improvised orally, as the artist explains:
"'The Fall of America' was spoken into a tape recorder in the back of a
Volkswagen bus crossing the country beginning Christmas 1965. The composition includes whatever I was thinking, what I saw out the window,
what came through the radio, newspaper headlines, comments in the
car."[51] Elsewhere he elaborates on the mechanics of the process and its impact on the graphotext:

> I dictated it on this Uher [reel-to-reel] tape recorder ["the state of the art for
> a small portable"]. Now this Uher microphone has a little on-off gadget here
> (click!) and then when you hear the click it starts it again, so the way I was
> doing it was this (click!); when I clicked it on again it meant I had some-
> thing to say. . . . So when transcribing, I pay attention to the clicking on and
> off of the machine, which is literally the pauses, as words come out of my—
> as I wait for phrases to formulate themselves. . . . And then having paid at-
> tention to the clicks, arrange the phrasings on the page visually, as some-
> what the equivalent of how they arrive in the mind and how they're
> vocalized on the tape recorder.[52]

The poem is a transcription of the voice on tape, with the arrangement of
the page "notat[ing] the thought-stops, breath-stops, runs of inspiration,
changes of mind, startings and stoppings of the car"; it is a product constructed out of the condition of secondary orality in which Ginsberg finds
himself,[53] and is intended as a score of himself.

Ginsberg's stunning illocutionary effects in the "Wichita Vortex Sutra"
utterance of *The Fall of America* are intended to counteract the official discourse streaming through the radio at the time it was composed (at the
height of the Vietnam War). In speaking out, he imagines bringing into being a new world order:

> I lift my voice aloud,
>   make mantra of American language now,
>   pronounce the words beginning my own millennium,
>   I here declare the end of the War!
>   Ancient days' illusion!

As Ginsberg believes, "the war has been created by language . . . & a Poet can dismantle the language consciousness conditioned to war reflexes by setting up (mantra) absolute contrary field of will as expressed in language. . . . 'I here declare the end of the war' is a fact, whether the war ends for everyone or not. I end the war in me and anyone who's affected by my gesture."[54] The act effected by his voice ironically is mediated (through his tape recorder), but it is not transmitted impersonally via the country's vast global telecommunications network, a network whose shadow falls ominously across the poem. Perceiving the war through the mass media, "in the center of America," Ginsberg pits his own manually controlled recording apparatus against a commercialized mass vocalism (*"Corporate voices* [that] *jabber on electric networks"* and general *"radio fear"*). The low-tech personal recorder—one that picks up the clicking sound of the on/off switch—captures Ginsberg's auratic voice; as Michael Davidson finds, "For Ginsberg the orality of the tapevoice stands in direct opposition to the reproduced heteroglossia of incorporated sound."[55] Ginsberg's "Poem-rant" against "chauvinist patriotism" ultimately mellows ("hear my soft voice at last"), as reduced audibility here stands as sign of a new, more enlightened citizenship.

"Wichita Vortex Sutra" was set to music in 1992 by Philip Glass and the full poem recorded on CD in 1994. The authenticating background noise on the original tape recording is reenacted in this performance: "The way the various instruments come in and out of the soundtrac [*sic*] on the composition tape—clarinet, banjo, the 'honkytonk tinkle' of a piano, and later the swirling electric piano on Dylan's 'Queen Jane'—is not unlike the way the instruments come in and out of the performance recorded here"; moreover, it comes in at the same length, a testament to "how this poem arrived, fully present, in the moment of its original, spontaneous vocalization." Ginsberg's performance of the poem in 1994 was experienced by many who heard it as cathartic. Cary Nelson observes that "Hearing Ginsberg read 'Wichita Vortex Sutra' during the war was exhilarating. In a large audience the declaration of the war's end was collectively purgative." Greil Marcus in the liner notes to the live recording of the poem at St. Mark's Church in New York (October 29, 1994) cites the mediumistic character of the performance, "There's a slight edge of the ludicrous in his voice, or maybe it's simply wonder, or surprise: the war is sending him a voice," and reports that as Ginsberg keeps reading, he "picks up a terrific momentum"—"the momentum of his own words, of panic in the face of war, speed on Kansas highways, whatever's at hand." The poem, he concludes, "could have been written today" "if one changes a few names, locations, and statistics to current events."[56]

Notwithstanding Marcus's claim, many of Ginsberg's poems could not have been written on any day other than the one (or ones) on which they were written, and throughout his career when Ginsberg published his poetry he included the date of composition beneath the final line. This technique indicates just how firmly yoked to a particular U.S. cultural moment his poems are. "Plutonian Ode" (composed on July 14, 1978) is a case in point—a poem that is not only date- but site-specific and pays homage to Whitman's oral poetic example. Ginsberg reports that it was written the night before he was arrested for blocking a train full of plutonium wastes from going out of the Rockwell Corporation Rocky Flats Plutonium-Bomb-Trigger Factory near Boulder, Colorado, and the lyric begins in thrall to Whitman, whose poem-chant thread Ginsberg imagines picking up:

> Father Whitman I celebrate a matter that renders Self oblivion!
> Grand Subject that annihilates inky hands & pages' prayers, old orators'
>   inspired Immortalities,
> I begin your chant, openmouthed exhaling into spacious sky over silent
>   mills at Hanford, Savannah River, Rocky Flats, Pantex, Burlington,
>   Albuquerque
> I yell thru Washington.
>
>   (CP, 702–3)

As in "Wichita Vortex Sutra," the performative utterances within the poem—"I vocalize"; "I chant"; "I speak"; "I roar"—seek to bring to an end nuclear proliferation: "My oratory advances on your vaunted Mystery!" (CP, 703). Ginsberg figuratively sets his voice in contrast to the inhumane technologies of the nuclear age, chanting, "My voice resounds through robot glove boxes & ingot cans and echoes in electric vaults inert of atmosphere, / I enter with spirit out loud into your fuel rod drums underground on soundless thrones and beds of lead." In the end, he commands, "Magnetize this howl with heartless compassion, destroy this mountain of Plutonium with ordinary mind and body speech," with the live vocal presence of the poet conceived as being able to neutralize Cold War technology dedicated to destruction through a Buddhist enlightenment. Appropriately, at the age of fifty-three, Ginsberg literally magnetized his howl, overseeing the production of a flexi-disc recording of "Plutonian Ode," which was inserted into a British literary magazine.

But Ginsberg sometimes did in fact change such indicators as names, locations, and statistics to current events in sync with his "spontaneous bop prosody" (always carefully noting the date of such changes), thus rejecting the notion of the static, autotelic text much as Whitman and Hughes had done before him: In the case of the written text as well as that of the oral there is no one original intention in relation to which other readings can be considered only variations. Although Ginsberg's credo, "First thought best thought," would point to the virtue of unretouched transcription of immediate idea, he often would revise a previously published poem in light of changed cultural and political conditions in the United States and the world.

Ginsberg updates a number of poems in an effort to keep tabs on the mounting corrosive effects of corporate capitalism. "Put Down Your Cigarette Rag," first published in *First Blues* (1975), gets revised when it appears in *Cosmopolitan Greetings* (1994): The cost of a pack of cigarettes rises from a "half buck" to "two bucks," and the amount of money that "Madison Avenue gets / t'advertise nicotine / & hook you radical brats" is upgraded from "275 Million in Green" to "Four billion dollars in Green." In the later version (in *Cosmopolitan Greetings* the poem is dated "1971; June 21, 1992"), a stanza appears reflecting the fall of the Soviet Union and the rise of the global economy:

> Communism's flopped
> Let's help the Soviet millions
> Sell 'em our Coffin-Nails
> & make a couple billions

In another stanza, "Senator Joe Fear / who runs the CIA" (i.e., Senator Joseph McCarthy) becomes "Senator Jesse Fear who pushes Tobacco subsidy / In the Senate Foreign Relations Committee" (i.e., Senator Jesse Helms). Ginsberg adds other parts to the poem in order to comment sarcastically on the "war on drugs" declared by Reagan in the 1980s:

> 20 thousand die of coke
>   Illegal speed each year
> 400 thousand cigarette deaths

> That's the drug to fear
> Don't smoke Don't smoke Don't smoke

Also, in *First Blues* the poem "CIA Dope Calypso" is set in the present tense, since some of the events narrated are happening in Indochina as Ginsberg composes; when it is republished almost twenty years later in *Cosmopolitan Greetings,* the word "today" is changed to "yesterday" a couple of times in the poem to keep it true to the moment. In the liner notes to *Holy Soul Jelly Roll,* Ginsberg indicates that "CIA Dope Calypso" was "written in New York City & elsewhere, 1972–1976," a range of years that denotes its status as a poem-in-process, a poem in a state of change, and one intent on performing a politically resistant counterpublic sphere ("Don't smoke don't smoke the official dope").[57]

"Hum Bom!"—another of Ginsberg's performance poems that is composed over a period of years ("Written in New York City & other places, 1971–1991")—first appears in print in the last section of *The Fall of America,* where it is dated May 1971 (*CP,* 182).[58] A second section dated "June 16, 1984" is added in the expanded rendition in *Collected Poems 1947–1980* (1984). In 1991 a third section is appended and published along with the first two sections in *Cosmopolitan Greetings.* The poem chronicles the recent history of U.S. militarism extending from Vietnam to Iraq and begins in the following sound-rich chant:

> Whom bomb?
> We bomb'd them!
> Whom bomb?
> We bomb'd them!
> Whom bomb?
> We bomb'd them!

The second section continues this style of frenetic back-and-forth:

> Whydja bomb?
> We didn't wanna bomb!
> Whydja bomb?
> We didn't wanna bomb!

As Ginsberg has said of the performance poem, "Part I codifies a longer improvisation in a Southern church at an antiwar rally marking U.S. carpet-bombing North Vietnam, early '70s. Performing this percussive bummer with me at Folk City a decade later, Don Cherry laid down his trumpet and protested squealing, 'We don't wanna bomb!?' so Part II evolved to alchemize the aggressive energy into something positive." After he thought he was finished with the poem, "the bombing of Iraq prompted another seven stanzas' blacktop analysis," including the lines, "Saddam said he hadda bomb! / Bush said he better bomb!"[59] In Ginsberg's performance of the poem to music on the CD *The Lion for Real* (1989), a saxophone intensifies the call-and-response pattern, constituting an additional layer in the poem's evolution.

On the Internet, the poem has taken on yet another life, heard as a chant against U.S. imperialisms in "the chorus of voices" of people who recorded a couple of lines of the poem and sent them into the host site as individual audio files, which then were assembled into the completed electronic version of the poem.[60] In this manner of mediatization, a truly collective voice is enabled to sound out in protest. As Ginsberg himself has noted of such venues, "in a world of demagoguery poetry can stand out as the one beacon of sanity: a beacon of individual clarity, and lucidity in every direction—whether on the Internet or in coffee houses or university forums or classrooms. Poetry, along with its old companion, music, becomes one mean [*sic*] of communication that is not controlled by the establishment."[61]

SAPPHIC SONICS

As Ginsberg tells us, he was inspired vocally early on (in 1948) when he experienced what he calls an "auditory hallucination" of Blake. In an unpublished poem about this peculiar audition, he writes that, having just masturbated and with "an open book of Blake on my lap," he turned to the poem "Ah! Sunflower" and heard a voice: "it was Blake's reciting / in earthen measure: / the voice rose out of the page to my secret / ear that had never heard before." It was, he insists, "a physical voice / not hallucination / except hallucinations be real," that is, it was heard as "a voice in the room," not a voice "inside my head," a voice separate from his own mind and body. Blake's "deep, ancient voice" reads several poems from the book out loud, and Ginsberg would come to believe that the mystical voice of Blake that he heard that day in Harlem was his own mature voice as it later would develop (he notes that he had "a higher voice" at the time that he had the vision, at the age of twenty-two): "I was imagining my own body consciousness, I think."[62]

Notably, the voice is heard following orgasm, a fact that links vocalization to ejaculation, and thus encodes vocal utterance as primitively masculine, notwithstanding Shepherd Bliss's sense of its androgyny. It is also heard in Harlem, a fact that points directly to Mailer's construction of the figure of the hipster: "The Negro could rarely afford the sophisticated inhibitions of civilization, and so he kept for survival the art of the primitive. The Black man lived in the enormous present, he subsisted for his Saturday night kicks, relinquishing the pleasures of the mind for the more obligatory pleasures of the body, and in his music he gave voice to the character and quality of his existence, to his rage and the infinite variations of joy, lust . . . and despair of his orgasm." Jack Kerouac, too, genders performance poetry, believing that what he advocates "is diametrically opposed to the [T. S.] Eliot shot, who so dismally advises his dreary negative rules like the objective correlative, etc. which is just a lot of constipation and ultimately emasculation of the pure masculine urge to freely sing."[63]

Beat poet Anne Waldman intervenes in this discourse, putting a feminist stamp on the male-gendered public performative mode, as she imagines herself enacting an empowered feminine deity through her ritualized performance of identity. She locates a female from which to trace her descent, stating that her attempt to realize "a public poetry—a communal poetry" is linked not only to "those dancer-shamans in the Paleolithic," but also to the Greek lesbian poet Sappho, and sounds the following charge (*FSW*, 129, 131):

> Women artists rise up. We are on the mound, which is our stage, our platform, a throne for the manifesting deity. It is Sappho's stage. It is an image of "becoming" in Prigogine's definition, a pattern or process which reoccurs and is in constant motion. Nor do we have to fetch for anyone else. This also serves as a paradigm for performance. Literally: taking center stage. (*FSW*, 158)

The reference to Ilya Prigogine's theory of dissipative structures, his term for open systems that "are involved in a continual exchange of energy with the environment—such as the ovum and seed or the various life forms and structures that make up a town," is foundational to Waldman's view of herself as a performance poet. According to Prigogine's theory, "At the deepest level of nature, nothing is fixed," thus "allow[ing] for spontaneity," which "is also the potential in poetry and in the performance of poetry" (*FSW*, 127–28). Waldman further attests: "The continuous movement in a structure results in new fluctuations, which is how I characterize the act or event of extending the writing back off the page. . . . I am interested in extending the written word off the page into a ritual vocalization and event, so that 'I' is no longer a personal 'I.' I enter into the field of the poem with my voice and body" (*FSW*, 128). In this way, she imagines herself enacting theatrically a communal cultural identity.

Waldman's conception of performance—and the political possibilities of performance—is conditioned by feminist multimedia "happenings" in New York in the 1960s, where, she sees, "A definite exchange of energy between poet/performer and his or her 'muse' as well as an exchange between poet and audience was taking place," as with performance artist Carolee Schneeman's *Meatjoy*, "in which naked bodies cover themselves with slabs of meat in a wild orgy of flesh and blood," "bring[ing] to mind Dionysian rites" where "The audience feels the event viscerally, energetically" (*FSW*, 141). She is also taken by the performance aesthetic of Karen Finley: "On stage, she immediately worked herself up into a frenzy. She seemed inspired by her own blasphemy as she peed on numerous venerable plaster saints. Her humor was both flagrant and foul. She intoned a kind of physic diatribe. . . . She had also covered her body with Mazola early on and 'performed' masturbation on stage. It was a cathartic and iconoclastic event to say the least" (*FSW*, 142). Contending that Finley "is most definitely 'writing the body' in much of her work," Waldman draws on feminist theorist Hélène Cixous, who "speaks of 'writing the body' as a kind of ritual practice for women," with such writing in close proximity to voice and desirous of obliterating hierarchical structures (*FSW*, 131, 134). Similarly, Waldman "writes the body" on page and stage in powerfully transgressive ways, mounting her own physic diatribe.

In her book *Fast Speaking Woman* the longer chants are motivated not only by Allen Ginsberg's poetry readings (as Waldman says, "his whole oral presentation was inspiring") but by the anaphoric Celtic *Song of Amergin* ("I am a stag: *of seven tines* / I am a flood: *across a plain;* I am a wind: *on a deep lake . . .*"), which was chanted by the chief bard of the Milesian invaders, Amergin, when he set foot on the soil of Ireland. In the poem the poet Amergin seeks to claim sovereignty over Ireland by becoming all of the elements of the land; it is thus a model for the performance of both self and

a new nation. When composing the title poem "Fast Speaking Woman,"
Waldman conceived of it as "a list-chant telling all the kinds of women
there are to be, interweaving personal details . . . with all the energetic ad-
jectives I could conjure up to make the chant speak of/to/for Everywoman"
(*FSW*, 35). Her catalog of the diversity of femaleness is syntactically similar,
regenerating, as she says, an "elemental modal structure to capture Everywoman's psyche" (*FSW*, 36):

> I'm the dulcimer woman
> I'm the dainty woman
> I'm the murderous woman
> I'm the discerning woman
> I'm the dissonant woman
> I'm the anarchist woman
>
> (*FSW*, 10–11)

She refers in the poem to her own acts of making as well ("I'm the cata-
loguing woman"; "I'm the woman with the refrain"), and in a reading of
the poem at Naropa (with Ginsberg) she ends the long poem with a humorous line not in any printed versions of the poem: "I KNOW WHEN TO
STOP."[64] Focused on her "own femaleness and, by extension, any
woman's," Waldman gives voice to a composite mystical female identity—
fully empowered and embodied—in a chant "to be spoken, or sung, or even
more interestingly, sprechstimme, spoke-sung" whose ritualistic energies
work to actualize that identity (*FSW*, 36).

Jerome Rothenberg, whose concept of an ethnopoetics bears directly
on Waldman's performance aesthetic and its anthropological rootedness,
has said of "Fast Speaking Woman" that "what she's doing is analogous
to certain kinds of chanting, certain repetitive patterns that are fairly
widespread in tribal and oral poetry"; he notes the relationship between
the poem and the Wasson recording of Maria Sabina, the Mazatec healer
and shamaness, hearing it as "almost like an extended translation."[65]
Waldman acknowledges the influence of Sabina in a note to the poem
and says of Sabina, "The sacred mushrooms speak through her as she
guides young female initiates to confident womanhood and into the
Mazatec healing lineage. Her litanies are of radical empowerment" (*FSW*,
38). Waldman seeks to tap into the "remedial power" of language that
Sabina's chants enact, their "transformational" energy, recovering the fe-

male sacred, Everywoman's ability to change the world. And, like Sabina, Waldman imagines herself as a medium: "I'm the instrument. My voice is the instrument. My voice is articulating the sounds which are coming through the imaginings and visitations in my head, and I'm making these sounds but I've selected them from an ocean of sound. I'm the go-between."[66]

"Fast Speaking Woman" is not a text that sits still on the page. On the back cover of the 1975 edition of *Fast Speaking Woman* we are told of the accretive nature of the title poem, the fact that "Earlier, shorter versions of this poem have been published but this is the latest, fullest text as it has evolved in her brilliant public performances of it. Also included are nine other 'chants' with which she has awakened many audiences, and they are worth cutting down trees to print." Elsewhere, Waldman comments on the state of change in which her poem resides: "Fast Speaking Woman is still going on, it's interminable. It began as a journal work, a list, fill in the blanks around the word 'woman' piece, but constantly playing with the sound of other words in my head."[67] In a note that she published with the poem in 1975, she observes that "Reading aloud as intended I can be more playful improvising new words & sound thus expanding the territory I'm in" (*FSW*, 2). Such an open-ended poem is capable of responding to new social and political contexts: as Waldman remembers of one public reading of "Fast Speaking Woman" for the "street people" of Boulder, Colorado, in 1974, in a park: "The organizers hadn't secured the proper permit for a public gathering. I was in the midst of reading the poem when I saw two cops approaching from a distance, and as they closed in I ascertained that they were both women! I immediately sprang to 'I'm the blue cop woman,' 'I'm the woman with the billy club,' 'I'm the powerful bust-cop-lady assigned to close this reading down,' and so on. I was able to dispel the tension of the situation and complete the performance" (*FSW*, 39). In one recorded reading of the poem, she says that she will be performing a "current realization" of it, a testament to the fact that each enactment of the poem is unique and of its historical moment.[68]

What Waldman calls her "rant poem" "Crack in the World"—a "ritual enactment" of "menses dementia"—stands as another prime example of her performance of a visceral gendered vocalism:[69]

I see the crack in the world
My body thinks it, sees the gaping crack in the world

My body does it for me to see
Blood flowing through the body crack
Body, send your rivers to the moon
Body twist me to the source of the moon

(FSW, 119)

Through her flagrant staging of female menstruation and its putative magical power ("My body enchanted me to this! / My body demented to this /
It is endometrium shedding"), she takes possession of herself, in full command of her surroundings: "I make up the world & kill it again & again / I
offer my entrails to the moon / Ovum not fertilized / Architecture haunt-
ing me." Near the end of the poem she issues an aggressive warning to men
to "keep your distance," insisting on her supremacy: "I will overpower you
with my scent / of life & death / You who came through the crack in my
world / You men who came out of me, back off."

This reclamation is enacted through what she finds to be the "intrinsic
power" of the sounds of words and their deep connection to ritual ("Seed-
syllables travel and carry certain efficacies"). Of the expressive, efficacious
phonetics that undergird her vocal performance of "Crack in the World,"
she reveals that

> I'm interested particularly in exploring the nuances of sound that mani-
> fest different states of being. I'm interested in the atmosphere created
> when I chant . . . "CR-A-A-A-CK in the world" so that the "crack" is actu-
> ally felt and activated, or taking the phrase "endometrium shedding" in a
> visceral way. I play with all five vowel sounds in the word "endometrium."
> The syllables also carry their own semantic message—"end" "o" "me"
> "trium" (which sounds like "triumph") paralleling the composite word
> (endometrium) which sounds like its literal meaning "the mucus mem-
> brane lining the uterus." As I intone the words "endometrium shedding,"
> I am reenacting that process. It is an "end" "of" "me" and yet a "triumph."
> I have been told by people in the audience that the enactment of this
> poem completely evokes the condition and the power of that condition.
> (FSW, 144–45)

Here she articulates what we might call a somatics of performance, what
she herself refers to as a "body poetics."[70] In her performance of the poem
off the page, she elongates the vowels in the words "Crack" and "en-

dometrium" ("The long vowel stretch downward of the word 'endometrium' led me into 'Crack' [which is also sounded as a literal crack or rip] in the World") with "an hysteria in the vocal presentation," as she describes her recitation mode. In *The Pleasure of the Text* (1975), Barthes, in his discussion of "writing aloud," links *actio* (the rhetoric of actorly expressiveness) to hysteria and ritual, and thus to feminization, with *actio* containing all of the elements Barthes feared about speech. It is, of course, this condition of hysteria that Waldman consciously and cannily performs, calling down its full political powers in her vocal writing. As Barthes explains, such "writing aloud" is carried "by the *grain* of the voice, which is an erotic mixture of timbre and language": it is a writing that aims for "a text where we can hear the grain of the throat, the patina of consonants, the voluptuousness of vowels, a whole carnal stereophony: the articulation of the body, of the tongue, not that of meaning, of language."[71]

In Waldman's poem "Uh Oh Plutonium!"—"a bold indictment against a radioactive future," as she terms it on the back cover of her book *Skin Meat Bones*—we find further evidence of her allegiance to "a participatory poetics, a transformative poetics" through oral writing.[72] She explains that one of her classes at Naropa Institute one year "tried out various enactments of words to create a force field of energy for protest demonstrations at Rocky Flats plutonium plant in Boulder. One evolved into an antinuclear work that was subsequently performed as a group piece. I also began chanting 'Mega mega mega mega mega mega mega death bomb—ENLIGHTEN!' the summer of 1978, later working the lines into lyrics for a 'new-wave' recording of 'Uh Oh Plutonium!'" (*FSW*, 41). Running the words together in a frenzied vocal decrescendo, Waldman performs gender and at the same time opens up a space from which to contest hegemonic design.

Waldman's body poetics connects her to her male beat peers, and Ginsberg himself hailed her as "a poet orator," judging her body "an instrument for vocalization" and her texts "the accurate energetic fine notations of words with spoken music latent in mindful arrangement on the page," thus hailing both her page and her stage work and the dialectical relationship between them. Indeed, when Waldman pronounces her belief in a transformative poetics, she speaks on behalf of all of the beats, who sought through ritualized poetic utterance to sound—and to reconfigure—norms of identity and nation.

HIS MASTER'S VOICE: PUBLIC POETRY AND
COMMODITY CULTURE

In 1957, with Kenneth Patchen, Kenneth Rexroth, and Lawrence Ferlinghetti at the helm, the poetry-and-jazz movement made headlines, wag-
ing a frontal assault against normative (consumerist) American culture by
infiltrating the culture's very forms. As we have noted, this was not the first
such collaboration between poets and musicians, but it does represent a
new phase in the commodification of that hybrid art form, as poets sought
to enlarge their audiences and reclaim lost cultural ground by performing
their work to musical accompaniment. As Lawrence Lipton reports, the
mainstream media found the form freakishly fascinating: "Poetry and jazz
was a two-headed calf. Better yet, it was a two-headed calf of which one of
the heads was an animal of some other species, which made the whole
thing a carnival side show attraction. A monstrous miscegenation." Lipton
goes on to remark on its historicity, stating that "Before the present revival
in the United States, there were two previous and abortive attempts to restore poetry to the oral tradition. The key figures in these two attempts
were Walt Whitman and Vachel Lindsay, and Lindsay was one of the first
poets whose voice was recorded on records."[73]

The scene received national attention in a *Time* magazine article (December 2, 1957) that rather cynically focused on the bottom line—that is,
the commercial interests entailed in the emergent form: "The poetry was
usually poor and the jazz was worse, but nobody seemed to care," since
"Record business was being done by dim little jazz spots." The reporter's
sarcasm depends on a view of "Poetry" as separate and distinct from the
cultural economy, and he clearly regards these artists as sellouts. To insinu-
ate, as he does, that the poetry-and-jazz movement was merely a money-
making scheme is to draw attention away from the fact that Patchen,
Rexroth, Ferlinghetti, and their cohorts conceived of jazz as a way to capture new meanings in poetry, and, ultimately, to return poetry to its roots
in public bardic performance. Rexroth asserts that "Poetry and jazz together return the poet to his audience"; likewise, Ferlinghetti explains, poets are in "competition with the mass media" and must innovate to succeed as artists: "We're trying to capture an audience. . . . The jazz comes in
as part of an attempt to get the audience back."[74]

In Rexroth's essay "Jazz Poetry" in the *Nation* (March 29, 1958), he worries that this fusion art will be deemed "freakish or faddish" if not well

done, and he is intent on hitting a mainstream audience as he reminds his reader that the art is really nothing new, tracing it back to black expressive culture—Big Bill Broonzy and Leadbelly ("some of their records are really more talked than sung") and certain "Rock 'n Roll 'novelties,'" which also "are recited, not sung." Further detailing its genealogy, he writes that "It has become a common custom in store front churches and Negro revival meetings for a member of the congregation to recite a poem to an instrument or wordless vocal accompaniment. I believe Langston Hughes recited poems to jazz many years ago. I tried it myself in the twenties in Chicago. In the late forties Kenneth Patchen recited poems to records. Jack Spicer, a San Francisco poet, tried it with a trio led by Ron Crotty on bass."[75] Expanding on these remarks, Rexroth emphasizes the public nature of his venture and makes clear that the poet must provide an entertainment that appeals:

> The combination of poetry and jazz with the poet reciting, gives the poet a new kind of audience. Not necessarily a bigger one, but a more normal one—ordinary people out for the evening, looking for civilized entertainment. It takes the poet out of the bookish, academic world and forces him to compete with "acrobats, trained dogs, and Singer's Midgets," as they used to say in the days of vaudeville. Is this bad? I think not. Precisely what is wrong with the modern poet is the lack of a living, flesh and blood connexion with his audiences. Only in modern times has poetry become a bookish art. In its best days Homer and the Troubadours recited their poetry to music in just this way.[76]

Understood as another form of amusement within the cultural economy, jazz poetry is an attempt to reorient the artist to the community, to vitalize the public sphere. At the San Francisco nightclub the Cellar, Rexroth and Ferlinghetti put on a series of performances of poetry and jazz in the spring of 1957; these sessions were recorded and later released by Fantasy Records as *Poetry Readings in the Cellar* (1958). In jazz critic Ralph J. Gleason's liner notes to that album, Rexroth is quoted as saying that "Homer, or the guy who recited Beowulf, was show business. We simply want to make poetry a part of show business."[77]

In competition to hold the ear of the public, Ferlinghetti's book *A Coney Island of the Mind,* published in mid-1958, includes a section of poems dubbed "Oral Messages." In the prefatory note to this section he informs

his reader that "These seven poems were conceived specifically for jazz accompaniment and as such should be considered as spontaneously spoken
'oral messages' rather than as poems written for the printed page. As a result of continued experimental reading with jazz, they are still in a state of
change." As he contends, the scripted poem is ancillary, and the poems are
only fully realized in individual acts of performance. By claming that the
poems remain forever "in a state of change," he calls attention to the radical instability of his printed texts, echoing the anthropologist Milman
Parry's finding that "the oral poem even in the mouth of the same singer is
ever in a state of change."[78] Ultimately, as readers, we are refused a fixed
aesthetic object open to traditional textual analysis; no matter how often
or how closely we read the poem on the page, there is no secure meaning,
because signifier and signified are susceptible to infinite revision. Or, to put
it another way (borrowing Saussure's terminology), the syntagmatic and
paradigmatic chains (the "framework of the grammar" and the substitu-
tions available to be made in that "framework") are in oral poetry never
finally closed. When Ferlinghetti says that these "oral messages" are "spontaneously spoken," he constructs a vocal equivalent to automatic writing
and opens them up to history.

Ferlinghetti's poem "Autobiography" in the "Oral Messages" section of
A Coney Island of the Mind yields meanings in performances of it that are
not fully available from a reading of the poem on the page. According to
the album notes to the 1958 Fantasy recording, "Autobiography" "developed right along with the cellar sessions," and this live performance version of the poem is different in a number of respects from the original
printed version. For instance, Ferlinghetti leaves out the phrase "Behind
the glib / farting trumpeters" in a description of a Columbus Day Parade
and another depicting himself as "blowing on a bugle in a tight platoon"
marching up Fifth Avenue. He also retracts the pun on Wordsworth's "I
Wandered Lonely as a Cloud," not delivering the printed lines that read, "I
have heard the sound of revelry / by night. I have wandered lonely / as a
crowd." Later, he leaves out another line, "I have travelled among unknown men," along with a four-line treatment of Lincoln and Columbus.
Ferlinghetti also adds material. Toward the end of the poem he notes that
he has "slept in mailbox overnight cabins," and announces, "I have heard
the loud lament of the disconsolate chimera." He also introduces in his oral
performance the lines "I have heard the tolling bell" and "I have made peri-
phrastic studies in worn-out poetical fashions, and my equipment is always

deteriorating." At one point, too, he transposes lines found in the printed version in his oral delivery of them.

Ferlinghetti improvises on the level of the smaller units of language as well: he changes "educated" to "ignorant" in his description of the army; "outhouse" to "men's room" in another part of the poem; and alters the tense of two verbs at the outset. As with other oral poetic forms (for instance, the oral epic or feudal ballad), the syntagmatic chain (grammatical sequencing) does not aim for tight closure and rigid subordination of elements in a linear development; rather it works through juxtaposition, addition, and parallel. In a poem that is meant to narrate the life story of the poet, this lack of closure is telling. For Lacan the coherence of the subject at any given moment—its place as intending meaning—is produced along the syntagmatic chain. Here the subject is developed as "a single voice" sustaining meaning and itself sustained in this linearity. When the "Other"— all language excluded from the syntagmatic chain, along the paradigmatic axis—is made readily available to that chain, the coherence of the subject is undermined: the discourses of the conscious and the unconscious commingle, and any authoritative statement is rendered impossible, just as any authoritative autobiography is impossible prior to one's death. In this way, Ferlinghetti performs a range of identities, seeking to lay bare the constructedness of each.

Ferlinghetti's use of allusions as literary and cultural cliches also has much in common with the traditional formula of oral poetry. Indeed, several lines in "Autobiography" are reproduced exactly from English translations of three ancient Celtic riddle poems—and so reach back to the bardic tradition of thirteenth-century Wales and beyond. One of the poems that he borrows from is *The Song of Amergin,* which, as we have seen, is designed to call forth a new nation. Ferlinghetti's poem is intent on bringing into being a new sense of self as that self is produced by the country: "I am an American." By invoking that precursor text, Ferlinghetti is able to fashion himself as a modern bard opposed to a tradition of officially sanctioned court poets (or academic poets, who appear in "Autobiography" as "a hundred housebroken Ezra Pounds"). "Autobiography," then, is not only constructed as an oral poem (in terms of its prosodic designs), but is itself about that construction. It is fitting that a majority of the improvisations Ferlinghetti works on the poem in performances of it, including his transposition of lines, occurs when he communicates his role as shaping poet.

The disposition of Ferlinghetti's voice in the 1958 *Poetry Readings in the Cellar* Fantasy recording of the poem—that is, *how* the words are presented: tempo, volume, timbre, and so on—opens up further meanings. In his recital we hear a distinct rise in pitch at the end of each sentence or line: It is a chanting voice, one that intones, with all sharp contours leveled out and few, if any, medial caesurae. The editor of *New Directions*, James Laughlin, noted this quality upon hearing the recording and remarked that he "didn't like . . . the monotony of the verbal tone. . . . I think some variation in pitch and force would help."[79] Of course, the "monotony of the verbal tone" that Laughlin does not care for is the tone of the chant, which Ferlinghetti consciously adopts to credential his performance as ritual event.

Also, in the Fantasy recording of "Autobiography," jazz accompanies the poet's performance, as musicians and poet trade statements in a fugue-like structure: Ferlinghetti will read a passage of his poem and then pause while the band improvises four bars of jazz on the chords of George Gershwin's "I Got Rhythm."[80] As tenor saxophonist Bruce Lippincott, leader of the Cellar Jazz Quintet, explained of the session, "We set up as the first rule—listen to each other. And second—respond with our instruments as emotionally as possible to the words of the poem and also the prearranged form. . . . if we listen to each other, we can get a kind of question and answer thing going underneath, all without any key." The concept of responding in what he calls "a relative pitch way, a very direct way" constitutes a contrapuntal arrangement, which highlights one of the central concerns of the poem: the dialectical construction of identity.[81] By engaging in a conversation with the poet, the jazz musicians stand in for the audience, who, though present, are articulated within the poem by these musical rejoinders. In this way, Ferlinghetti stages himself in the act of being heard (that is, he figures himself in the poem as an oral poet actively engaging an audience). The decision to use as musical accompaniment "I've Got Rhythm" further signifies Ferlinghetti's effort to establish his poem (and his poetics) as improvisational, as it is a popular song that jazz musicians have often favored as a basis for improvisation. Although in retrospect Ferlinghetti did not think highly of many of his poetry and jazz performances, at their best these sessions brought out new dimensions in the poems through successful fusion.[82]

In his poem "Dog" in "Oral Messages," Ferlinghetti's improvisational ethos also functions as trope, as he analogizes the freedom of a dog—a freedom he encourages us to grab in "Junkman's Obliggato" (another poem in

this grouping)—to the freedom from social constraint that is the preroga-
tive of the poet. His initial description of the title figure, "a real live / bark-
ing / democratic dog," begins to look like a famous mediatized dog, as we
watch and participate in the process by which sound-recording technology
threatens to co-opt the live and impact our sense of it. At the end of the
poem, in syncopated lines, the dog is seen

> with his head cocked sideways
>
> > at streetcorners
>
> as if he is just about to have
>
> > his picture taken
> >
> > > for Victor Records
>
> > listening for
> >
> > > His Master's Voice[83]

Here the iconic RCA Victor dog, Nipper, expresses a freedom, or spontaneity, that resists packaging (in neat left-justified lines) even, ironically, as he
is imagined as on the verge of being packaged by "free enterprise." The fact
that the dog is seen poised before a gramophone about to have his picture
taken for the purpose of publicizing that device suggests the dilemma of
the public poet, who speaks to the masses but must be wary of being cor-
poratized and thereby "standardized" (to use Vachel Lindsay's term) in the
process.

In a recording of *A Coney Island of the Mind* in 1999, with music by saxophonist Dana Colley of the rock group Morphine, the liner notes suggest
that the poet's view of these poems as unfinalizable has not changed:
"Lawrence considers these poems in flux, even changing a few words about
in his performance." As one reviewer of the CD put it, "Strongly rooted in
the American 'scene' when they were first published, many of these poems
now speak to issues more global and, therefore, more than half a century
later, seem more urgent. Ferlinghetti's reading brings to the fore the irrev-
erent, bawdy, heartfelt longing in his poetic gospel. The music, a jazz- and
rock-influenced accompaniment, expands the listener's experience without
upstaging the words." Greg Beets, writing for the *Austin Chronicle* (December 31, 1999), also points to the "bawdy" (carnivalesque) aspect: "Lawrence
Ferlinghetti's carnival-like set of poems . . . lends itself to the music/poetry
medium in an uncommonly rich way. The 29 poems that comprise *A Coney
Island of the Mind* read at times ranging from 30 seconds to four minutes—

perfect lengths for ad jingles or pop songs. And what better way to offer an eloquent, often-hilarious critique of the emerging plastic culture than to bastardize the tools of commerce in the name of 'a new rebirth of wonder'?"[84] These critiques point up the way in which the poet has used American commodity culture against itself in his construction of a vibrant counterpublic sphere.

Ferlinghetti's commitment literally to have us hear him materializes vividly in his book *Starting from San Francisco* (1961) in the form of a 45 rpm vinyl record of the poet reading the poems "Starting from San Francisco" and "New York-Albany" on side 1 and "Overpopulation," which was "Recorded during a reading at the University of California, Berkeley, on April 22, 1960," on side 2; indeed, it may be the first time a book of poetry was packaged with music.[85] On the back cover, we encounter this description: "Ferlinghetti's poems are written to be read aloud; he conceives of them as lucid oral messages. To this end, an LP recording of the poet reading some of the poems will be found in a packet at the back of the book." Alan Dugan reviewed the book when it came out:

> Mr. Ferlinghetti documents his claim to being an oral poet by including, flapped in the back cover of his new book, a 7" LP record of himself reading his poems. (This is a good thing to do, I think, even though it must result in square books which are larger than the record, or else pamphlets which are smaller.) Oral poetry has to fit the speaker's voice. At its best it can be true of the poet, his audience, and their common situation. At its worst it can be flashy or empty, since the poet can jazz up nonsense by means of vivid performance and not tell, from his local audience's reaction, whether or not he is saying anything worth repeating except as a party piece. Mr. Ferlinghetti's verse is perfectly suited to his style of delivery, and his style of delivery is effective and engaging.

As Dugan finds, Ferlinghetti's style is largely comic: "He makes jokes and chants seriously with equal gusto and surreal inventiveness"; in keeping with this judgment, another critic refers to Ferlinghetti as a "vaudevillean persona," but his brand of comedy clearly is meant to challenge the status quo and its repressive ideologies.[86] In the *San Francisco Sunday Chronicle* James Schevill predicts that *Starting from San Francisco* will be "controversial," since it represents Ferlinghetti's "turning away from his more lyrical, earlier poems to a direct, topical, colloquial tone"; he further alleges that

These poems are written to be read aloud, and they lose a great deal on the page unless one conceives of the phrasing and emphasis of the author's voice. They demonstrate perfectly the difference between hearing and merely reading poetry, a difference which might be characterized as the warmth of inflection. The voice creates a warmth and a pulse which the eye alone cannot conceive. Consequently, New Directions has wisely included in the book a phonograph record of the author reading several of his poems . . . The phrasing which often seems repetitious and oversimplified on the page takes on a new color and dimension in terms of the dramatic intent of his voice.[87]

The literal voice of the poet in performance proves the poetry on the page, adding to it an authentic humanizing presence.

The importance of utterance and audition that Dugan stresses (he also worries about the ephemerality of effect, observing that "The danger of poems conceived as 'oral messages' is that they communicate directly, but often do not have the depth of image, of metaphorical reverberation, to remain in the mind and ear") is not lost on Ferlinghetti, whose metaphors reverberate in that direction. For example, "Tentative Description of a Dinner to Promote the Impeachment of President Eisenhower" (dated May 1958) in his book *Starting from San Francisco* in a section titled "Broadsides" (the poem first was published as a broadside by Golden Mountain Press) is about the politics of hearing and not hearing, and one line in the poem particularly points up that politics, with "the Voice of America," the official external radio and television broadcasting service of the federal government, imagined to be "really the Deaf Ear of America," since the president is "unable to hear the underprivileged natives of the world shouting No Contamination Without Representation." The cover notes to Ferlinghetti's Fantasy recording *Tentative Description of a Dinner to Promote the Impeachment of President Eisenhower and Other Poems* (1959) make plain the essential performativity of the poem: "All the poems on this record are, in one way or another, protest poems, written to be heard. Oral messages. And without jazz . . . Let the poet carry it, if he can." Striking here is the sense that the political protest, or resistance, that these poems mount necessitates an oral delivery, deemed the most effective way to move the message into the hearts of men and women. On the record we hear "slowly mounting kennel drums" fueling the political tirade, and a voice that is "often laconic," laced with irony, one that speaks volumes about the disaffection that the speaker feels.[88] Paul Blackburn judges *Tentative Description* to be "comic art, with sincerity taking a back seat," but also finds that the humor makes its mark: "He exaggerates (the subject is usually serious) and finally his most serious statements have the quality of hyperbole with the cornball delivery. But his control is perfect, and one is resentful that it works so well."[89]

Starting from San Francisco, the book in which this poem first appeared, highlights its distance from print technology in a number of ways and establishes Ferlinghetti's closeness to Whitman (he reworks Whitman's poem title "Starting from Paumanok"). First, it comes with a 45 inside the covers. Then, ironically, the typography itself seeks to enforce that distance. In the book, titles of poems are facsimile reproductions of handwritten words, scrawled in capital letters and in bold black ink, as are the page numbers in the lower corners, by "the author," with credit at the front of the book duly given. That Ferlinghetti literally had a hand in the shaping of the printed characters suggests his Whitmanic desire to create an illusion of unmediated presence—and of authenticity through handicraft—in his careful attention to the book as material object.

The mediatized voice that the book encases becomes a powerful trope in later poems, too, where Ferlinghetti pays homage to modern performance poets and their distinctive, if not always live, vocal presence. The speaker of "Belated Palinode for Dylan Thomas" in *These Are My Rivers* (1994) listens to Thomas's disembodied voice on a visit to that poet's "cliff-perched writing shed" in Wales:

> And in his tilted boathouse now
> a tape of himself is playing—
> his lush voice
> his plush voice
> his posh accent
> (too BBC-fulsome, cried the Welsh)
>
>   (42)

In these stepped lines we sense the linguistic play on Thomas's sound quality (with the resonant words "lush," "plush," "posh") and the degree to which that quality performed nationality. When, later in the poem, Dylan's "great recorded voice runs out / (grave as a gravedigger in his grave) / leaving a sounding void of light / for poets and herons to fill," Ferlinghetti indicates the irony of a mediatized orality that does not endure and so must be replaced by future poets.

Not surprisingly, Allen Ginsberg's vocalism also attracted Ferlinghetti's poetic attention. In the poem "HE," in *Starting from San Francisco,* Ginsberg is depicted in full-blown orality: "He has a microphone around his neck / at a poetry reading / and he is more than one poet." Here his mediatized voice and stage presence are imagined as filling up the room, creating a multiple illusion. In a later poem, "Allen Ginsberg Dying," "Written on Tuesday, April 8, 1997," Ginsberg's voice again claims center stage. The public poet ("Allen Ginsberg is dying / It's on all the papers / It's in the evening news") lying on his deathbed phones each of his friends to say good-bye, and the disembodied voice already is heard as separating from life: "'This is Allen' the voice says." Notably, Ginsberg does not say "This is Allen"; rather, "the voice" does, "the voice" made famous in his time through his performances, but one that has been rendered mechanical and strange on the phone. Paradoxically, though, a trace presence is preserved, and audibility extended, by virtue of mediatization: "But his voice won't die / His voice is on the land / In Lower Manhattan / . . . His voice goes by satellite over the land / over the Sea of Japan."[90]

The embodied and disembodied voices of the beats are central to the tradition of an American performance poetry and represent a crucial hinge between earlier populist-minded poets and later identitarian and countercultural poets. Showing off once again his improvisational chops, in *Americus: Book I* (2004) Ferlinghetti riffs on a warning that he uttered nearly thirty years before in "Populist Manifesto," adding to his list of those poets who "should be / gadflies of the state" ("All you far-out freaked-out cut-up poets, / All you pre-stressed Concrete poets, / All you cunnilingual poets, / All you pay-toilet poets groaning with graffiti . . .") a couple of groups that did not exist in 1975: "You Nuyorican slammers and gangsta rappers." This time the warning is issued not by an anonymous poet-speaker, though, but by none other than "great rapper Homer," as Ferlinghetti draws a line under the ancient bardic roots of performance poetry and warns these more recent public poets of bowing to the corrupting forces of market capitalism.[91] Updating his poem in this way (he recasts other earlier published poems in *Americus* as well), Ferlinghetti extends its life and his own cultural relevance. In a statement on disk he claims that "The trouble with the printed word is, it is so silent. Let poetry return to its first purpose—the oral message. Let there be a law against writing poetry. It should be spoken, then recorded."[92] In this oral message Ferlinghetti speaks for all beats, as he harps on the supreme value of the spoken word and its broadcastings throughout the populist public sphere.

CHAPTER 5

"Rappin' and Readin'":
The Frequencies of the Black Arts

shall I scream
shall I scream
a loud / scream
a long / loud / scream
of blk / ness over
chalk / colored A MU RICA

   —SONIA SANCHEZ, FROM "LIFE / POEM"

The pen is not the main tool of the poet; the poet's tongue is.

   —ETHERIDGE KNIGHT

A NETWORK OF BLACK POETS of the 1960s and 1970s were as insistent on the spoken word and its public effects as their precursors had been, even if their politics of performance radically differed. Larry Neal, a prime agent of the Black Arts movement (what he termed the "aesthetic and spiritual sister of the Black Power concept"), insisted that "the poet must become a performer, the way James Brown is a performer—loud, gaudy and racy. He must take his work where his people are: Harlem, Watts, Philadelphia, Chicago and the rural South." He further observes (with Africanist emphasis) that "Poets must learn to sing, dance, and chant their works, . . . be a kind of priest, a black magician, working juju with the word on the world."[1] Don L. Lee (later Haki R. Madhubuti) pledged his allegiance to "art for people's sake," and Etheridge Knight, maintaining that "poetry is an oral art," hailed the holy trinity of "the poet, the poem, and the people."[2] Similarly, Nikki Giovanni attests that "When the black poets started reading poetry in the early '60s—LeRoi Jones (later Amiri Baraka), Don L. Lee, Sonia Sanchez—we read at places like Liberty House in Harlem. That's what—as I understood it—we were about: doing readings. Getting the poetry to the people. We were doing readings for a dollar."[3]

These Black Arts poets believed in the importance of publicity and designed their delivery of poetry in response to an expressive black political soundscape. As Neal alleges,

> We can learn more about what poetry is by listening to the cadences in Malcolm's speeches, than from most of Western poetics. Listen to James Brown scream. Ask yourself, then; Have you ever heard a Negro poet sing like that? Of course not, because we have been tied to the texts, like most white poets. The text could be destroyed and no one would be hurt in the least by it. The key is in the music.[4]

Thulani Nkabinde Davis, who has said that it is the job of the poet "to close the distance created by printing and to give the audience a sense of community not possible in the individual experience of reading," hears in the new black poetry the dissonances of racial strife and struggle: "These sounds, tones, cries, songs, even noises [in the poetry] rang of recent and distant people and events. Their pace and volume matched the intensity with which the poet could feel these often traumatic moments: Malcolm's speeches and the gunfire of his death; Nat Turner's rebellion; Emmett Till's tragedy; Orangeburg, S.C.; Martin Luther King's life and death; the riots across the country; Fred Hampton's murder; the Algiers Motel; Franz Fanon; Cinque; and the life, times, and work of numerous black musicians." Davis even ascribes to the poetry reading (in a resounding fiction of performance) the power to "conquer the alienation promoted by urban education, housing, unemployment, experience with violence and war": poetry, she argues, has to "reach out of printed pages and become physical," to enact community at the grass-roots level.[5]

The Black Arts poets, like their forebears, sought to unearth (or at least to make visible to others) the performance traditions upon which their work is based. On her spoken word CD *In Philadelphia* (1997), Giovanni pays homage to Hughes, as does Sonia Sanchez in "For Langston / I've Known Rivers" on her CD *Full Moon of Sonia* (2004). (Sanchez also looks forward on her CD to the new generation of rap and hip hop artists, paying tribute to, among others, Tupac Shakur.) In addition, Sanchez, in "A Poem for Sterling Brown," hails that poet's oral mastery, dubbing him "griot of fire."[6] Baraka also cites Hughes as an influence, and remembers in his poem "Why Didn't He Tell Me the Whole Truth" his grandfather urging him to commit James Weldon Johnson's "The Creation" to memory.[7] In his Broadside Press–published pamphlet *Black Pride* (1968), Lee praises Hughes (along with Malcolm X and musician John Coltrane) as innovator, and blues and jazz poet Jayne Cortez professes admiration for Hughes's "oral qualities."[8] Neal, who faults the Harlem Renaissance for having "failed to take root, to link itself concretely to the struggles of that [the African American] community, to become its voice and spirit," that is, for having failed to address squarely enough a black audience, nonetheless models his publicity in part on Hughes: "I used to refuse to sell my books myself. I was hung up in that European artistic thing, until I found out that Langston Hughes used to pay his way from campus to campus by selling his books. When I discovered what Hughes did, I did not have that kind of art-for-art's-sake hangup anymore, because the duty of the artist is to communicate with people."[9]

Overlapping as they did with the beats, it is perhaps not surprising that many of these new black poets were disposed to draw similarities and distinctions between the two groups. Nikki Giovanni effectively dismisses the beats, and points up the racial politics involved in reception, when she finds that "Those people [the beats] sat down in their coffee houses, read their work to each other but if you go out into the street and say 'Jack Kerouac' no one knows who the hell you're talking about. The only way they have survived is they have become the pets of the new generation of white people. . . . Their intent was to avoid people. And we consider the intent to reach people a positive—which is what we should be about."[10] Giovanni reads the beats much as Sterling Brown and others read certain poets of the Harlem Renaissance: as white-directed and, thus, not sufficiently "public." On the other hand, Baraka, who early on associated with the beats, appreciates that they were "trying to put forward a more mass-oriented kind of art, a more people-oriented kind of art"; he notes that in the 1950s "readings became more important. People wanted to actually read poetry and the whole oral tradition was reinvoked to get poetry off the pages. . . . When the Black Poetry Movement picked up after that, readings were its principle [*sic*] form. Then the oral tradition became principle and the printed word secondary."[11] Indeed, Baraka has cited Allen Ginsberg and "Howl" as instrumental in opening up the mouth of poetry.[12] Etheridge Knight also builds a bridge to the beats, believing that both the beats and the Black Arts poets "have brought back the oral aspect to poetry": "For a long time poetry was mainly on the page, was mainly analyzing and blah blah blah on college campuses. And there was poetry going on in the streets. But I think that Black poets and the Beats have brought the general public into poetry more than especially the Forties and Thirties."[13]

Black beat poets other than Baraka, it should be noted, also exerted an influence on the Black Arts generation and its insistence on orality in poetry. Ted Joans, who was himself shaped by Hughes, is recognized for his virtuosity as an artist of the spoken word in Sonia Sanchez's January 1972 poem-review of Joans's 1969 book *Black Pow-Wow: Jazz Poems* in *Black World;* there she reports meeting Joans at a conference and attending a reading he gave where he was "blowen his poems":

> if u EVER git a chance to see/hear
> ted joans asks him to read [his poem] "the nice colored man" cuz the way
>   he
> be dooooooooen it is a gasssssss.

Later in this chapter, we will look more closely at Sanchez's expressive typography and its performative cultural effects; it is enough to note here that she prizes this elder poet's delivery style and live presence. Bob Kaufman similarly is pictured by a fellow poet in terms of his distinctive and forceful vocalism, based on his reading in San Francisco at a North Beach nightclub:

> The dynamite volcano is not extinct
> We heard you at Vesuvio's
> singing Hart Crane
> You blew America from your mouth
> and smiled your ancient vision
> round a shocked barroom[14]

In the figure of Kaufman blowing the country through his mouth, we see how thoroughly entangled the relationship is between the oral performance of poetry and the performance of nationhood and nationality for these midcentury artists.

Casting back even further, June Jordan recovers the significance of Walt Whitman's democratic ethos to Black Arts poets laboring to secure a public audience for their work. As she sees, Whitman arrived on the scene at a time when "the phenomenon of a people's poetry, or great poetry and its spontaneous popularity, could no longer be assumed"; she credits him for bypassing "intermediaries—critics and publishers—whose marketplace principles of scarcity would, logically, oppose them to populist traditions of art," and for taking his art directly to the people. Jordan feels that her generation of black poets "suffer[s] from the same establishment rejection and contempt that forced this archetypal American genius to publish, distribute, and review his own work—by himself": "within the Whitman tradition, Black and Third World poets traceably transform, and further, the egalitarian sensibility that isolates that one white father from his more powerful compatriots." Moreover, she appreciates the fact that Whitman's poetry is not obscure ("nothing an ordinary straphanger in the subway would be puzzled by!"), that it is "intimate and direct," whether read silently or aloud.[15]

The poetics of the Black Arts movement are shot through with the tension between speech and text. As Knight reminds us, recalling perhaps the West African griot tradition (griots typically perform alone, accompanying themselves on a stringed instrument), "poetry is an oral art; there were poets long before there were printing presses."[16] He explains that he writes poems to be published in order to make a living, but that his primary commitment is to live performance, the poem off the page ("My real poems are for people. What happens at a reading is very important to me"). In *Black Pride*, Lee, who, Dudley Randall reports in his introduction, "writes for the man in the street," is shown in a photo on the back cover reciting to a black audience from *For Malcolm X* (1967), the first anthology published by Broadside Press, at the dedication of Malcolm X Shabazz Park, formerly Washington Park, in Chicago. In this visual image, an authentic blackness is purchased through the graphic depiction of the poet's twin regard for publicity and orality.

The racial politics of publishing—the whiteness of the page—troubled a number of Black Arts poets. A stark hostility to the white publishing industry comes across in a note in the first paperback edition of the anthology *Black Fire*, where the editors (Neal and Baraka) apologize for the omission of the work of several black poets in the hardcover and, again, in the first paperback edition: "We hoped it [the work of these excluded black poets] wd be in the paperback, but these devils claim it costs too much to reprint. Hopefully, the 2nd edition of the paperback will have all the people we cd think of. The frustration of working thru these bullshit white people shd be obvious."[17] The publishers literally are demonized here, and there is no room to doubt the antagonism of the relationship between black writer and white capitalist holding in his hands the means of textual production. Against this backdrop, Lee insists that black poets sign on the line with black publishers, like Broadside Press, if they want to authenticate themselves as black public artists:

> One way to look at the publishing scene is to look at some of our most vocal militants—talking Black and sleeping white: or, in the writer's case, writing Black and publishing white. We can rationalize for days the many reasons for this, but we have to question the racial validity of the writer's work when we see him legitimizing his Blackness in the pages of *Evergreen Review* rather than *Black World* (formerly *Negro Digest*), in the *Nickel Review* rather than *Freedomways;* in *Commentary* rather than *Liberator,* in *Poetry Magazine* rather than the *Journal of Black Poetry.* In essence, his publishing in the white market not only raises doubts about the audiences he is trying to reach but lend support and legitimacy to white organs, as if they were the vehicles Black people should respect and read.[18]

Lee invokes the model of minstrelsy in asserting that the black author who teams with a white publisher is illegitimate, "a white poet in blackface trying to write Black." He even slyly adopts a trope of minstrelsy (the thieving "darky") to account for the racial politics governing sales of black poetry in the United States, stating (with humor) that in the late 1960s "the books of Imamu Baraka and Don L. Lee were being sold in bars, taverns, churches, and street corner news stands. The books were being refused by white bookstores for many reasons, but mainly because the Black books were being *liberated* by the brothers who didn't have money to pay as fast as the shelves were being stocked."[19]

Of course, it is theft from a different direction—the white co-optation of black music—that quietly stands behind these remarks. Lee specifically decries white imitators of black music in his Broadside-published critical study *Dynamite Voices: Black Poets of the 1960's* (1971), as does Baraka in his book *The Music,* where he points up the racial dynamics—and problematics—of authenticity as it relates to such imitation: "Elvis Presley and company" are, he alleges, "written about as if they had actually *originated* something rather than copied." In light of what he calls "the Great Music

Robbery," he alerts us to the threat of the racist appropriation of the spoken word as well: "The black arts poetry movement of the sixties with its emphasis on the declamatory oral tradition can quickly become 'Performance Poetry,' with 'Performance Poets,' dominated by whites."[20]

Fear of co-optation led Black Arts poets to seek to control to the extent that they could the construction and dissemination of their printed voices. While some poets self-published in the style of Whitman (Nikki Giovanni, for example, published *Black Feeling, Black Talk* [1968] herself: "I decided to take my poetry to the people, and if they rejected it, that would be that. Why not be rejected by the people and not some authority figure who might not know anything?"), others threw in their lot with one of the emergent black presses: Lee, with four hundred dollars and a mimeograph machine, founded Third World Press in Chicago in 1967, and Amiri Baraka started Jihad Productions the same year. More such presses followed. As Marshall McLuhan and Quentin Fiore have observed, "Xerography—every man's brain-picker—heralds the times of instant publishing. Anybody can now become both author and publisher."[21] With this revolution in print technology, speedy transmission became the priority and increased circulation was made possible; thus, it was felt, the groundwork for a broad-based black cultural revolution was being laid.

Dudley Randall, founder of Broadside Press—a small black press that published more than four hundred poets in more than one hundred books and recordings—in Detroit in 1965, remarks in the introduction to Sonia Sanchez's Broadside book *We a BaddDDD People* (1970) on that poet's admirable and fierce resistance to white publishing houses: "Sonia Sanchez is black, and it's a blackness that can't be bought. A nationally known critic advised her to let a 'professional' publisher do her next collection of poetry. Sonia commented, 'The critics don't know that Broadside Press is the ba-a-a-dest motherfucken press today.'" Sanchez elaborates that, with the exception of Gwendolyn Brooks and Langston Hughes, "none of the big publishing companies thought about publishing black writers," and she, too, points to the publicity lesson of Langston: "we were publishing and our books sold in the hundreds of thousands because our books were affordable to people. Because, when we went on trips, we would take our books with us, like Langston. Langston would travel from New York to the South and he had suitcases. In those suitcases were his books, because he said the big publishing companies would publish him, but they wouldn't promote his books." She goes on to say that when she traveled south for the first time for readings and went into people's homes, the two books she found there were the Bible and a collection of Langston Hughes's poetry.[22] For all of these poets, a primary goal was to connect with an audience that had not been reached by poetry before and to connect those audience members to each other, to forge a politically potent black counterpublic sphere, "a nation within the belly of white America."[23]

This chapter will explore the ways in which black cultural nationalism and subsequent phases in the ideological evolution of prominent poets within the Black Arts movement find expression through the practice of their art. For these poets, the performative symbolism of speech and text is crucial to their negotiation of relations of power in the United States, with the paralinguistic features of their oral messages and the encoding of these in inscriptional practice key to a thorough understanding of their enactment of an identity politics. Their performance and deformance of tropes of blackness and nationhood—and, within those, of manhood and womanhood—point to the complicated politics of poetry recital in America, at a time when black poetry was intent on becoming physical.

DISSONANT DISSENT: SCRIPTING BLACK NATIONALISM

Even as Black Arts poets sought to communicate on the page, they often worried about whether the effects of a poetry primarily based on the launched voice could be conveyed adequately in print (a concern that we have heard raised before). Leaving the question open, the black literary critic Stephen Henderson in 1972 observed that "The central problem again is the printed page. Perhaps it will remain with us as a reminder of our compromise with a cold technology. Perhaps not."[24] In *Dynamite Voices* Lee observed of a poem by Nikki Giovanni, master of the "fast rap," that while "Orally this is cool, . . . it doesn't come across as printed poetry."[25] As Henry Louis Gates, Jr., has noted, "So much of our [African American] literature seems dead on the page when compared to its performance," and Barbara Johnson, in reply to Gates, agrees, going against the grain of her own theoretical presumptions: "Trained as I am in deconstruction, I have always been suspicious of the privileging of the spoken word as a sign of presence or authenticity. But this attitude clearly cannot account for the *signifying* dimensions (precisely, the inflection) of performance. If Afro-American literature is sometimes, as Gates puts it, 'dead on the page,' it may be that the dimension it inhabits is not primarily visual or spatial."[26] While such a statement may ring true, it is also the case that Black Arts poets sought every means at their disposal to allow their work to succeed on the visual and spatial field of the page, even if that appearance is sometimes a secondary effect, and even if its transcription did pose a certain "problem."

In his introduction to Sanchez's book *We a BaddDDD People*, her publisher Dudley Randall notes the oral aesthetic that Sanchez shares with Lee and other Black Arts poets and the dialectic between orality and print established by her texts; believing that "Much of the new black poetry depends on sound for its effect," and that "some of it, alas, when written down on the page becomes merely banal," he concludes that Sanchez's does not, that it "has a notation that preserves much of the sound of an actual oral reading": "Perhaps the best way to solve this problem would be to place all lines flush left and to select such inevitable words that the silent reader would be forced to vocalize them in his mind just as the poet wanted them to sound" (10). The "problem" that he refers to here is that of representing the full set of expressive effects that the poet wants to get across. Sanchez's strategy to overcome the deficit of the printed page is to encode on it the politically discordant sounds of blackness, as she breaks through the hegemony of a script-centered poetics by violating the integrity of the script itself.

Indeed, central to the success of Sanchez's black revolutionary poetry are her tonal semantics, which work to validate her "blackness." The title poem, "We a BaddDDD People," is scored on the page in such a way as to indicate a particular vocalization; as performed out loud (or silently), it is meant to sound in a staccato patter (or stutter): "We a Bad-Bad-BaD-BaD-BaD People." Within the poem we also encounter the following notation four times in quick succession: "aaa-ee-ooo-wah / wah." Her poetic transcription of scat, the imitation of musical instruments and production of nonsense syllables, is meant to authenticate her blackness and symbolizes her own improvisational racial performativity. Indeed, in Sanchez's "a/coltrane/poem," also in *We a BaddDDD People*, we encounter such a blitz of sound effects that the page is transformed into a chaotic field of black on white (dislocated orthographics, lower- and uppercase lettering alternating within a single word, hyphens, dashes, slashes, parenthetical performance directions):

(to be   rise up blk/people
sung   de dum da da da da
slowly   move straight in yo/blackness

to tune	da dum da da da da
of my	step over the wite/ness
favorite	that is yessss terrrrrr day
things.)	weeeeeeee are tooooooooday.

(71)

It is in this graphic figure of utter deformity—a radical racialized dissonance—that Sanchez locates political empowerment, mounting her assault
on textual whiteness. She transforms acoustics on the page much as John
Coltrane transformed "My Favorite Things" in his jazz interpretation of it
ten years earlier, nodding in his direction in the marginalia.

Ironically, it is in many ways the white poet Charles Olson's essay
"Projective Verse" (1950), an essay that Baraka recognized as important
and edited for his Totem Press series, that opened up these avenues of expression. As he states there, "Verse now, 1950, if it is to go ahead, if it is to
be of *essential* use, must, I take it, catch up and put into itself certain laws
and possibilities of the breath, of the breathing of the man who writes as
well as of his listenings"; he calls his method "COMPOSITION BY FIELD."
Lamenting that "What we have suffered from, is manuscript, press, the re-
moval of verse from its producer and its reproducer," Olson credits the
typewriter for allowing the sort of scoring that he desires (fully noting the
irony that a machine would pose a solution to a machine-made problem),
and urges that contemporary poets pick "the fruits of the experiments of
Cummings, Pound, Williams, each of whom has, after his way, already
used the machine as a scoring to his composing, as a script to its vocali-
sation":

> It is the advantage of the typewriter that, due to its rigidity and its space pre-
> cisions, it can, for a poet, indicate exactly the breath, the pauses, the sus-
> pensions even of syllables, the juxtaposition even of parts of phrases, which
> he intends. For the first time the poet has the stave and the bar a musician
> has had. For the first time he can, without the convention of rime and me-
> ter, record the listening he has done to his own speech and by that one act
> indicate how he would want any reader, silently or otherwise, to voice his
> work.

Olson goes on to recommend a range of devices that will enforce the poet's
breath as the primary prosodic unit, including blank space between

phrases, enjambment, the backslash and solidus, which are to be used when a poet wants "a pause so light it hardly separates the words, yet does not want a comma—which is an interruption of the meaning rather than the sounding of the line," ellipses, and "multiple margins."[27]

Such methods of typographic inscription are fundamental to Black Arts verse. As Knight avows, "My lines, my form, everything is simply meant to approximate the spoken words. When I leave out periods, or use slash marks, or jam words together, or pull them apart, or leave a space, it's simply meant to try to help the reader say . . . [the poem] the way I say it."[28] Even so, his prosodic practice is tame compared to that of Sanchez, with his slashes appearing typically at junctures in syntax, as in "The Idea of Ancestry" from his Broadside-published *Poems from Prison* (1968):

I walked barefooted in my grandmother's backyard/I smelled the old
land and the woods/I sipped cornwhiskey from fruit jars with the men/
I flirted with the women/I had a ball till the caps ran out
and my habit came down.[29]

Nikki Giovanni similarly has remarked that "you should write the way you breathe," and of the pervasive ellipses in her 1983 book *Those Who Ride the Night Winds* ("Trees are never felled . . . in summer . . . Not when the fruit . . . is yet to be borne . . . Never before the promise . . . is fulfilled"), she remarks, "I thought it was a good way to have human breath breaks on the page, without intimidation to the reader."[30] Her fear of overloading the page with notation—of creating a text that is not easily read and thus precludes an immediate, sensory, and preanalytical perception of the performance—is telling, as she sees her own standing as a public poet possibly compromised by creating illegible text.

Sanchez's postprojectivist inscriptions are radically deformative, as she seeks to mime the runs of the revolutionary voice through her use of the slash, idiosyncratic spacing and spelling, "speedwriting" (the contraction of words, as "cd" for "could"), and capitalization. Her pace and volume keep the politics present to us, and are in keeping with her fierce black nationalism. As a result, *We a BaddDDD People* was criticized by some for its shrillness and "noisy exhortation." Others, though, found her racialized "blue/blacksound" militant *and* melodious, hearing on the page a "surprised softness," a voice with the "ability to be forceful without force." Consistent with these claims, a review of the book in *Black*

World (April 1971) describes the poems paradoxically as "shout[ing] softly."[31] Sanchez's performance of her message of social protest is also a canny performance of gender, of an empowered, but not unsexed, black womanhood.

Sanchez's carefully modulated vocalism sounds throughout her liberationist performance-centered texts. In "blk/chant" in *We a BaddDDD People,* we are instructed,

> (to be sed everyday.
>> slowly)

(33)

The poem is presented as a liturgical script, as a poem meant to be incorporated into the ritual performance of cultural identity in everyday life. In the poem, Sanchez chants in order to alert her people to the crisis of their situation and exhort them to action, to sow the seed of social revolution:

> Yes. brothas & sistuhs.
>> repeat every day
> (as u reach
>> for that scag
>>> reefers
>>>> wine
> that send u spinnen into witeness
> forgetten yo / blackness.)

(33)

In "a chant for young / brothas & sistuhs" in the section of the book entitled "Love/Songs/Chants," Sanchez hails her audience through the deictic

>> yeah yall
>>> rat there
> listen to me
> screeaamen this song.

thereby attempting to wake black Americans up and out of their drug-induced haze, their "wite / highs," to the crucial task of self-determination:

listen to this drummen.
this sad / chant.
                    listen to the tears
flowen down my blk / face
                    listen to a
death/song being sung on thick/lips
by a blk/woman

                                                    (42)

It is through the figure of black womanhood—the recognition of the black man's need to find his voice through her ("once I loooved a man / still do looove that man / want to looove that man again / wish he'd come on home again")—that power resides. What Carolyn Rodgers states in a 1971 article in *Black World* about black political struggle goes to the heart of the poem: *"the survival of a nation rests with its women."*[32]

In the next poem in the section "Love/Songs/Chants," "blk / wooooomen / chant," the speaker is again foregrounded, and here, too, typography registers intensity, shifts in emphasis, rhythmical beats and breaks, as a distinctly black female voice plaintively wails:

waiten. waiten. WAITEN. WAITENNNNNN
            A long AMURICAN wait.
Hurrrrreeehurrrrreeehurrrrreeeeeeeeeee

                                                    (45)

The woman calls on "blacKKKKKKKKKKKKmennnnnnnnnnn" to recognize the "plain ol blk/wooomen" standing before them, urging,

            pro tect us
    treat us rite
                looooovvVVE us
    yeh. here. now.

The speaker believes that it is through such behavior—that is, by plugging themselves into these "hi/voltage" black women—that black men's standing as "warriors" can be secured. The caressing tonalities of the poem-chant (a "rite") are intended to empower black men through its performance of a sexual politics, where black womanhood is posited, paradoxically, as both protective and in need of protection. Notably, Sanchez is not working in the blues mode, however; indeed, in "liberation / poem" in *We a BaddDDD People,* she pointedly rejects the blues as "sounds of / oppression," with her emphasis all on preparing the ground for the coming black revolution: To the question "am I blue?" she answers "no. i'm blk / & ready" (54).

Other performance-centered texts in *We a BaddDDD People* thematize the mastery of acoustics in expressive black America, with both utterance and audition spotlighted as acts of public consequence. In "life / poem," for instance, the speaker wonders whether she will be able to raise her voice when the time for "the death cry" ("ah—eh—eee—ooo—AH") to effect black liberation is at hand:

> shall I scream
> a loud / scream
> a long / loud / scream
> of blk / ness over
> chalk / colored A MU RICA

In "listenen to big black at s.f. state," she stages herself as auditing a speaker denouncing whites to no effect: The only solution, she feels, is to start beating the drums of revolution, "maken warriors / out of boys" and "blk/woooomen / outa girls" so as to be strong for the struggle. At the end of the poem, she scats a tribute to her black political heroes:

> aree-um-doo-doo-doooooo. MalcolMmmm
> aree-um-doo-doo-doooooo. ElijahHHH
> aree-um-doo-doo-doooooo. Imamuuuu
>
> just the sonnnng of chiefs.
> loud with blk/nation/hood
> builden.

(48–49)

As Sanchez finds, building a black nation requires more than just speaking up (as "big black at s.f. state" does); it calls for a war cry. In her citation of three black fiery orators, she performs according to her own poetics of modulated "loud-soft"ness, connecting herself to the public power that these men symbolize through chant.

In addition to the carefully considered typographical noises by which she declares herself, the choice of font for Sanchez's black nationalist poetry confirms her status as a public poet. Dudley Randall has noted that "All the Broadside books were letter pressed in sharp, offset letter type. I would choose the type to harmonize with the book, and I would design the cover to harmonize with the contents of the book."[33] For *We a BaddDDD People,* he decided to use a dark sans-serif, with titles in bold, a typeface typically used for headlines, and, therefore, one that insists on the contemporaneity and public relevance of her political poems. The effect of the font is one of oral insistence, with the words seeming to leap from the page in a way that undergirds the assaultive political message that runs through them.

Like Sanchez, Don L. Lee "joins words together or splits syllables into fractions for greater expressiveness," as Randall observes in the introduction to Lee's *Black Pride.*[34] In Lee's first book, the self-published and self-distributed *Think Black* (he sold over 700 copies on street corners in Chicago in a week in 1966), we find these effects first on display, as in his poem for the political activist H. Rap Brown, "Re-Act for Action":

> re-act to whi-te actions:
>> with real acts of blk / action.
>> BAM BAM BAM

In his third book *Don't Cry, Scream* (1969) (the very title announces its refusal of the tears that Sanchez's female speakers sometimes shed), vocalization serves as an agent of and figure for political resistance, and Lee spells out (in self-descriptive fashion) in the preface the political opposition mounted by such a discordant poetics: "Blackpoetry in form/sound/wordusage/intonation/rhythm/repetition/direction & beauty is opposed to that which is now (& yesterday) considered poetry, i.e., whi-te poetry."[35]

Pitted against what he sees as a racist mass media, Lee highlights the disruptive revolutionary power of the unmediated black voice, as this densely ideophonic passage from "DON'T CRY, SCREAM," a performance-centered text in memory of John Coltrane, demonstrates:

> naw brother,
> i didn't cry,
> i just—

Scream-eeeeeeeeeeeeeee-ed	sing loud
SCREAM-EEEEEEEEEEEEEEEEEE-ED	& high with
we-eeeeeeeeeeeeeeeeeeeeee ee	feeling
WE-EEEEEEeeeeeeeeeEEEEEEEE	letting
WE-EEEEEEEEEEEEEEEEEEEEEEEE	yr / voice
WHERE YOU DONE GONE, BROTHER?	break

(29)

Other passages similarly entail recital cues in the margins alongside the wailing and screeching ("sing / loud & / long with / feeling"; "improvise / with / feeling"). Toward the end of the poem, the speaker, sotto voce, puts across his radical politics, one ready at any moment to explode through the surface:

can you scream—brother?	very
can you scream—brother?	soft
i hear you.	
i hear you.	

The repeated reply, "i hear you," suggests that listening to the ideological message is as important as the sounding of it in the project of nation build-ing. These same figures of utterance and audition shape Lee's lyric "Mal-colm Spoke / who listened?" where the failure to heed Malcolm's insurgent words ensures continued oppression, and his poem "Assassination," in which it is reported that Martin Luther King, Jr., has been hit by a bullet in the "throat-neck," a sign of the silencing of a politically defiant vocalism.[36]

Lee's own resistant voice was in high demand: it is reported that by 1971 he had sold "more books of poetry (some 250,000 copies) than probably all the black poets who came before him combined"; moreover, his "unique delivery" of his poetry in performance secured him "a popular appeal which is tantamount to stardom."[37] Two of the most popular tapes in the Broadside Voices series were "Don L. Lee Reads *Don't Cry, Scream!*" and "Don L. Lee Reads *We Walk the Way of the World.*"[38] As liner notes attest, Lee's project of "culture building" leads him to "his explosive, annuncia-tory kinetic rap style," and, we are told, he is "one of the most imitated po-ets among young artists seeking to develop a performance style."[39] In his percussive delivery, he intends to pound into people the reality of the American racial situation. Lee was a popular reader on college campuses and at political conferences (Broadside Press produced just one album—as opposed to cassettes and tapes—of recorded poetry: Lee's *Rappin' and Readin'* (1970), which was recorded live at Wayne State University). Typically, he would talk politics between poems, for instance telling black students in the audience that they "were being processed into want-to-be-white people, an accusation that echoed the charges of H. Rap Brown."[40] Indeed, like Brown, who got his name "Rap" based on his verbal dexterity as a youth (a dexterity that helped him win when playing the dozens), and the Last Poets, a popular group of poets and musicians who formed in the late 1960s and proved to be an early influence on hip hop, Lee would challenge his audience to disavow white nationalism—the nationalism that they all had learned growing up and unwittingly were passing onto their children. This intense dialogism, with Lee challenging and provoking his audience in direct ways, goes hand-in-hand with the seamless conjoining of poetry and public discourse that I will examine in the chant work of several of Lee's female peers, where aggressive tones yield to more mellow, though no less refractory, ones.

One side of *Rappin' and Readin'* features Lee rapping (that is, informally talking) the preface to his 1970 book *We Walk the Way of the New World*. It is a politically potent statement that seeks to bring into being a new black consciousness. His delivery of it is quick and easy, a verbal display in the style of repartee. When we hear him read his poems on the other side of the album, the same speed and plosiveness obtains: he talks the poems as he would sound off in casual conversation or discussion. Between poems he speaks out on issues related to black life in America and black nationalism, for instance, homophobically denouncing "fags" as wholly unhelpful in the building of a black nation, and enacts his masculinity at the same time. As opposed to poets like James Weldon Johnson and Langston Hughes who were intent on sounding a more formal English, Lee's racy recorded street conversation aims to reach a general black audience in familiar tones meant to narrow the distance between the patter of poetry and the politics of public life.

Broadside Press was all about bringing poetry to the people. In *Black World* (December 1971), Dudley Randall articulated the public thrust of his venture: "Broadsides are poems printed on single sheets of paper. I started with $12.00, and that amount paid part of the printing costs of the first broadside. I had noticed how people would carry tattered clippings of their favorite poems in their billfolds, and I thought it would be a good idea to publish them in an attractive form as broadsides."[41] The Press also sought to authenticate print and mediatized performances of its poets by way of signs of their unique subjectivity that in turn would boost their publicity. Posters showcased a single poem, a limited number of which were signed by poet and artist. In 1968, the Press inaugurated the Broadside Voices series, cassettes and reel-to-reel tape recordings of black poets reading their own work, and, between 1968 and 1975, twenty-five Broadside books were recorded on tape. Having gotten the idea for a series of tapes from John Martin's Black Sparrow Press of Los Angeles, Randall decided to set the price of the tapes at five dollars apiece, as opposed to ten dollars (Martin's price), "because our audience does not have as much money as the Black Sparrow audience has"; as he went on to explain:

> I thought it would be very good if you could hear the voice of the living poet reading his tape. . . . We do not publish many of these because we haven't found a large audience of people that have tape recorders and buy tapes. Our original plan was to publish fifty tapes that would be autographed, and that would be that.[42]

The autograph was meant to serve as a sign of presence, supplementing the disembodied voice of the poet. Randall's recognition of the fact that sound recording and playback technologies were not as affordable as they would become suggests the shifting nexus of oral and print modalities during these racially turbulent years.

Although the Broadside tapes did not sell as well as the books and broadsides, no doubt for the reason that Randall gives, they suggest the importance of the spoken word in Black Arts verse and the value accorded sites of performed blackness. Etheridge Knight's Broadside tape *Poems from Prison,* made in 1968 in Indiana State Prison, where he served eight years, sold sixty copies at five dollars each between 1968 and 1976.[43] (Over the same period, the book had total sales of $4,766, at one dollar a copy.) As one writer has noted of the Broadside Voices series, "There are interesting sound effects in some of the tapes," including in *Poems from Prison.* Dudley Randall recalls that Knight at first was intimidated by "the precise diction" that he heard when Randall played a tape of James Emanuel, an African American college professor, reciting from his book *The Treehouse,* and that Knight had to make four tapes before he was satisfied with his performance. Randall reports that the first tape was "realistic," the background gritty with ambient "sounds of iron doors slamming, radios playing, and prisoners yelling" (13).[44] Of course, such sounds authenticate the poetry in ways that the printed page cannot do (or typically would not do), pointing to the black public sphere of the jail and the performance of black masculinity entailed there.

Knight points up both the oralness of his poetry and its ritualistic aspect when he explains that he "understand[s] poetry and the poet as a song—as a chant. . . . When you say things in a chant, they take on a different meaning from what you say—and you may be saying the same words—in everyday speech."[45] Insisting on the need for the poem to be activated in vocal performance, Knight further alleges that "none of it [poetry] stands up on the page as well as it does out loud," that his own blues poems "are written down for somebody to read aloud. . . . The written word is an extension of the spoken word. What the fuck is a word other than something that represents sound . . . That's all that is . . . and it's not ended until it's said aloud. A poem isn't finished unless the reader reads it aloud. That's where that's at." Knight's pages are less busy with recitation cues than the pages of many of his Black Arts contemporaries. He does not need an elaborate notational field in his blues poems, he argues, because he "can hear the blues on the page unlike perhaps a scholar who didn't live it": "it's a matter of hearing." In holding this view, Knight stands with those who believe that the vocal effects of poetry need not be scored for the cultural outsider, that the sounds are there on the page to be heard by those in the know.[46]

CHANTS OF A NEW BLACK WOMANHOOD

In the wake of the commercial experiment of Broadside Voices, and with the availability of more affordable stereophonic technology throughout all segments of the United States, a long string of audio recordings, including on cassette, LP, and CD, has poured forth from Black Arts poets into the twenty-first century. In some cases, these recordings strive for dissonance, much as some of the printed texts themselves do; in other cases, though, an effort has been made to engineer a more melodious sound that would appeal to a wider black audience. Some of these performances include musical accompaniment; with others, the performer's voice stands alone. Of particular interest are recordings made by virtuoso black women artists of the period, women like Sonia Sanchez and Nikki Giovanni, who, through their vocal arrangements, serve up a trenchant political critique in ways unavailable to a printed poem.

Nikki Giovanni, who recorded one Broadside tape, puts music to her spoken words in later studio sessions to activate a transgenerational community of black Americans, especially reaching out to an older audience, who, she says, "usually do not attend militant rallies or street activities" and who may not be receptive to the inflammatory rhetoric of black nationalism. She recites her poems to the accompaniment of gospel music— the New York Community Choir under the direction of Benny Diggs—on her first album *Truth Is On Its Way* (Right On Records, 1971). (The poems were first performed live at a free concert at Harlem's Canaan Baptist Church in the summer of 1971 before a crowd of 1,500.)[47] As Giovanni explains of her musical selection, "I wanted something my grandmother could listen to and I knew if gospel music was included, she would listen. I have really been gratified with the response of older people, who usually feel that black poets hate them and everything they have stood for. The record demonstrates that this isn't so." She goes on to say, "The album also 'converted' a number of listeners who previously had some difficulty relating to Black poetry because they found it to be offensive and antagonizing." Taking the edge off of the discordant notes of a group like the Black Panthers, Giovanni resonates familiarly (and so unthreateningly) in an attempt to widen the revolutionary circle, and looks at the situation—and her role as public poet—pragmatically: "Let's say that old people have bad eyes, or, we don't like to talk about it, but a lot of people, first of all, cannot read. These people can put the album on and listen to it and really understand its message. . . . I wanted them to be able to sit down and hear (the spiritual) *Peace Be Still*, and they would be able to relate to what Aretha Franklin went through and say, 'Yes Lord.' But more than that, they would say to themselves, 'She's not going to jump on me.'"[48]

The music on *Truth Is on Its Way* does more than simply tap a new audience; as Giovanni reveals, it offers up "a valid comment on my poetry." Each song on *Truth* is chosen carefully to pair with a poem. The album opens with "Great Pax Whitey" read to the strains of the hymn "Peace Be Still," a song that tells the story of Jesus calming the sea during a storm and presents a powerful allegory for black communities in upheaval. On later tracks, Giovanni notes, her poem "Nikki-Rosa" "matches well with the song *It Is Well With My Soul*[,] and the poem on Rap Brown, one of my fa-

vorite people, goes well with *This Little Light of Mine,* which expresses how
I feel about him."[49] In the case of "Nikki-Rosa" (the poet's childhood nickname), the gospel singing preludes her reading of the poem, which is about
her happy childhood, a thing, she says, her white biographers never understand, as they presume that the life of a poor black girl could entail only
misery. The spiritual ("It Is Well with My Soul") announces, along with the
poem, that she is in a place of contentment and is imbued with a feeling of
empowerment (as she told an interviewer, "I like it 'cause the song leaves
me in charge").[50] In the case of the poem about Black Panther H. Rap
Brown, the gospel song "This Little Light of Mine" with its dulcet tones
shines a different light on that political figure, whom Sanchez mellows for
her audience, seeking to make him and his message more palatable. Her
own "soft voice" on the record plays into this project, as she tones down
the revolutionary rhetoric but not the revolutionary message.[51]

   Giovanni's album was immensely popular, and the artist credits its being played on the radio as "absolutely key" to its success. (It sold more than
100,000 copies in its first six months.) The phenomenon that it became
earned her the scorn of Baraka, who believed she was a sellout, a mass-marketed flash-in-the-pan. Indeed, one reviewer of the album suggested that
Giovanni was exploiting black people through it: "It is the responsibility of
black artists to be Seekers-of-the-Truth in the tradition of Douglass and
Dubois [sic] and not to become moneychangers in the Temple of black
people's future."[52] Such a finding, fair or not, points up the peril that comes
with the entry of poetry into the cultural economy, and the conversion of
artist into celebrity in the public, or even counterpublic, sphere.

   Giovanni's *Like a Ripple on a Pond* (Niktom Records, 1973), released a
couple of years after *Truth Is on Its Way,* was met with a tepid response by a
reviewer for *Black World* (July 1974), who worried further about the commodification of the spoken word and the politics surrounding it:

> The sound has none of the aliveness of *Truth Is On the Way* [sic], which was
> Nikki's first album. The addition of bass and drums to the regular piano and
> organ make for a slickness and a commercial sound that is not appealing to
> this reviewer. Instead of helping the choir to get down, it obtrudes.
> Nowhere here does the choir move as authentically as on the earlier set. The
> arrangements do not allow them to stretch out. (I concentrate on the choir
> because, basically, they are three-fourths of the record.)[53]

Most of the time, poems and music do not "mesh," the reviewer notes, and, in terms of its revolutionary charge, he laments that "the feeling of fire and commitment is gone. As absent from this work as it was flaming, scorching hot on the last album." A *New York Times* review of a reading that Giovanni gave at Alice Tully Hall on July 25, 1972, a reading that included some of these new poems, deems the poet "cool in tone and presence" and senses "a sharp modulation in tone" from "the militancy and strident note of protest in her book, 'Black Feeling, Black Talk, Black Judgment'": "Last night, her poems seemed more conciliatory, more understanding, militant but in a muted way."[54] Here her soothing vocalism stands as a sign of a partially lapsed politics, or at least a retreat from vociferousness into a quieter persistence. However, the reviewer also points out the enduring bond that the poet forges with her audience, "the feeling of kinship, nay communion, between Miss Giovanni, the New York Community Choir and the musicians who assisted her, and the audience. . . . The sense of communion was palpable, a canopy that enveloped everyone in the hall. It was a hand-clapping, foot-tapping, body-swaying audience, mostly black, mostly young and it filled the hall. . . . If there was a line between those on the stage and those in the seats it was not visible to this observer." Refusing the "propriety" of customary poetry readings, Giovanni works to forge an expressive dialogic counterpublic sphere through ritualized authenticating performance that will allow her message to gain a full hearing.[55]

Of her recordings, Giovanni says she is interested in trying "to make use of all media" to get her message across:

> It would be ridiculous, the only word I can think of, that I would live in an electronic age and not choose to electronically transmit my voice. . . . I think that our obligation is to use whatever technology is available, because whether or not art is able to be translated tells us something about whether or not it's, in fact, living, whether or not it's part of us. . . . So if I were a poet when Gutenberg invented his press, I would say, "let me recite this, and you write it down, and we'll get it printed. And we'll see what this becomes," because you don't want to ignore the possibilities.[56]

Although Giovanni was criticized by some for her multimedia packagings, she clearly saw her mission as a public poet realized in crossover appeal. Her eagerness to adapt new broadcasting technologies to her poetic purposes substantiates the oral basis of her art and the running dialectic in it between speech and text.

The resonance that Giovanni strives for in her effort to build a transgenerational black political community resembles the liquid sounds of Sanchez's performance style. Sanchez began by reading her poetry in bars, refining her style in San Francisco, where, she says,

> we really, many of us really got out, began to get our teeth into that whole reading bit. And you must remember, when we were reading poetry at that time, there was not that interest in poetry. Period. People had their ears tuned to radios and whatever, et cetera, and you know, something with a beat. So you had to engage people in a dialogue to draw them into what you were going to do. So I began to, when I got an audience that was like really rough or loud, or perhaps saying, "Well, what is this?" before someone comes on the scene, or "Where is this poet coming from?" before the dance or whatever, I began to talk about the poem which would lead right into the poem. And then you had people, they'd listen to what you said, and then, when you had their ear, you'd take them into a poem.

Indeed, in public performance, her discussions surrounding her poems blend seamlessly into the poems themselves, as she discovers that, with the move toward black themes in poetry in the mid-1960s, there is a need "to integrate the talk with the poem," such that "you didn't know where one began and where the other one left off," and in that way bring more people to poetry by refusing to mark it off as some sanctified discourse. Along with Giovanni, who notes that at poetry readings "at least half of what I'm doing is talking with the audience," Sanchez too comes into close communion with her audience, speaking *to* them in an effort to forge a solidarity that will be capable of mounting effective political resistance.[57]

Sanchez's ambition to integrate the talk with the poem is met in her recording *A Sun Woman for All Seasons Reads Her Poetry* (Folkways, 1971). She announces at the outset that "This record is gonna be talking about love. A black woman's love for her children, man and nation," and it is in these overlapping commitments—and her performance of these commitments—that she begins to redefine her identity and the identity of a larger African American community.[58] The first set of poems on the album includes "Black Magic," an intense erotic lyric about her love for her man, and his for her:

magic
>   my man
is you
>   turning
my body into
a thousand
smiles.

The final word of the poem, "breathe," is not drawn out typographically in *Home Coming* (1969), the book in which the poem appears. On *Sun Woman,* however, Sanchez elongates that word in such a way that it might have been scored "breeeeeeeeathe." The opening up of the vowel sound at the center of the word re-creates, or mimes, the effect of sexual release that the speaker describes. In this case her refusal of a kind of eye dialect, for so long seen by African Americans as a means of misrepresenting and minstrelizing black figures in literature by whites, would appear to be an effort to come across in print, not to disfamiliarize her speech, in her first collection of poetry. (It is not until her second book, *We a BaddDDD People,* that the elongation of words on paper as a cue to pronunciation becomes standard practice.)

In many of her love poems on *Sun Woman,* Sanchez records her longing for her man and the satisfaction he provides in the carefully orchestrated inscription of words on the page. In "last poem i'm gonna write about us," for instance, her painful yearning is scored in the following way:

>   cuz I waaannNT
>   neeeeEEeeD u so
>   baaaaAdDD.

On the record, Sanchez's voice activates these expressive words via a mid-word stutter: "I wa-ant you; I nee-eed you." The erratic use of lower- and uppercase letters is meant to signify the pitchiness of the lover in the throes of desire. In the liner notes to the album, Sanchez (or an editor) corrects errors in spelling by hand—the typed word "toouch" is amended to read "tooouch," and the typed word "naturrral" in two places is amended to read "naturrrral"—thus suggesting the interest in scoring precisely the sonic contours of each word as orally performed.

A poem in *Home Coming* titled "to ChucK" indicates Sanchez's under-

standing that her unconventional poetic formatting is not without precedent, as the speaker tells her lover in that poem,

    i'm gonna write me
        a poem like
           e. e.
      cum
          mings to
             day. a
  bout you
      mov
          ing iNsIdE
            me

Here she imagines intercourse and the lines of her own body as mediated,
"rul / ED" on lines of paper, the field of the page capable of expressing in
its way the ecstatic gropings and gyrations of sex. Her self-consciousness
about doing it on the space of the page, with her lover 3,000 miles away,
colors the entire poem, as the event of

    scr
       EW
   ing
      on WH
         ite   pa   per

impresses a sense of the page as authoritarian in its patrolling of the limits
of appropriate discourse and of her own capacity to disrupt that authority,
skirting the limits (à la Cummings) through an unruly typographic inscription. That the intermediary agent is white strongly suggests a racial politics
that steers away from Cummings, with black expressiveness deforming, by
making almost illegible, hegemonic discursive practice and that for which
it stands.[59]

   Sun Woman includes two versions of the poem "a/black/woman/
speaks," whose title points to the agency that comes with public articulation, the entwinement of oratorical and political mastery. That there are
two poems with the same title on the album further indicates the improvisatory nature of Sanchez's performance aesthetic, as she offers dual

takes on the same theme. The version she delivers first begins in a bold conceit:

> i am deep/black soil
> they have tried to pollute me
> wid a poison called amurica

Sanchez as speaker expresses her antagonistic relationship to her nation, which in its misspelling suggests her disidentification from it and its racist practices. Later in the poem, Sanchez again performs herself, this time through a more expressive typography:

> i am deeeeeEEEp
> blue/black/soil

Continuing in this vein, she again locates herself according to race and gender, with indentation, slashes, and orthographic irregularities marking her out as her own woman, a rich field in which to cultivate a subaltern black American counterpublic:

> i. be/en blk.
> woooOOMAN
> know only the way of the womb
> fo I am deep/red/soil
> fo our emerging/black/nation.

As heard on *Sun Woman,* the poem is nested in talk that is crucial to the overall effect Sanchez is trying to achieve. Leading up to her reading of it on the record, she states, "One of the most important words that we don't say, black people don't say, they don't say we love each other. We have to start dealing with ourselves loving ourselves, dealing with each other. Loving each other because it do be about that. Because as a black woman: . . ."[60] At this point, she segues into a reading of the poem, the boundary between the two in oral performance fully dissolved, her rap perfectly consistent with her public poetic voice.

In her informal discourse leading up to the second poem by that name, she tells her audience, "Black women especially have been many things in this country and quite often when I talk to people I always tell young sisters you have to be more than your mama was. You have to be more than people think you be; you have to be. Because in the past we have been this: . . ."[61] Once again, without skipping a beat, she reads the poem, this version fashioning a series of metaphors that call attention to the untapped oracularity of African American women:

> we are songs
>> yet unsung
> we are music
>> yet unplayed
> we be black/women
>>> yeh. yeh. yeh. yeh.
>>> (singen in the night)

The chorus sounds differently when it is repeated later in the poem ("yeh. yehhhHH. yehhH"; "yeh. yeh. yehhhhHH"), as does the sentence "we be black/women," which becomes "we be/blk/women," then "we be black woomen," and, finally, "we be blk/woooomen." These improvisational turnings suggest the free-form expressiveness of Sanchez, whose ecstatic patter at the end of the poem celebrates the dawning of a new sense of self and agency:

> YehhhhhhHHHH!
> (moven in the sun)
> sun.   sun.
> sun.   sun.
> sun.   sun.
> sun.   sun.
> sun—n—n—n—n—n
> Yehhhh!

The line "sun—n—n—n—n—n" is sounded by the poet in oral performance as "sun-sun-sun-sun-sun," a tympanic delivery that calls her into being as the eponymous "Sun Woman," center of the solar system. As Dudley Randall observes, pointing to her well-timed and well-modulated recitation style, "She has a unique way of reading, giving each syllable equal weight, sometimes breaking into a chant or a song. The contrast between her bold words and her soft feminine voice makes her words even more effective."[62] It is this gendered clash that symbolizes Sanchez's effort to perform ideological dissidence through an oral resonance.

THE SUBALTERN AND THE STATE: MAGNETIZING BLACK POWER

With the growing pervasiveness of sound recording technologies, male Black Arts poets in the 1960s also were led to figure mediatization and its effects into their evolving semiotics of performance. Indeed, access to the airwaves became a crucial public political concern. In one amusing story, the white poet Ted Berrigan reports running over to another white poet, Frank O'Hara, to tell him that "Amiri Baraka's on the radio . . . and he's talking about killing white people"; in response to that news, O'Hara, like Berrigan a friend of Baraka's, calmly replied, "Well, . . . I don't think he will begin with you or me. Now sit down and have some wine."[63] Although O'Hara was nonplused, many worried that the broadcasting of the black nationalist message could spark racial violence. The magazine *Black World* noted that black music could—and had been—banned from communication over radio. Sanchez, who was inspired by Max Roach and Abbey Lincoln's inspirational jazz composition *Freedom Suite* (1960), observed that "you couldn't hear [it] . . . on the radio. It was that aggressive piece, belligerent piece, and they literally—I don't know if they banned it consciously. They probably banned it, but they wouldn't say they had; they just didn't play it." In light of this censorship, she and other black poets were determined to perform on the lower frequencies and thus turn these media to their poetic and political advantage.[64]

In addition to the radio, Black Arts poets eyed other communications technologies in their effort to oppose the dominant white culture and construct a separate nation. A speaker in Larry Neal's *Black Boogaloo (Notes on Black Liberation)* (1969), under the heading "Notes for Black Musicians," pronounces, "Get yourself some tape recorders, Cecil. Get back what they stole, Archie," urging black artists to retaliate for the white theft of black music by going to clubs where white artists are performing and recording the sound on magnetic tape. He also exhorts them to "knock off" television and radio stations in revenge for that theft.[65] When he signs off in the poem, his mediatized voice is charged with a sense of mission: "Calling all Black People. Calling all Black People. Come in. Come in. in. in. in. in. in." A wide hearing of this revolutionary call-to-arms relies on a technology capable of disseminating it electronically, and the speaker's plea for reception indicates the felt importance of making contact with the black masses. In Lee's poem "'Stereo'" in *Directionscore* (1971), he asserts confidently, "I have Power, / BLACK POWER," locating that power in a device of home music reproduction that uses two speakers to re-create the left-right sound-stage image of a live performance. His use of capitalization ("BLACK POWER") indicates the force and energy inherent in a mediatized presence, and by enclosing the title in quotation marks, he calls forth the metaphorical possibilities of "stereo," with black empowerment seeking to correct the balance, all on the side of a hegemonic whiteness.

The mediatized voice of a hypermasculinist Malcolm X serves as a crucial trope in a range of Black Arts poems that comprehend the politics of orality and aurality, both of which, as we have seen, are deemed essential in informing a black revolutionary consciousness. In *We a BaddDDD People* Sanchez plays with the dynamic prophetic charge lighting up Malcolm's speech:

for we have
                    hearrrd   Malcolmmmmmm's
blood/
      letten/
                    words   and
been born a gine.

(61)

In a later book, *Under a Soprano Sky* (1987), her poem "on listening to Malcolm's Bullet or The Ballot," a speech that is recorded and that she can play and replay, directly addresses that assassinated leader ("malcolm sweet singer") and the artifact of his disembodied voice:

    wrap me in your
  red orange rage
  til I ripen in your black field.
  O masculine man of words
  your words run down
  and no one can wind
  you up again.[66]

His voice preserved on LP, Malcolm attests through the manly mediatized word to his enduring power, even, ironically, as the expenditure of that voice on record ("your words run down") signifies his passing from the world ("no one can wind / you up again"). In Knight's *Poems from Prison,* he, too, paints an image of Malcolm's oracular brilliance, his revolutionary blaze: "His throat moans / Moses on Sinai and cracks / stones."[67] Neal's "Morning Raga for Malcolm" likewise elegizes that speaker's oral insurgency: "the voice tears at blood / streaked faces"; it is "a gnawing, pounding skin ripping voice / that does not back down," a "blue free voice."[68] If, as the critic Houston Baker, Jr., claims, the voice of Martin Luther King, Jr., brought into being "a new black publicness" ("only King's voice metaphorically and expansively imagined could have achieved such publicity"), Malcolm X's violent voice heralds a new black counterpublicness.[69]

The symbolic conflation of vocal amplitude and ideological resistance defines the poetics and evolving politics of these poets. As we recall, Vachel Lindsay, after first turning the volume up, then wanted to turn it back down (to the level of the whispered college yell) to save "Poetry" from the contamination of mass culture. Male Black Arts poets also work to pump up the volume in their performances on page, on stage, and on record and cassette, but begin to see, for different reasons than Lindsay, that a more fine-tuned voice can be efficacious for the cultural work that they intend to carry out. (Of course, the women, as women, were skirting this line all along.) For example, the epigraph to Madhubuti's *Don't Cry, Scream* when it is reprinted in *Directionscore* in 1971 states, *"a scream can be silent / pick your own time & place / and part your lips softly."*[70] In his *We Walk the Way of the New World,* we again find that a strange sort of diminuendo is key to a new emphasis on creating a common consciousness: "As indicated above, we are much louder, but softer, a logical progression, still screaming like supersonic wind tuned to a special frequency, but hip enough to realize that even some of those brothers and sisters tuned in will still not hear."[71] As an ad inside the front cover of *Home Coming* asserts, "Don Lee's fourth book [*We Walk*] is 'softer, but louder,'" but such a reduction in volume does not mean a change of agenda; it simply signifies a change in tactics in tune with the maturing of the movement.

Amiri Baraka is a bellwether with respect to the ethics and aesthetics of performance throughout the black nationalist era and after. His commitment to the spoken word becomes, he says, "increasingly more orally con-

ceived rather than manuscript conceived" as his career unfolds, and he attests that his poetry "is much more intended to be read aloud, and since the
mid-sixties that has been what has spurred it on, has shaped its line. . . . The
page doesn't interest me that much—not as much as the actual spoken
word."[72] Despite Baraka's professed desire for a romantic immediacy of expression that would bypass any technological interface, he does rely often
on typographical formatting to encode his vocalism and its attendant ideological message. In "Black Art" in his 1969 book *Black Magic,* he cleverly
tropes Archibald MacLeish's definition in "Ars Poetica," "A poem should be
palpable and mute," when he sends out the call,

> We want a black poem. And a
> Black World.
> Let the world be a Black Poem
> And Let All Black People Speak This Poem
> Silently
> or LOUD[73]

This proclamation returns us to Whitman's formulation that "America itself is the greatest poem," but with a difference: Baraka is expressing a pan-
Africanist vision, not a nationalist one, and imagines the black-centered
world as spoken into being, just as in the early national period vocal utterance frequently served as a figure for the making of the United States. The
world as poem, he says, will be spoken "Silently / or LOUD," with the letters of the word "LOUD" capitalized self-descriptively. What exactly a silent
speaking of the poem would be, we are not told, but perhaps Baraka is suggesting here the importance of internalizing the black nationalist creed, its
activation within the body and mind of the black citizen no less a performance than if that same person were to utter it on the street. In the same
poem, Baraka states, "We want live / words of the hip world live flesh & /
coursing blood," and it is through such a poetics of liveness, a cool pulsing
presence, that he locates maximum political energy.

Baraka's 1969 preface to Neal's *Black Boogaloo* entitled "Sound for
Sounding" lays out in its own hip way the oral emphasis that, he believes,
male black poets must cultivate, and he praises Neal for charting in the
book "the kind of nationalistic direction committed to blackness we must
have in the post 'literary' world." Likening art to "a street loud conversation," he explains,

Post "literary" because we are *men* who write. Black Men Black Artists. Literary sound like somethin' else . . . sound like it ain't sound. And sound is what we deal in . . . in the real world . . . sound for sounding.

These words are to be spoken. These songs are to be sung. Sound. They are sound. Real. Make (it to & with) sense![74]

The sounds of the new black poetry are explosive and revolutionary, authenticating not only the blackness of the artist but his masculinity ("we are *men* who write"). As he insists, he and Neal (and others like them) are of "the real world"; they are not precious poets enthralled by the printed page. Like Whitman, who distanced himself from the conventionally "literary," Baraka demands that his poetry be heard not as parlor art, but as raw, "Real" sound, as part of the social soundscape where black men perform their masculinities every day.

Baraka's construction of performance-centered texts speaks to his desire to activate the voice on the page, to get those real brute sounds into the poem. Expecting that some day people primarily will be listening to audio recordings of his verse, not reading it, he views his inscriptions on the page as "a score": "the whole wave of the future is definitely not literary in a sense of books and is tending toward the spoken and the visual. . . . I think that page will be used by people who want to read it aloud."[75] In his books *It's Nation Time* (1970) and *Spirit Reach* (1972), we witness his effort to translate something of the presentational fullness of performance to the print medium, with, for example, a poem like "PEACE IN PLACE" in *Spirit Reach* in all capitals in the first half to signify the raised voice to be applied to the sun-worshipping chant, which yields to a quieter register in the second half, one that nonetheless includes expressive utterances like "Listen to the brother yahhhoooooeeeeeeeayayayayayayayayay"; "can you diiiiiiiiiiig it??"; and "space blackness waaaayyyyy dig it dig it yeh." Some of his other poems specify the music to play during a recital of it, as with "Reggae or Not!" (1981), *"A piece to be read with Reggae accompaniment."* His poem "JIM BROWN ON THE SCREEN" in *Spirit Reach* even entails kinesic notation: "(hand/slap, stomp, wheel)."[76]

Baraka ties his poetics of vocal performance to his politics directly when he says that he admires the "singing quality" of Larry Neal's and Askia Touré's voices, which influenced his own reading style, as did "the music [of Monk and Coltrane] in combination with the [political] activism." As for his own politics of sound, he remarks that he and others were after a "new music poetry, that would scream and taunt and rhythm—attack the enemy into submission. . . . An art that would educate and unify black people in our attack on an anti-black racist America. . . .We wanted an art that was as black as our music. . . . We wanted a *mass art,* an art that could 'Monkey' out the libraries and 'Boogaloo' down the street in tune with popular revolution. A poetry that people could sing as they beat Faubus and Wallace and Bull Connor to death!" In "Three Modes of History and Culture" in *Black Magic,* he portends that at some point, "when I will be re-laxed," "my songs will be softer," and in his book *Hard Facts* (1976), where we sense a marked ideological shift away from black nationalism and to-ward international socialism, he describes his early black nationalist writ-ing as having been at the time necessary, and necessarily loud, arising as it did out of "an enraptured patriotism that screamed against whites as the eternal enemies of Black people, as the sole cause of our disorder + oppres-sion."[77]

Along with his political beliefs, then, Baraka's delivery style changes over time in accordance with them. Recordings tell the story of the ways in which he uses scat rhythms along with musical backgrounds to perform an evolving black cultural nationalism and to extend his publicity. On *Black & Beautiful* (Jihad, 1963), featuring Yusef Iman and the Jihad Singers with Baraka (then LeRoi Jones), the poem "SOS" (in *Black Magic*), as Werner Sol-lors explains, "becomes, with the accompaniment of the Smokey Robinson sound of Freddie Johnson, a light and memorable appeal for Blacks to 'yoo-hoo-nite.' 'Beautiful Black Women . . .' . . . similarly evokes images of love and peace against a 'Detroit sound' falsetto" (the Jihad singers humming Smokey's "Ooh Baby, Baby"). The track of "SOS" includes text additional to what appears in print in *Black Magic,* a testament to its improvisational sta-tus. Kalamu ya Salaam reviewed *Black & Beautiful* in *Black World* in July 1971, judging Baraka's to be "the first album to my knowledge that was cut as a nationalist Black poetry recording. Langston Hughes had done some things of his own readings and Charlie Mingus cut a side that is out of print now. But both of those were simply artifacts lacking a strong ideology."[78] In his melodies, Baraka is able to make tonally pleasing that radical and stri-dent revolutionary program, to make black (cultural nationalism) beauti-ful.

As with other Black Arts poets, Baraka was highly attuned to the black spoken word on record. When he read his poem "It's Nation Time" at the First Modern Pan African Congress in 1970 (Baraka coordinated the event), in his speech leading up to his recital of the poem he too refers to the disembodied voice of Malcolm X on LP, a voice for careful study by the black community in its quest to unite: "Think about Malcolm. . . . Listen to that record again. I don't mean at a cocktail party, I mean by yourself. Listen to it. By *any* means."[79] As Baraka finds, by reactivating the words of Malcolm, ingraining them into yourself through repeated playback, you can be recalled to your duties as a black citizen. Notably, too, in the poem as read at the Pan African Congress, Baraka adds several lines toward the end of the poem ("get up Roy Wilkins / get up Diana Ross / get up Jimmy Brown") that are not in other printed versions in an effort to keep it current, to keep the list of those co-opted by white America up-to-date; it is, of course, a strategy that harks back to Whitman and Hughes, among others, and that stands as further proof of his radical performance of race and nation.

"It's Nation Time" is infused with the percussive qualities of the black music of Baraka's day (James Brown's funk idiom, etc.), as he performs through it as well a new black masculinity ("the black man is the future of the world"):

Boom
Boom
Dada
      Hey aheee   (soft)
      Hey ahheee   (loud)
Boom
Boom
Boom[80]

Listening to the 1972 Visionary Music (Black Forum Records) LP recording of "It's Nation Time" to drum accompaniment, Meta DuEwa Jones notes the different tempos at which Baraka recites, occasionally miming local meaning as he does so, and observes that Baraka's "work engages in a process of revision modeled upon the improvisatory ethos of jazz"; as she finds, Baraka's "onomatopoetic approximation of a drumming chorus counterpoints the drummer, Idris Muhammed, who interjects and echoes his utterances."[81] He then trades screams with the saxophonist. As Nathaniel Mackey explains, "as a deliberate affront to the dominant culture's canons of musicality, 'honking' [or screaming] challenges and delegitimates that culture's distinction between music and noise, its imposition of hegemonic expectations as to what constitutes acceptable sound."[82] Baraka understands "honking" well, stating himself that the practice entails trying "to make the instruments sound as unmusical, or as non-Western, as possible. It was almost as if the blues people were reacting against the softness and 'legitimacy' that had crept into black instrumental music with the advent of swing."[83] His style owes much to James Brown (whom he alludes to in the first poem in *It's Nation Time*, "The Nation Is Like Ourselves": "please come back / as james brown says / please please please"): Brown's extensive vamps in which he would use his voice as a percussive instrument with frequent rhythmic grunts and with rhythm-section patterns resembling West African polyrhythms present Baraka with a useful musical mode. As opposed to Giovanni, whose resonance is designed to build black community by bridging generations, Baraka here vocalizes a dissonance that symbolizes his antagonistic relationship to dominant white culture, his refusal to be heard on its terms, and through it an intransigent Africanist identity ("Christ was black / krishna was black shango was black").

As reviewed in *Black World* in 1973, *It's Nationtime* (on Motown's Black Forum label at the price of $4.98) is cast as an album "under siege": "Won't find it on no record rack hardly no where in the country. Certainly few if any radio stations playing it. Why? Cause the powers that be, mainly the distributors, have decided that nobody wants to hear it. To my knowledge this is the first commercially produced Black poetry record that those who control the record industry have taken seriously." As Kalamu ya Salaam comments, the effective "ban" on the record is a "problem," "Not cause of no money or nothing, cause it wasn't going to sell a million in the first place, but rather cause we can cut records and publish books but we can't effectively distribute them!" Of one track, "Peace In Place," Salaam notes that Baraka's voice is "jumping octaves and finding weird notes past pain."[84] Together, the amped-up vocal performance and the attempted squelching of that performance by corporate America point up black oppression. Of the book *It's Nationtime*, we are told, "The words are to be read aloud and the listener would be well advised to just surrender to the sounds." However, simply surrendering is not always such a simple matter, as another reviewer discovered, finding that when Baraka read "tricky typographical poems . . . beautifully" on one occasion, he made "admirable oral sense of what often looked like chaos on the page."[85] These are by now familiar formulations concerning the nexus between oral and print modalities in a state of secondary orality.

Baraka's stature as public poet landed him at the Geraldine Dodge Poetry Festival in Waterloo, New Jersey, in 2002, where he read "Somebody Blew Up America," a poem written a month after 9/11 with (some have charged) anti-Semitic lyrics ("Who told 4000 Israeli workers at the Twin Towers / to stay home that day / Why did Sharon stay away?"). The recital of the poem caused an uproar in the state, leading to the governor's attempt to strip Baraka of the mantle of poet laureate of New Jersey, a mantle that he had bestowed on him the previous year. Baraka's published self-defense reveals the ways in which new technologies have expanded the scope of public poetry but also pose a threat to it. As he explains, "Almost immediately I circulated it [the poem] around the world on the Internet," and in readings and printings of it across the United States and around the world, it "has become one of the most circulated of my poems," receiving "thunderous applause" when it was performed at the festival:

> So why now and Who, as the poem asks, is behind it [the backlash]? Perhaps the forces which have dishonestly tried to characterize the poem as "venom" or merely "a harangue" (just as they called John Coltrane's music "Barbaric Yawps") are simply, the Charlie McCarthy voices for Bush & Sharon's Edgar Bergen's. Empty-headed devilish dummies constructed of wood and painted and costumed to look like it is real people speaking, when all the time it is imperialism [that] is the ventriloquist speaking through their mouths,
> NO, I WILL NOT APOLOGIZE, I WILL NOT RESIGN.

Baraka's citation of critics of Coltrane, who draw on Whitman's "barbaric yawp" to term what they hear as unartful noise, is telling, as he insists that a dissonant or discordant poetry cannot be dismissed simply as hateful, vulgar political speech, as crude polemic. When he goes on to imagine his critics as puppets of the imperialists Bush and Sharon, "dummies" who do not speak for themselves but are spoken through by those in power, we see just how powerfully subjectivity and agency are tied to individual utterance. Baraka further declaims that he will continue to perform his duties as poet laureate, to "Publicize and Popularize poetry and poets throughout this state": "We will ask that poets POET-ON! That they begin to produce at least one poem or publish a poem monthly, in the most modest forms, Kinko style, and give them away if they have to. That they begin to set up readings not only in the places we mentioned but also in parks and restaurants and in neighborhoods." As he insists, a counterpublic sphere (this time not an exclusively black one) built on recital and xerography will enact us as citizens, awakening us to "the deepest and most profound human values that poetry can teach" and effectively pit us against those who mouth but make no sounds themselves.[86] That such a large controversy could be provoked by Baraka's public reading suggests the continuing power of the physical performed word and its contentious politics.

CHAPTER 6

Slam Nation: Immediacy, Mediatization, and the Counterpublic Sphere

the Purpose of SLAM!
being to fill your hungry ears
with Nutritious Sound/Meaning Constructs,
Space Shots into Consciousness
known hereafter as Poems, and
not to provide a Last Toehold
for Dying Free Enterprise Fuck 'em
for a Buck 'em Capitalism'em.

—BOB HOLMAN, FROM "DISCLAIMER"

Poetry lives on page as words in type, poetry lives on stage as words in body, challenge of CD is to let poetry live as words in air.

—EDWIN TORRES

PERHAPS TO OVERCOME THE CHARGE of trendiness, contemporary artists of the rap-meets-poetry scene have constructed for themselves a family tree, one with many arcing branches, to authenticate their performativity and affirm their identitarian politics. Bob Holman, a slam poet and one of the poetry slam's best-known impresarios (he led the effort to reopen the Nuyorican Poets Cafe, a main slam venue, in New York City's Lower East Side), whimsically situates Whitman as progenitor when he "turn[s] on the Walt Whitman Lite-Brite on the side of the stage" at the Bowery Poetry Club, his slam site, and gushes, "'Oh, Walt! I love you!'"[1] Other slam aficionados track back to Walt as well, finding his pluralism appealing: "When I came to the Green Mill [the Chicago birthplace of the slam] that first night, I remember feeling exhilarated by some of the poets on stage and saying to my friend that old familiar refrain from Whitman, 'I hear America singing—its varied carols I hear'" (*SWR*, 141). In his review of the film *SlamNation* (1999), which chronicles the progress of several poets to the national slam championship, Roger Ebert cites Whitman's successor, Vachel Lindsay, as a precursor to these poets, finding that "Most of the material exists halfway between rap music and Vachel Lindsay"; he specifically points to a scene in the film of a New York book editor sighing over a pile of slam poetry manuscripts as he notes that such poetry does not always translate well to the page, a charge that plagued Lindsay.[2]

Others locate affinities between slam and beat aesthetics, even as they make certain distinctions. Slam poet Lisa Martinovic finds that "Slam is a movement, reminiscent of its Beat generation predecessor, but one that has already more deeply permeated the culture. It is a social phenomenon that—not coincidentally—embodies one of the most diverse communities on the planet. People of all ages, races and sexual persuasions come together to compete on a level playing field."[3] A reporter for *Newsweek* makes a similar point about the democratic ethos of the form: "Unlike the Beats, this [the poetry slam] is not just a bunch of white boys riffing on the meaning of life. There are 'womanist' poets, rapper poets, gay poets, lesbian poets, neo-Beatnik poets, deaf poets who use sign language, Afro-Caribbean immigrant poets, Latino poets, Asian-American poets, cowboy poets and cyberpunk poets."[4] Marc Smith of the Green Mill observes that "We started [the slam style] with contributions of democratic origin, a focus on the community and the audience, the poet as the servant of the people." The function of poetry, he argues, is "not to glorify the poet, it's to serve the community."[5] Bob Holman agrees: slam has "created . . . a community of poets who have democratized an art that was suffocating under a false perception of elitism."[6]

Jessica Care Moore, a black performance poet and slam artist, is quick to disabuse us of the notion that the spoken word is in any way a new phenomenon, preferring to see it as a sequel not to the beats but to the Black Arts poets: "We've traveled the ocean on Amiri Baraka's Blue Ark and sang to Jayne Cortez's Blues while listening to what Nikki Giovanni was gonna do to her lover with a full orchestra in the background. Ain't nothing new ya'll."[7] Yusef Komunyakaa also sees the slammers descending from this previous generation of black artists, even as he recognizes a distinct change in tone: "It seems that some of these voices were directly transfigured from the Black Arts Movement. . . . The aesthetics are similar, almost down to the uncapitalized personal pronoun *i*. But the ideological conceits and transparent rage are less on the surface of this poetry of the 1990s."[8] One of these "voices"—Tracie Morris—invokes "reverend amiri," "seer sonia," "monkess jayne cortez," and "uncle etheridge," claiming that they, among others, "are the runway from which I go!"[9] Slam poet Reg E. Gaines likewise reveals that "'I try to stay true to the oral tradition I come out of. . . . You know, people like Muhammad Ali, Gil Scott Heron, the Last Poets, Malcolm X, Sonia Sanchez and every Baptist preacher I've listened to.'"[10] Asserting that "our generation of Black Arts poets began to show poets how to read," Sonia Sanchez in *Bum Rush the Page: A Def Poetry Jam* (2001) recalls that "When I first heard some of the older poets in the anthology [Cortez, Mad-hubuti, Baraka, etc.] read, their words sped from the paper to our ears and back to their pages," revealing her sense of the permeable boundaries between text and performance; she credits the new generation of hip hop poets for keeping the tradition alive, doing "the same thing we did with poetry and sound, they did the sound, the pace, the pace of sound, the swiftness of sound, the discordant way of looking at the world of sound, the blackness of sound, the color of sound, the beat of sound."[11]

In his introduction to the slam anthology *Aloud: Voices from the Nuyorican Poets Cafe* (1994), a title that foregrounds the oral art that the book showcases, Miguel Algarín travels farther back to what he sees as the classical multicultural roots of the slam format, arguing that it "grows out of ancient traditions of competitive and/or linked rhymes between orators—from the Greek mythological tale of Apollo and Marsyas to the African griots, from the Sanjurokunin sen, or imaginary poetry team competitions, of tenth-century Japanese court poet Fujiwara no Kinto to the African American 'dozens'" (16). In these historical scenes, he points up the entertainment value of poetry as staged in predominantly oral societies. But as intriguing as Algarín's slam genealogy is, it is the immediate American cultural context out of which the slam grew that establishes its contours and purchase on publicness.

SPECTACLES OF IDENTITY

Likening the slam to popular sporting events such as "boxing, rodeo, surfing, demolition and roller derby," Bob Holman pinpoints its emergence in a poetry bout between the poets Ted Berrigan and Anne Waldman—both of them decked out as boxers—in 1979.[12] The next year, in an unrelated occurrence, the Chicago poet Jerome Salla was challenged by a musician, Jimmy Desmond, who previously had gotten drunk and created a disturbance at one of Salla's readings, to what was billed by Al Simmons, the contest's promoter, as "a ten-round poetry fight to the death." The poet Elaine Equi's description of that event highlights its spectacular nature: "They had a stage like a boxing ring. . . . Girls in bikinis, holding up cards for the number of the rounds. . . . And judges. . . . Each round Jerome and Jimmy reading one poem. Jerome won. . . . They had a rematch and he won again." At the rematch, Salla reports that he "read in leather boxing shorts, and had a robe that said Baby Jerome" and that Jimmy [Desmond] had a nickname too." Equi surmises that Simmons got the idea for the contest from professional wrestling, which was enjoying a resurgence of popularity in America at the end of the 1970s.[13] The influence of professional wrestling would seem to be confirmed by performances in 1986 at the Green Mill, where, Anna Brown recalls, she created a character named Rambolina (a clever gender-bending takeoff on the hypermasculinist movie hero Rambo), who was a ballerina in camouflage with weapons; her competitor, Jean Howard, showed up in leather shoulder pads and studded leather gloves with spikes. Brown reports that "Marc [Smith] wanted us to do battle. We worked together on it. We came up with poems we could battle with."[14] Judges were picked from the audience and held up cards with a score from 1 to 10 to register their opinion of the performances.

Just as the slam is predicated on interaction between poets and audience (as Algarín attests, the slam "demands an involvement from the audience," whose backtalk becomes an intrinsic part of the performance), in professional wrestling both the wrestlers in the ring and the fans in the stands contribute to the action; players are exposed to the view of audiences who judge their performance (*Aloud*, 19).[15] Wrestlers elicit responses from the crowd and react to the yelled comments of fans seated nearby; fans are encouraged to support their heroes by cheering loudly when they are in a temporarily compromised position. On television one notices that the audience at these events is lighted as deeply as possible, indicating that they, too, are conceived of as performers in the ritual. In this way, communitas is enacted, with audience members brought closer together through their common understanding of the events transpiring in the ring. But if American professional wrestling is a "dramatic ritual . . . communicated through the use of instrumental symbols, composite symbols, and stereotypes whose meanings act to reinforce cultural myth and to reinforce inequalities," the dramatic rite of the slam seeks to dismantle cultural myths of identity and to abolish (if temporarily) inequalities.[16] In effect, it works to escape from its own status as commodity spectacle.

In addition to the professional wrestling scene, which stamps the dialogic poetics of the slam, punk, which came to America in the late 1970s, also set the stage for its rise. Equi has noted the influence of the punk scene on prototypes of the slam (such as the boxing matches in which Salla participated). Salla supports this linkage, observing of the performance culture of the early 1980s: "It was the end of the punk age. Everybody was throwing stuff, swearing, insulting, and loud. It was a more verbally confrontational time, not just with us on stage but also with the audience, back and forth with the poet. . . . Just that constant thing where you'd assault people verbally."[17] Kenneth Bindas has described the contemporary punk music scene similarly: "Fans showed their appreciation by 'gobbing' (spitting) on the performers, who usually countered by telling them all to 'fuck off' and calling them stupid or mindless."[18] The erosion of the boundary between artist and spectator in punk performance points toward the interactive relationship between audience and poet that is central to the slam. Indeed, the conception of these poetry bouts as "anti-art" (Salla's words) further suggests a linkage to the slam, which Harold Bloom lamented as "the death of art."[19]

As Bloom's judgment suggests, the poetry slam and its players often get no respect. In 1996 the *Wall Street Journal* rather snidely wrote off slams as "the hybrids of performance art, Gong Show and verse that are making poetry accessible to the MTV generation," observing that judges are randomly "plucked from the audience" to rate the performances on a scale of 1 to 10. Two years later, in an article on the annual national slam competition in Austin, Texas, the newspaper described the slam as "a populist, slightly cultish offshoot of the fast-growing spoken word movement. . . . Reminiscent of the old Ted Mack Amateur Hour, pumped-up audiences watch pumped-up poets alone, or in ensemble, perform their own edgy work—no props or scripts—in styles ranging from the slick and the searingly funny to the 12-stepper's wrenching confessional." Algarín attests to the "pumped-up" world of the slam, but perceives it not as "flimflam" ("There are those who recoil at the thought of hooking that which is prodded by the gentle Muse to an applause meter," so the *Wall Street Journal* duly notes) but rather as the grounds on which to build community and effect social change (*Aloud*, 15).

Bob Holman refers to the slam scene as a "carnival," with much of the poetry performed there heard as searingly funny (*SWR*, 166).[20] As we have noted, such a subaltern space shapes what Bakhtin calls a "second life"—one alternative to (and subversive of) the official culture and its orderings—as it unwinds ethnic, racial, gender, and sexual stereotypes. As with medieval carnival, the slam "does not know footlights, in the sense that it does not acknowledge any distinction between actors and spectators," and its laugh-inducing, unfinalizable (improvisational) poetry counters the dogmatic and repressive "seriousness" of the official culture.[21] On the back cover of *Aloud,* a blurb highlights the profane nature of the poetry awaiting the reader inside: "It has the vitality of vulgarity." In the introduction, Algarín notes the "bawdy atmosphere" of the Open Room—the performance space in the Nuyorican Poets Cafe that serves as a trial ground for slammers—and the "literate humor" on display there. While it may be a literate humor, though, its connections run to folk humor. In his description of the emcee function, Algarín insists on the element of laughter that is integral to the slam, remarking on the "short tight monologue" that begins the show and "releases anxiety as it makes people laugh, both at themselves and at the competition that we are about to engage in" (*Aloud,* 28, 16, 17). This ambivalent laughter is in line with Bakhtin's notion of the "ambivalent," utopian character of carnival laughter, which is neither negative nor unidirectional and does not pass authoritative judgments: "It is gay, triumphant, and at the same time mocking and deriding. It asserts and denies, it buries and revives. Such is the laughter of carnival."[22] It should be noted here that indisputable social and ideological differences exist between the slam and medieval carnival, and that, while for Bakhtin "true laughter was always ambivalent and two-way, a vehicle of freedom for all sides and thus unencumbered by practical politics, a settling of scores, or the residue of real historical events," for slam poets parody often is a prime mover of political consciousness.[23] Nevertheless, we can learn much about the cultural work of the slam by viewing it through the spectacle of carnival.

While recognizing the slam's liberatory potential, some spoken word poets also have expressed concern about the vogue of that form, its commodification of a set style. For instance, the slam poet Paul Beatty told *Newsweek* that he "worries that the move [of the slam] into mainstream venues will dull the critical edge that poetry should have. . . . 'The real hook of poetry is that it turns things inside out, and I'm not sure all this trendiness meshes with that'" (qtd. *Aloud,* 22). As quoted in a 1995 *New Yorker* article on the poetry slam, Amiri Baraka conveyed a similar concern: "I don't have much use for them [slams] because they make the poetry a carnival—the equivalent of a strong-man act. They will do to the poetry movement what they did to rap, give it a quick shot in the butt and elevate it to commercial showiness, emphasizing the most backward elements." Here Baraka presses his belief that such poetry is mere entertainment, a sideshow spectacle that may attract an audience, but does not necessarily have artistic merit. His pejorative use of the term "carnival" is especially noteworthy, since organizers of the slam consciously have sought to promote such a "rowdy," "raucous," "riotous" second culture, a milieu in which new social relations might be created (*Aloud,* 16–17).

In a sense, the slam lives a double life: even as it appeals to the masses through a slick commercialism, much of its poetry defines itself against commodification, and often in sharply satirical ways. As Holman explains, although slam is an "experiment in community" beyond the pale of mainstream society, it is also, he admits, "a marketing ploy" that resembles in its way Lindsay's "Higher Vaudeville": "An emergent form in this Triumph of Capitalism means being able to find a way through the billboard blitz to the tender public. Slam is a way to ease an anti-poetic era into an ear of plenty." Later in the same piece he states that "By taking on the competitive model in this horrendous (burp) era of The Triumph of Capitalism Over Everything, poetry can demand parity with other competitive events, like football."[24] In these remarks Holman faces the fact of the commodity spectacle and does not flinch, as he imagines turning "the billboard blitz" against itself, to the end of performing resistant cultural identities and the counterpublic spheres in which they form.

In light of the pluralism of the slam scene, it perhaps is not surprising that the spoken word in the United States in recent decades has been tied up in powerful social movements that have reframed—and validated—cultural identities of minority citizens, a fact that prompted Marc Smith to proclaim the form itself "a social movement" (*Wall Street Journal,* September 10, 1998). Algarín affirms in *Aloud* that "The poet of the nineties is involved in the politics of the movement. There need be no separation between politics and poetry" (10). In his preface to *Listen Up!* Yusef Komunyakaa also reads the oral performance of a new generation of poets in public political terms, as a refusal on the part of oppressed minorities to remain silent: "These young voices have witnessed the voicelessness of loved ones (family and community)." Just as many of these poems, he contends, "can only come alive through the human voice," so, too, it is suggested, the poets and their communities can only remain alive by speaking out against those who would deny them their civil rights.[25] Through strategies of counteridentification and even disidentification, slam poets in performance both on and off the page work to transcend the boundaries of socialized roles and come into solidarity.

As with earlier generations of U.S. performance poets, slam artists wrestle with the problem of the relationship between the printed text and oral performance, between the figurative and literal voice, creating fictions of vocalism that address a condition of secondary orality. We are interpellated in the preface to *Aloud* by the figure of the self-performing book: "DO NOT READ THIS BOOK! You do not have to. *This book reads to you*" (1). *Aloud* is not a book that comes packaged with a CD, as some print spoken word compilations do, but the reader is nonetheless enlisted to listen to the poems "speaking" from the page. The quick shifts in font in the passage symbolize a range of registers, the expressive soundings of a literal (not figurative) voice, thus subverting the alleged fixity of the written word by investing it with the ephemeral polysemy of the voice in performance. Holman pictures the paradoxical condition of unmediated voice inscription in one of the bullet points in his "Praise Poem for Slam: Why Slam Causes Pain and Is a Good Thing": "Because performance is a see-through page, and the oral tradition a hidden book" (*SWR*, 170). In *Poetry Nation* (1998) we again are made to believe that slam poems do not sit quietly on the page in the book in front of us, that they only are activated fully in our utterance of them: "it is the *Saying* of these poems which allows them to be heard." Of course, one could "hear" the poem, too, in a silent reading, but such a reading would not realize the ideal of unfettered access, of sincerity and integrity, that orality is imagined to possess: As the editor of the anthology explains, we are meant to enact "a dynamic pulling of the poem from the page into the *honest* air" (emphasis added), and, in that unfixing, to experience a release from old orders: "The poem resting in, but not confined to, this or any book, now twirls Rumi-esque as spoken or sung, on television or the Internet, direct or mediatized, feminine, marvelous, tough."[26]

This urgent politics of vocalism informs the prolegomena to slam poetry in other collections as well. In *The Spoken Word Revolution: (slam, hip hop & the poetry of a new generation)* (2003), which comes with "over 70 minutes of electrifying live poetry on 1 audio CD," Billy Collins, at the time U.S. poet laureate, states, "To hear a poem is to experience its momentary escape from the prison cell of the page, where silence is enforced, to a freedom dependent only on the ability to open the mouth—that most democratic of instruments—and speak" (*SWR*, front cover, 3). Of *Poetry Nation*, the editors boldly proclaim, "This anthology is a grenade to borders between generations, gender, sexual orientation, race, class, formal training, academic degrees, aesthetics—these divisions dissolve herein"; in its "breaking down of borders," it effectively "zaps nationalism . . . , naming a new all-inclusive Nation of Poetry in the process" (23). Holman likewise suggests the trans- or counternationalist identities that are performed in and by the slam: "Multi-culti was energizing. The Nuyorican was an open platform for these voices. Hip hop was poetry here; performance was poetry too. The Nuyorican aesthetic was open, street, loud. It was the perfect patria dish for slam" (*SWR*, 165). The sly substitution in that last sentence of "patria" for the expected "petrie" hints that the grassroots slam movement is about the coalescing of a new nation within the belly of America.

In *Burning Down the House: Selected Poems from the Nuyorican Poets Café's National Poetry Slam Champions* (2003), Holman similarly confirms that "If you've learned your poetry from hip hop and slams and television, it's obvious the book does not 'contain' the poem—it transmits it. . . . A poem isn't written until it is read, and heard."[27] Here (in a case of strange bedfellows) he joins with Yvor Winters in insisting that a poem cannot be said even to exist until it is orally performed (as Winters avows, "without audible reading, and adequate audible reading, you simply do not have poetry"), and, going one step beyond Winters, actively audited. Likewise, in *Bum Rush the Page* (a title that itself plays on the slippage between page and stage), the editor, Tony Medina, believing that the anthology brings a socially responsible poetry "back to the people," also notes that it "exists in a paradox": "While it will be closely related to what some are calling the spoken word—that which lives in performance—the poetry gathered here, for the most part, maintains the integrity of the page, of the written word. . . . Collectively, and individually, this is our mouth on paper, our heart on our sleeves, our refusal to shut the fuck up and swallow our silence. And if you hold the pages of this book up to the light at an angle just so, it's as close to an autopsy on capitalism as you're gonna get, for now."[28] The paradox of "mouth on paper"—of utterance on the page—is one that the poets turn to artistic advantage, and by which they are able to extend their political critique to audiences beyond the reach of live performance.

This chapter will reveal more fully the dialectical relationship between stage and page in the work of leading slam poets and the fictions of performance that they create along the way—fictions that are directly tied to the performance of race, class, gender, sexuality, and nationality in the United States in the late twentieth and early twenty-first centuries. It also will show how a politics of authenticity and integrity, an ideal of the "real," is reimagined by and for the slam. And while our recognition of the slam as implicated in the cultural economy may seem to complicate certain of its claims to alterity, it properly acknowledges the ways in which the mediatization of voice changes its sound and our history.

TREACHEROUS LAUGHTER

Bob Holman's "DisClaimer," a poem that he reads at the start of slams that he emcees, announces the antagonism between slam poetry and "official" discourse through a billingsgate rhetoric that gets directly at the issue of commercialization and its corrosive effects; the purpose of the slam is, he announces, "not to provide a Last Toehold / for Dying Free Enterprise Fuck 'em / for a Buck'em Capitalism'em" (*SWR,* 168). The resistant ideology of the slam ("We disdain / competition and its ally war") is not without irony, though, as artists contest in a world where entertainment—and the cash it brings—is king. The ritualized conditions surrounding the poem are cited in the second line, "We are gathered here today," the first words of the celebrant's preamble to a ceremony featuring the illocutionary speech act par excellence, the phrase "I do" that constitutes the act of marrying. Through such language, the poet assures us not only that something is about to happen but that something new will be brought into being by the poems about to be performed.

The organization of the verbal idiom of slam poetry bespeaks not only its illocutionary power (what Holman calls "poetry's cocoon of action" in "DisClaimer") but its essential publicness. At carnival, Bakhtin explains, a "special kind of speech was heard"—one that was "unlike the tongue of official literature" and marked by freedom, frankness, and familiarity: "The temporary suspension, both ideal and real, of hierarchical rank created during carnival time a special type of communication impossible in everyday life. This led to the creation of special forms of marketplace speech and gesture, . . . permitting no distance between those who came in contact with each other and liberating from norms of etiquette and decency imposed at other times." "The familiar language of the marketplace," then, "became a reservoir in which various speech patterns excluded from official discourse could freely accumulate," including such billingsgate forms as abuses, curses, profanities, and oaths.[29] Through such "low" forms the prescriptive, monovocal, official language of ordinary power relations is disrupted and, thus, put in a position to be critiqued.

Such billingsgate speech also shapes the art of Edwin Torres, whose parents are Puerto Rican and who grew up in the Bronx; he, too, relies on the transgressive mode of the carnivalesque to parry American-style capitalism. His slam poem "Mission-Fuckin'-Impossible" repeatedly interrupts an "official" language with the obscenity "Fuck" in an effort to derange the commodified comic teams and media superstars that have become our history. Torres is laughing as much at himself and his listeners as he is at those agencies and institutions that have marketed our history to us:

Hey . . . Spank-Fuckwheat & AlFuckya.
Hey . . . AbFuck and Fuckstello.
Hey . . . WilFuckma, Fuck, BetFuttyFuck'n-ArneyUck.
Hey . . . Nort'n-Trick-Fucksie-RalphFuck.

(*Aloud*, 163)

His hailing and defacement of pop icons (many of them harking back to the 1960s and 1970s, but continuing into the present with such deformities as "Dan Ra-Fuckather" and "Farbra-Falters-Falter-Fucktite") goes on without interruption, as we are bombarded with a vulgar parody of our own revered, electronically broadcast touchstones. Through the prosodic device of tmesis—where a word is cut in two by an intervening word—and other disruptive linguistic strategies, the poem symbolizes the speaker's own politics, with each line beginning with "Hey" trying to awaken us to the reality of our ideological interpellation as consumers. By way of these techniques, Torres incites an ambivalent laughter, one directed not only at commodity culture itself but also at his own attempt to contravene capitalism—seemingly (as his title indicates) a "mission . . . impossible," but, ironically, one that Ethan Hunt, central character of the movie *Mission: Im-*

possible, always accepts. Ending with the truncated one-word line "Hey!"
the poem offers up a space for us to fill, as it urges us to action.

Everton Sylvester's "Well?" likewise relies on carnival insults as he challenges the dominant Yuppie paradigm that would seek to deny, because it
feels fundamentally threatened by, any assertion of privilege or power by
someone outside of that social group. The brash assault of the speaker is at
once funny and poisonous:

> I got cash in fuck-you quantities
> Now what?
>> that makes you uncomfortable?
> Fuck you
>> and the Range Rover you drove in on
> Fuck your Saab convertible

(Aloud, 488)

Parodying the pretensions and conspicuous consumption of the upper
class, the speaker flaunts his cash in an effort to beat the elite at their own
game, to make them submit to his authority. His braggadocio is reminiscent of what propels the African American street game the dozens, where
insults are crafted in order to gain victory over opponents; here, though,
his is the only voice, the voice that for so long has been silenced by a white
majority. The parodic inversion at the end of the poem positions the poet
as heir to the slave master and the white addressee as offspring of chattel,
with the black poet daring his white listeners to dispute his claim that his
family has grown fat off the slave trade, that he can buy and sell them. This
discourse of transgression and inversion is not ambivalent and utopian, as
in carnival, since Sylvester places himself above the object of his mockery;
however, the poet's reordination of the world—his rearticulation of what is
high, what is low; what is us, what is them—allows black subjects to imagine another world, a utopia where traditional hierarchy has been upended.
In the end, Sylvester curses his white listeners as too dumb to know how to
take his claims, thereby undermining the stereotype of the ignorant black
man in his critique of everyday life, of "normal" power relations.

The refusal to perform according to essentialized notions of race likewise shapes Andrea Thompson's performance poem "Fire Belly," in which
she stages a self that transcends the boundaries of her socialized roles, stick-
ing a finger in the eye of those who want her to accept the status of erotic
"exotic":

I am not
a hot chocolate
sweet ginger
coco, oreo
honey dipped
brown sugar
butterscotch
coffee, caramel
cinnamon girl

(PN, 33–35)

Thompson invokes the epithets that white male culture uses in its construction of her as a racialized and sexualized "Other," humorously ticking off the edible delicacies that have helped metaphorize her out of existence. She repeatedly rejects ("I will not"; "I am not") the idea that she would perform as expected, and lays claim to a self fired by history—not a "cinnamon girl," but rather a woman with one white and one black parent. Describing herself as in part "from the land of Buckingham / marmalade, BBC, Royal Brigade / and a little / nosh with tea," she also declares forthrightly her African Americanness; her legacy is double, and at root conflicted: "I am slave / and I am slave master." Refusing to be colonized to satisfy someone else's sex fantasy, she highlights her fate of "exile" and lays claim to middle-class American citizenship by virtue of her "belonging" to "a land / of strip malls, snow tires / backyard barbecues, Safeway." In defiance of "the heart of pre / judice" where the rule is "assume first / think later," Thompson undermines racist stereotypes, insisting that she does not hail from the Dark Continent—a myth generated by a white imperialist culture—but rather "from here," where "the natives / are brown" and there is no identifiable "Other."

Another poem that laughs treacherously at the performance of race in contemporary American culture is Reg E. Gaines's "Thomas the Burnt English Muffin," which speaks out with force against Clarence Thomas's nomination—and ultimate confirmation—to the U.S. Supreme Court. Gaines berates Thomas for his adoption of mainstream white American values and identities in billingsgate speech forms that show no respect for Thomas or the politicos who would promote him to power. The poem as printed in *Aloud* is centered on the page, rather than justified left, in imitation of Thomas's modeling of himself—and conservatives' modeling of him—along the lines of the cultural (if not ideological) center:

you son of a . . .
Georgia sharecropper the
brand nubian showstopper
flip floppin from left to right
afro/saxon fly by night and we know
your wife's white

(Aloud, 67)

The initial curse in the poem is muted ("you son of a bitch") in favor of a
mythic personal history of Thomas—a history harped on by his white Republican proponents to hide the fact that he is in fact a product of the
affirmative action system that they would like to see destroyed. Playing on
the brand name Thomas' English Muffins, Gaines shows how Thomas has
blurred his racial identity in his effort to market himself—and allow himself to be marketed—as a Horatio Alger "success story," a minstrel ("bojan-
gles") playing to please white America and to further the agenda of the
George H. W. Bush administration. Exposing the hypocrisy of Thomas's position, Gaines claims that the judge ("satan disguised as a catholic") has
been "brainwashed" and that he is being used; as he jokingly warns
Thomas: "smell the smoke wake the fuck up man / your ass is on fire." With
an unwitting Thomas stereotyped for political expediency and, ultimately,
to the detriment of all African Americans, the point of this final salvo is to
expose the racial masquerade and subvert the regnant political order
through a string of abuses meant to deride a "scam" that cynically feeds off
of "racial muck and mire."

Like Gaines, who in performance often will sound off between poems
on political matters much as the Black Arts movement poets did, other
slam poets strive to deny the legitimacy and challenge the claims to authority of racist myths in American popular culture. In "Rock Me, Goong
Hay!" Alvin Eng performs an ulterior identity for himself and other Asian
Americans that is at odds with disabling cultural stereotypes ("So don't diss
me as some ping pong, ching chong, / Mah-jongg, egg foo yung, bang a
gong, muh fuh fuh") through the fictional Chinese rapper, Kid Goong Hay
(*Goong Hay* is Cantonese for "congratulations"):

Lose that shit—this ain't the mainland
I'm the Goong Hay Kid hope you understand
Don't do no kowtowing or no rickshaw

So don't be talking no dragons or the Great Wall
I ain't good in math, don't know kung fu
Ditto for Confucius and Fu Manchu

(*Aloud*, 59–60)

Eng's humorous citation of racist images and his sense of triumph over the forces of oppression (he calls himself "The defest C-town B-boy you ever saw") also involve his renunciation of a stereotyped "Oriental" manhood. He refuses to be treated as a sexual curiosity, and his use of metaphors from the world of the Chinese restaurant suggests how confined he feels by attitudes of the dominant culture derived from it. Hitting back with self-defined images, Eng makes clear that he is rapping into being a new future—a utopia where he is not limited by prejudice and, yet, where he is not required to renounce his ethnic heritage. The final line of the poem is in Cantonese, "Goong hay fat choy!" (Happy new year!), and it effectively wipes the slate clean, as he resolves to revamp cultural identity through rap and its transgressive politics.

Beau Sia's "The Horse Cock Manifesto" also holds Asian stereotypes up for ambivalent laughter. Countering the stereotype of the poorly endowed Asian male, Sia turns it on its head and gives the inversion force by virtue of his own frantic, ultimately futile effort to deny its legitimacy:

some menace, villain, nemesis, enemy, threat
to the asian community as i know it,
has been spreading around that
"asian men are hung like horses!"
and i hate the idea of the fact,
as the word has spread farther than i can control.

(*PS*, 173–74)

Claiming that men in other cultures are cursed with "miniscule proportions" and so are unable to satisfy their women, who look for fulfillment in Asia ("i cannot stop them, / a flood of people swarming into asia, / fucking around the clock with asian men!"), Sia jokes (with a straight face) that the rumor has had global impact: "this has ruined the ecological, sociological, sexological / breeding patterns of the whole world." He claims in mock serious tones that the rumor is "humiliating," that he "can't live like this anymore, / with sex five times a day, / sex eighteen hours a day" with requests for casual sex mounting ("it is always so uncaring, / as it is name, number, place, time. // no list of hobbies, interests, or favorite colors") (175). The entire poem is fueled by exaggeration, and it is the poem as tall tale, but vigorously denied as tall tale, that generates laughter: it is the disjunction between reality and the poet's paranoid fancy that is so hilarious here. Of course, Sia is laughing as much at himself as he is at the world where such rumors define and delimit, and the laughter that he inspires is utopian insofar as it makes room for the performance of new ethnic identities apart from the racist scaffolding of the old.

Filipino poet Regie Cabico in his slam poem "Game Boy" puts yet another spin on the Asian myths promoted in Western culture, as he seeks to deconstruct stereotypes of the submissive male "Oriental" sexual partner—the "boy" who is game to play his part as scripted in a gay white erotics. The poem begins with Cabico's assault against those who would try to fit him into a category designed to strip him of power and provide others with sexual pleasure at his expense, especially as such racist desire is encoded in the language of personal ads. Akin to the rhetoric of Thompson's "Fire Belly," "Game Boy" interrogates the exoticized racial image that gay white men have constructed for their titillation and, in abusive tones, refuses the designation:

> you can just quit orientalizin'/ cause i ain't
> gonna change my cotton-knit calvins for you or my mother/
> if i lose
>
> i ain't gonna fry you an emperor's meal or throw you eurasia/
> or butterfly you an opera/
> i'm thru givin sex tours of unicef countries/ 3rd world is for hunger/
> & fat sally struthers

> (*Aloud*, 49)

Here Cabico's penchant for puns comes through in his use of the word "butterfly" to denote a cutting method in cooking as well as the opera *Madame Butterfly*, which revolves around a sexual masquerade. His bitter denunciation of his oppressor, those men who "for fun" "spit" racist words at him and "rape" his boyish body, culminates in his relinquishment of his role in the charade: "i forfeit the game / remove my makeup/ & call you the winner." The note on which the poem ends is a necessary prelude to the reclaiming of personal identity and integrity, as he slips the yoke of sexual imperialism and searches for new grounds on which to love and be loved.

Carol Diehl's feminist performance piece "For the Men Who Still Don't Get It"—described by Algarín in his introduction to *Aloud* as "a semiserious comic release that drives the Open Room [slam] audience crazy"—similarly undermines the power structure promoted by, and underwriting, the dominant culture (27). In the poem she speculatively shapes a world in which women and their bodies are for once recognized as capable and powerful, and in the process she successfully challenges patriarchy and its terms of worth:

> What if
>> the ability to menstruate
>> was the prerequisite for most high-paying jobs
>
> What if
>> your attractiveness to women depended
>> on the size of your penis
>
> (*Aloud*, 417)

In a long sequence of "What if" bursts, Diehl operates according to "a characteristic logic, the peculiar logic of the 'inside out' (a l'envers), of the 'turnabout,' of a continual shifting from top to bottom, from front to rear, of numerous parodies and travesties, humiliations, profanations, comic crownings and uncrownings. A second life, a second world of folk culture is thus constructed; it is to a certain extent a parody of the extracarnival life, a world 'inside out.'"[30] Diehl's topsy-turvy does have a sharp-edged politics to it, as she works to imagine a public space in which female identity is not crippling but enabling, and where men are put in their place. The title makes clear her target audience ("For the Men Who Still Don't Get It"), and her resort to parody is meant to carry her message across to those men who cannot see the double standards and harassment to which women are subjected every day. By laughing at the scenarios she describes—scenarios where women and men exchange places in the hierarchic order, that is, where women are crowned and men are uncrowned—she is able more easily to get her audience (or at least the men in it) to feel what it is like to be intimidated and dismissed ("What if / the doctor who examined your prostate / was a woman / and called you 'Honey'"), with her object being to effect social change.

Just as Diehl imagines gender "turnabout," other slam poets act out gender transgression—or a personal desire for it—on stage, with women performing as men and men performing as women in an effort to expose the cultural coding of sex and gender in American society. In "I Want To Be a Woman" Evert Eden strives to cross the gender divide in order to tap into feminine power and projects a range of female identities from femme fatale to lesbian to mother as being open to him. At the end of the poem he calls attention to and seeks to defuse his own hard-wired, American-branded masculinity:

> I want to be a woman
> so I can understand why
> I'm such a fucking . . . guy
>> heavymetal hardline
>> hangtough hotstud
>> take-no-prisoners
>> duck, scud!
>>>> (*Aloud*, 427)

Eden's fantasy of gender inversion points up the machismo that fuels misogynistic references to male sexuality and heterosexual conquest and the entwinement of sexual and national military might. As his list of epithets grows, lines move further to the right of the page, symbolically representing the "hardline" conservative, hypermasculinist self ("be-a-man") that he wants to shed. From the opposite direction, but ideologically akin, Lisa Martinovic's slam poem with props "If I Were a Man, I'd Have a Big Dick" satirizes the cult of American manliness that she sees as a symptom of American jingoism:

> So how do I know I'd have a big dick?
> Because I'm an American, damnit!
>
> Male or female, I was born macho
> outfitted with a certain confidence
> a swagger even
> an attitude
> that befits a man with a well hung slab o ham
>>>> (*PS*, 182)

Here the poet imagines phallic power in militaristic terms, with "A Colt 45 shotgun M-16 MX missile of a dick" bent on "World domination / one inch at a time." Her imperialistic claims are meant to call attention to the ideological constructs on which American masculinity rests, and the extent to which "our national dick"—America's "cock-sureness"—is not just a sexual tool but a tool of political and corporate control. Ultimately, to the bravura statement "If I was a man / I'd have me a / big ole / American / dick," a papier mâché "simulacrum of an exceptionally healthy male organ" with an "American flag protruding from urethra" takes the stage (*PS*, 179, 183). In this, we are meant to laugh at the illusion of American male identity and to see that gender is itself an act, and, in seeing that, to realize that, as Judith Butler attests, "The possibilities of gender transformation are to be found precisely in the arbitrary relation between such acts, in the possibility of a failure to repeat, a de-formity, or a parodic repetition that exposes the phantasmic effect of abiding identity as a politically tenuous construction."[31] In other words, if gender is not essential but performed, then it can be performed as well "outside the restricting frames of masculinist domination and compulsory heterosexuality," a fact that Eden's and Martinovic's parodic enactments highlight for us.

Similarly focused on the performativity of gender, Maggie Estep inspires an ambivalent laughter in her slam poem "Sex Goddess of the Western Hemisphere," showcasing at once her own psychotic behavior and the psychotic sexual politics of patriarchy that have informed it. In the course of the poem, she boasts repeatedly, "I AM THE SEX GODDESS OF THE WESTERN HEMISPHERE," and in her recital of it she adopts a languid air, which stands in ironic counterpoint to the outrageous claim that she makes and that shapes the entire parodic performance. Estep's definition of herself in effect robs the dominant order of its power, and the disjunction between what she says she is and how she behaves poses a serious challenge to culturally defined gender roles:

> "Hey,"
> you may say to yourself,
> "who the hell's she trying to kid,
> she's no sex goddess,"
> But trust me,
> I am
> if only for the fact that I have

the unabashed gall
to call
myself a SEX GODDESS

(*Aloud*, 63)

Estep sends herself up as vamp, the woman who uses her sex appeal to en-
trap and exploit men, and her tone becomes testy when she describes the
perversion of female sexuality by pornography and her alienation from
that mass-marketed image. Her satiric portrayal and recognition of the
ideological dimensions of sex and gender constitute a subversion of the efforts of those in charge to subordinate her sexually and disenfranchise her
politically. The poem ends with the hilarious assertion, "I AM THE SEX
GODDESS OF THE WESTERN HEMISPHERE / and you're not," as her denial
of power to others mocks as it performs the competitiveness of female-fe-
male relationships bred in patriarchy. Although her statements would seem
to reinscribe attitudes of a hegemonic, misogynist culture, they in fact are
"denaturalized and mobilized through their parodic recontextualization,"
as Judith Butler would have it; the poetry slam provides Estep with a context and reception in which her imitation of an imitation of the female is
truly troubling.[32]

Both the slam and its festive poetry are intended to evoke our laughter,
but that laughter does not mean that either is insignificant or trivial. As
Bakhtin argues, laughter in a carnival context is therapeutic: "laughing
truth" is valuable, he suggests, not because it conveys a concrete set of ideas
but because it never worships, commands, or begs. For this reason, it can
banish fear, mystic terror, and guilt. In any given historical situation,
Bakhtin concedes, laughter is ephemeral, for everyday anxieties and terrors
always return. Nevertheless, carnival images offer an "unofficial truth,"
"the defeat of fear presented in a droll and monstrous form, the symbols of
violence and power turned inside out." Laughter may rarely alter actual
material conditions, but it can free people "to a certain extent from censorship, oppression, and the stake" if not by eliminating those realities
then by liberating people from "the great interior censor . . . from the fear
that developed in man during thousands of years: fear of the sacred, of prohibitions, of the past, of power."[33] The laughter inspired by the poetry slam
likewise frees participants from the prohibitions and norms of a dominant
culture, allowing them, if momentarily, to construct a "second" or

"unofficial" culture in which to perform new identities and to contest those to which they would be subject.

SIMULATIONS OF LIVENESS

When Lisa Martinovic says, "In a world where everything from sex to reality itself is virtual, where being passively entertained is lauded as a way of life, slam bucks the trend by providing a venue for authentic creative expression," we see that, for her, the slam is an oasis of the genuine and real.[34] Her use of the word "virtual" is striking, though, as it leads to the question of what happens when slam poets go digital, when something taken to be authentic and real performs in an environment that is founded on simulations of the real. "Anyone who has ever worried about the future of literature in a media-mad, electronic rock'n'roll era must take heart from the National Poetry Slam." This remark from the *Chicago Tribune* plastered on the back cover of Gary Mex Glazner's primer-anthology *Poetry Slam: The Competitive Art of Performance* (2000) similarly positions the slam and its "live" voices as antidote to the digital, a live pulsing presence in an increasingly mediatized society, notwithstanding the fact that, as Kurt Heintz points out, "The rise of connectedness among slam poets, and slam poetry's rapid ability to jump across national frontiers intact, was never before enjoyed and practiced so widely by any preceding movement of writers," with e-mail and the web providing "a kind of cultural glue for the slam movement."[35] Moreover, the pervasive digital distribution of poetry audio and the development of archives and portals raises issues of transcription and editing, of how performance documents are displayed in digital media, and what effect that has on the overall performativity of the poem.

Of course, as I have noted before, the harnessing of emergent communications technologies by spoken word artists is not new, but it does intensify in the mid- to late twentieth century. One artist who was instrumental in the mediatized poetry revolution is John Giorno. As he explains, in the 1960s he "hung out with young artists like Andy Warhol, Bob Rauschenberg and Jasper Johns, as well as with members of the Judson Dance Theatre," and it was "the use of modern mass media and technologies by these artists [that] made me realize that poetry was 75 years behind painting and sculpture, dance and music. And I thought, if they can do it, why can't I do it for poetry. Why not try to connect with an audience using all the entertainments of ordinary life: television, the telephone, record albums, etc? It was the poet's job to invent new venues and make fresh contact with the audience." He developed a record label, Poetry Systems, and, by his own account, "eventually built up a catalog of 40 titles, ushering poetry onto the radio alongside rock, jazz, etc. for the first time."[36]

In addition, Giorno pioneered the transmission of poetry over the phone lines, a service begun in 1968 called "Dial-A-Poem" that allowed people to place a phone call and listen to a recording of a poem being read—a mediatized verse performance. Its successor, Poemfone, used the technology of voice mail so that people dialing up a poem could then interact, leaving a message (sometimes in the form of a respondent poem) on the answering machine. In *Verses That Hurt: Pleasure and Pain from the POEMFONE Poets* (1997), a print anthology of Poemfone art, the creators of Poemfone credit Giorno's Dial-A-Poem as "the first time poetry versified the phone lines," claiming that Poemfone "continue[s] the tradition of populist rebellion" by "using poetry to illuminate the technological void"; they imagine the electronic dissemination of the spoken word as in keeping with the spirit of previous performance poets: "Would Walt Whitman have participated in the Poemfone? . . . Langston Hughes? . . . Sappho? . . . You Betcha!"[37]

Bob Holman has led in the effort to expand performance poetry into electronic mass media. Seemingly at home live, on page, or on screen, he assures in his "Praise Poem for Slam" that there need be no privileging of any one mode, "Because cool mediaization of poetry is rooted in hot live performance of poetry" (*SWR*, 170). That is, Holman claims, the unmediatized spoken word is in dialectical relationship with any recorded version of it: If it wasn't originally "hot," it won't work once it's cooled, now a step away from the live (and thus won't be "cool"). In "Rock'N'Roll Mythology" in *Panic DJ!* (1987), Holman invokes a range of mediatized forms in dramatizing what the contemporary poet is up against, using contractions in his score that point back to the Black Arts poets, and, in the process, rolling out a series of fictions of writerly performance that undergird his inscriptional practice:

open up the book w/ yr finger hook
& scan it w/ yr television eyes
(televisionize televisionize televisionize televisionize)

ah, stick it with your eyes
stick out yr tongue & memorize
it's just you reading
the book is breathing![38]

The speaker understands the battle for the airwaves—and thus for the people's attention—that the poet in the digital age must wage, and insists on electrifying the poet's voice to cut through the culture's white noise; as Holman remarks elsewhere,

> In order to be heard now, you have to shout through the megaphone and the megaphone is a system of electronics and technology that poets have wanted to move away from. Ever since Plato kicked the poets out of the polis, out of the city, out of the Republic, we've been very content to stay outside and have a beautiful view of things. It's only that now we're so far away from them that whatever we say can't be heard. How do you get heard in 1994? . . . That's the question. The universal remote control is being passed into the hands of a new generation. Click! Poetry!"[39]

Noting the short attention span of the citizen-consumer and the concomitant need for loudness in an effort to try to hold her interest, Holman scripts his verse accordingly and would capitalize on every device at hand to reinvade the republic.

But such "cool mediatization" hinges on an originary poetics of liveness, as Holman himself tells us, and so even when he is not operating live he insists on the authenticating force of unmediated vocalism and creates fictions about it. In his poem "57 Gazillion Lung-Tongue Varieties" in *The Collect Call of the Wild* (1995), a book title that shuttles in its word play between the telephonic voice and the voice unenhanced by electronic amplification, he seeks to collectivize the wide diversity of Americans, and in doing so figures a powerful populist oral presence. Riffing on Bob Marley's famous anthem, he exclaims:

Hey, US!
Get up!
Stand up!
Pay up
The Bill of Writes!

In these lines Holman performs a particular idea of authorship and citizenship, with the poet asserting his "rights" when he "Writes," but, in order fully to exercise and validate those rights, needing to make his actual voice heard: "You gotta speak it up to keep it up! / You have the right to noisy!" In a boisterous performance of identity, the poet imagines the nation being rechristened "The United States of Poetry," with "57 Gazillion Varieties / Of newly-free voices raised as one / From top shelves of Dust Museums!" Whitman's "multitudes" disseminate into the open air ("Millions of tiny voices freed"), and the power of the people is thereby ratified. With Gil Scott-Heron's creed, "The Revolution Will Not Be Televised," ringing in our ears, Holman insists in the poem that "The revolution will be LIVE," with capitalization sounding the urgency of the unmediatized event, an event grounded in direct political action.[40]

Ironically, "The United States of Poetry" morphs later into the mediatized product *The United States of Poetry*, a compilation of video-poems that Holman produces in 1996 as a five-part series for airing on PBS. *TV Guide* blares that the program "tosses aside the textbook approach to poetry and drags it, kicking and screaming . . . into this wired world . . . it's poetry as you've never experienced it."[41] In this description, one senses the writer's belief that poetry is not naturally suited to the circuits of mass culture. Holman, however, describes the setup of the poet Robert Creeley for his appearance in the series in a way that reveals his view of the fruitful embodiment of the poetic text in this "wired world": "Creeley, in his signature jeans and flannel shirt, looking much younger than seventy, stands in front of a seamless white background. His body is the text, black print on white page" (*SWR*, 65). Here the poet becomes the poem, a presence, albeit mediatized, to be read and interpreted; the fact that Creeley has a "signature" style invokes the celebrity culture that poetry has entered, or reentered. Holman concludes his reflection on Creeley by alleging that "when presenting the poem aloud, the poet is not performing the poem, maybe that's what an actor does. The poet *is* the poem" (*SWR*, 66). Performance is imagined as materializing both text and author, and, in the case of Creeley in particular, conjuring the look of a book ("black print on white page"); it is publication by the body.

Another television event starring the spoken word—HBO's *Def Poetry Jam*, the brainchild of Russell Simmons and emceed by rapper Mos Def—is built around a simple stage, microphone, and occasional podium, a relatively low-tech affair. The print anthology *Bum Rush the Page* features poetry from the series, and in the introduction, the editor comments on the rhetorical range within and among the poems, noting that "They shout, they curse, they whisper and sing."[42] When the show was translated to the live space of Broadway in the form of *Russell Simmons Def Poetry Jam on Broadway,* the question of the relation of speech to text reared its head. Ben Brantley of the *New York Times* (November 15, 2002) noted that certain lines "sound better than they read. You need to experience firsthand the body language that makes the verbal language spin and the voices that seem to get high off their own inflections. This is poetry for the stage, not the page, and it exists completely only in the moment it is being performed." But Brantley also makes clear that while the poetry may not take off in print, the intensity of the performance does not "require the intimacy of a club or the magnifying closeness of a television screen": "All of the performers are radioactive with stage presence, conferred partly by the hormonal glow exclusive to the young and unwrinkled, partly by polemical righteousness and partly by the immortal showbiz urge to show off."[43] Here a compelling "presence" is measured against the standard not only of the venue where performer and audience stand in close proximity but also, ironically, of the televisual event and the related camera work of close-up, as would shape the same performance on an HBO episode of *Def Poetry Jam.*

Patricia Smith, a four-time individual champion of the U.S. National Poetry Slam and in 1997 cowinner of the prize belt at the Taos Poetry Circus World Heavyweight Championship of Poetry, appeared on an episode of *Def Poetry Jam* performing her poem "Skinhead," which is included in her book *Close To Death* (1993). The book was inspired by interviews she conducted while working on a *Boston Globe* article about black men in Boston ghettos, and is based on tape-recorded voices of black men talking; in her performance poetry she rearticulates those voices through her own body. Assuming the form of the dramatic monologue, the poems that she builds out of these voices are what she calls "persona poems," "in which a poet passes his own power to the subject of the poem" and the "neutral voice" is eliminated (*SWR,* 180). Her sense of herself as a medium or channeler of disparate voices is apparent: "The poet, whether on page or stage, is simply a conduit for the story. . . . I let him [my subject] tell me who he is—but, more important, I forget who *I* am. I speak as my subject, not for him." In "becoming someone else," the voice, she finds, "is both immediate, and immediately engaging" (*PS,* 71). She dwells on this ideal of immediacy, contending that "those ephemeral and uncomodifiable [*sic*] aspects of live performance—the voice, the body on stage, the intimacy between the poet and her audience—infuse the poem [she is speaking of her persona poem "The Undertaker"] with an immediacy and urgency that cannot be captured on the page."[44] Whether or not these aspects are or are not commodifiable is beside the point: Smith's fiction of performance positions them outside of the cultural economy, where she believes communion is possible and authenticity is served.

This immediacy of voice can be particularly shocking when the imagined speaker of a poem is so different physically from the actual performer, as with "Skinhead" (Bob Holman barks of that persona poem, "hear the voice of a white supremacist skinhead come from the mouth of this black woman"). Smith has observed that "those moments of slipping on his voice . . . trapped me in his hatred. I felt as if I were losing myself. It was a struggle to write my way out. Even now when I perform the poem, audiences are jolted by his voice coming from the mouth of a black woman."[45] Such an effect is at an angle to what many regard as the dominant mode of the slam: the relentless focus on the ego. Figuratively speaking, such vocal impersonation can be said to represent the social repositioning of the subject herself, not simply an assertion of unique subjectivity.

In scoring the voice on the page, Smith often relies on italics and capitalization to register shifts in speaker (when there is more than one represented in the poem) and the interior thoughts and vocal expressiveness of a single subject, but we do not encounter the radical discordant effects that we come across in the print texts of the Black Arts poets. In *Close to Death* we note attempts to represent intonation and emphasis through typography in such statements as "Hey *chill*, Terrell. Chill"; "'Bitch, you *could* speak'"; and "'What YOU doin' here.'" The encoding on paper of oral features shapes character, and, on stage, by assuming in her verbal and bodily movements a range of different characters, Smith is able to perform an immediately visceral polyvocality, giving the marginalized a voice.

MTV's *Spoken Word Unplugged* series (1992; 1994) also made celebrities out of some slam poets. As Caryn James observes in her review of the series in the *New York Times*, "The distance between rap and poetry has always been as thin as the page of a book. That gap disappears in 'Spoken Word,' an energetic and wry all-poetry edition of the smash MTV series 'Unplugged.'"[46] The very title, "Unplugged," suggests the oppositional stance it takes, the acoustic pitted against the amplified electric enhancement of instrumental and vocal sound. The show is meant to strip poetry bare, to leave nothing on stage except the unmediated voice, a raw presence, in an effort to create greater intimacy between artist and audience, to foster a feeling of sincerity. Of course, the scene is not ultimately unplugged (it is, after all, on TV), which may suggest just how thoroughly the live and the mediatized crisscross in contemporary culture; in the case of Maggie Estep's performance, "Lights flash in the background, bass-heavy backup music plays," and "The camera swirls and tilts," leading Caryn James to declare, "Here is poetry as Performance, poetry as video. And though most purists would prefer to ignore this truth, here is poetry returned to its roots, in song and chant. There's nothing to say an MTV moment can't be poetic, as long as you don't think Matthew Arnold and T. S. Eliot own the poetry franchise." James credits a politics of presence for the form's success: "By focusing on the persona of the poet who takes the stage, spoken word poetry seems at times to exalt the authoritative presence of the poet's body and the esoteric aura of the poem's voiced body prior to any technology of reproduction (whether the printed page or a tape recording)"; she claims that "the oral roots of the lyric tradition require the poet to conjure the 'voice' or 'presence' of an authentic and representative self with which the reader can identify, even to the point of total, or absorptive, identification."[47] More modern is the identity politics on which this spoken word poetry is based, as it seeks to reclaim, redescribe, or transform previously stigmatized accounts of group membership through consciousness-raising.

In Miguel Algarín's poem "Nuyorican Angel of Wordsmithing," he cites this MTV program and its cultivation of a poetics of presence in his articulation of a new performance ethos for the digital age:

I. Nuyorican Aesthetics:
It is a moral imperative to give poetry to the people. It is a media twenty-first-century picturetel event when a young poet can read on *Unplugged*, transferring via MTV the heat of passion. Electronic verse has changed the craft of writing poetry. We can interact *live* with Tokyo, London and Rome simultaneously; once the poet reaches millions, he / she learns how a verse can heal human pain. (*PN*, 65)

Notably, Algarín's conception of liveness does presuppose an unmediatized state: a poet can interact live, he finds, on television or in cyberspace, with none of the heat of emotion lost. Philip Auslander has shown with respect to *Unplugged* (it was conceived as a showcase for musicians) that it "takes acoustic performance and liveness as its twin imperatives," promoting the values of "authenticity, sincerity, and rootsiness" that have been associated with acoustic playing since the early 1960s, even though it is staged through mass media; as he finds, "the abundance of signs insisting on MTV Unplugged's status as live event contributes to the simulation of liveness, the creation of a live-effect that appears to denounce simulation while actually furthering its dominance."[48] This "regime of simulated liveness" (*Unplugged* distracts us from the media of its own communication) is crucial to the spoken word poets who appear in that format, poets seeking thereby to authenticate themselves and their (often subversive) messages.

Tracie Morris, Nuyorican Grand Slam Champ in 1993, appeared both in MTV's *Spoken Word Unplugged* pilot and in Holman's PBS series *The United States of Poetry*. Her featured hip hop poem "Project Princess" serves as a prime example of her insistence on liveness and her enactment of a visibility politics. The poem appears in print in Morris's first book, *Chap-T-Her Won* (1991), which was self-published. The foreword to the book charts a quick history for the poem and its companions that passes through the Black Arts poets all the way back to spirituals and sermons: "Hawk back to the days at night, the last poets. On stage, radio and screen. Scream, Jay Hawkins, Quincy Troupe, Sonia Sanchez, Jayne Cortez, Ntozake Shange, the Gumbo Girls. The Last Poets. Those *unknown bards*. *God's Trombones*. Sing ev'ry voice and risk." Holman states on the back cover of *Chap-T-Her Won*: "For those who haven't heard Tracie Morris live—fear not. This book reconstitutes into the rill thang, the living word. Just add mind and time and mix: sublime." Here Morris's stage work is imagined as recuperable in her page work (we need not have heard the poem performed by Morris to appreciate its power), as Holman insists on the performances as "rill" (or "real") and as a consequence of their authenticity worth the price.

Morris's performance poetry extends from her early slam work to a more dadaist sound poetry that is not syntactically standard. It was, she says, in her hearing of Sonia Sanchez in particular that she was "subconsciously pushed . . . along the sound trajectory." Morris marks her move from one performance modality to the next with "Project Princess," which she says she began "deconstructing" in 1993 at a reading at the Apollo Theater; to her mind, the "improvisational life" of the poem—her sonic manipulations of it in performance—allows it to resist commodification ("the dead recording that is understood as object"): "I consider these poems to be living entities that invite a live moment between the listener and utterer."

Christine Hume asserts that "Project Princess" "hints at the half-spoken, half-sung recitative style that will go on to inform her sound poems, yet the intonation patterns and rhythms exist so fully within a predetermined slam style that the work comes close to feeling commodified." But which "Project Princess" does she refer to? Although she argues that Morris's later sound poetry "stand[s] against reified notions of authenticity and sincerity," in Morris's articulations of "Project Princess" she also is seeking to resist the reified as she enacts a gendered and racialized subjectivity and authenticity in a precise moment.[49] Indeed, when recording other poems for audition in a "non-live format," she is careful, she says, to work with her engineer to make the poems sound "viscous," with a "very live feel to it." When she needs to edit a printed poem for recording, she reads the edited version aloud first to make sure that it sounds "organic, authentic."[50] Morris's simulation of liveness bears directly on her performance of a nonpredetermined, improvisational self.

In her oral performance of "Project Princess" Morris delivers the words rapid-fire, building up a momentum that blurs lexical boundaries. She acknowledges the influence of hip hop, in particular the qualities of rhyme (assonance, consonance, and end rhyme) and "flow" ("Part rhythm, rhyme, timing, and technique, flow is almost intangible but refers to the musicality of the artist's delivery") in that popular musical form.[51] In addition, her orality is shaped by interruption, an effect analogous to the practice of hip hop DJs whose manipulation of sound involves the use of cutting—"the systematic interruption of the conventional musical pattern with another record or sound to create a new pattern"—and looping or scratching—"using the sound of a vinyl album (or digital sound equivalent) being interrupted within the groove to create the distinctive sound of the amplified needle literally scratching the recorded pattern." Her interruptions happen differently in each performance, as they would at the hands of a DJ. As Morris explains, her poems "evolve through repetition and performance," and three different iterations of "Project Princess" exist on tape.[52] One of these instantiations is part of PBS's *The United States of Poetry*.[53] Her performance there is framed by an epigraph by Walt Whitman ("I hear America singing, the varied carols I hear!"), and the video sequence is structured entirely around low-angle shots of the housing projects, of young black girls who live there, and of Morris herself, with the camera swirling in circles around her. We watch Morris, her eyes closed and her hands gesticulating in air according to the rhythms and emphases of her poem. The poem on PBS ends with the line "It's all about you and living in your world," a line not in any of the printed versions of the poem. Indeed, none of those printed versions seek to capture the oral or kinesic properties of the poem as she has performed it on tape, no doubt as a result of her sense that any version of it felt to be perfectly full, and thus authoritative, would contribute to its commodification ("the dead recording that is understood as object").

Another poet who unplugged on MTV but who is nonetheless a master of the mediatized, remastering verse in the recording studio to arrive at his final product, is Edwin Torres, whose poem "Mission-Fuckin'-Impossible," as we have noted, takes aim at the commodity culture in which the mediatized reigns. Holman describes Torres's CD *Holy Kid* (1998), released on the label Kill Rock Stars, as "the el classico combo po dj CD," and Torres acknowledges it as "an important step for me. . . . working with studio technology to realize a vision of hearing." He tells Holman that the poems on *Holy Kid,* in various styles ("acoustic, electric, homemade, a capella"), were recorded over a period of two years, and that he enjoys its "lo-fi feel": "I think the 4-track tapes give it a recurring homemade groove." As Torres finds, such a feel allows for the realization of his poetic ideal, which is to perform "truthfully" and with "sincerity": "From the quietest piece to the loudest shriek, a poem delivered from the heart will always register." Just as Ginsberg harks back to the graininess of an early recording of *Howl,* and just as Morris works toward a rough density in her recorded work, Torres seeks to simulate liveness in a mediatized environment in order to push humane values through. While digital technologies may afford the artist with certain performance opportunities, the struggle against marketplace pressures is thereby heightened: "Challenge for recorded poetry is to utilize the medium, to not just be words documented but to be as linear or non-linear as poem dictates. . . . Possibilities are as possible as creator creates, or as business-types allow poetry to be recorded and distributed . . . fat chance." Torres instructs that a poetics of realness depends on "poeticizing the sound studios. Poets who understand subtlety and bravado need to start handling production. . . . [P]oetry as CD has barely penetrated the universal hear-drum!"[54] He sees, too, how it must work in the opposite direction, with live performance transcribing the printed page: "The music, sound, actions onstage are all part of the poem, performing an evolution within the audience's reception—equating a subtle turn of lyrical phrasing into a delicate lighting change. The stage is the sheet of paper, the poem is each theatrical element—a physical manifestation of the poem's language, brought to life."

Torres's performance-centered texts recognize this dialectical relation-ship between the literate and the oral, with the poem (as he puts it) taking "an elaborate graphic treatment on the page, echoing its live dynamic on-stage with inventive typography on page."[55] For instance, in "Entrancielo," the affective pace of the poem is negotiated through graphic forms that represent signs introduced as notations for oral performance:

> . . . and all I mention
> is understood . . . and no more invention
> in this tongue, there is
> > . . . no more invention in this tongue, there is
> > . . . no more invention in this tongue

(Bum Rush, 181)

The cues that he embeds in "Dig on the Decade" are more variegated and orchestrate his aggressive expressive bravado:

> I GOTTA MADDENING PACE TO KEEP! DO YOU *GET-SO* MY, SWEEP!?!
> Look at me! LOOK AT ME! Take-my-thumb-out-of-your mouth-and-LOOK-
> AT-ME!!!
> 'Cause I KNOW the guy with the big eyes who's been lookin' at you.
> *bare . . . skin . . . back . . . . my patience . . . . . . your bridle . . . . . .*
> *. . . riiiiiide . . .*

(Aloud, 153)

Through texts such as these, Torres can be heard as one of the most recent in a long line of poet-performers who have sought to capture qualities of liveness in their print art and at the same time create figures of vocalism that ironically reveal a tongue full of "more invention."

In their attempt to establish a nation within a nation—what the 1999 documentary dubs "SlamNation"—these poets wear their identities on their sleeves: they embody their resistance to the dominant culture on stage and page and through the transmissions of new media, even as they look to undercut, or at least complicate, the ideological effects typically as-sociated with those media and their spectacles. Operating across a range of registers, the poetry of the slam (and its outgrowths in the later work of Smith, Morris, and Torres) reconstitutes selfhood and America itself by sounding through the public sphere the varied carols they hear.

Afterword

Because rap is poetry, and hip hop is culture.

—BOB HOLMAN, FROM "PRAISE POEM FOR SLAM:
    WHY SLAM CAUSES PAIN AND IS A GOOD THING"

As DANA GIOIA POINTS OUT in his 2004 book *Disappearing Ink,* we currently are living through a cultural revolution, one in which "print has lost its primacy in communication"; as he observes, "the most surprising and significant development in recent American poetry has been the wide-scale and unexpected reemergence of popular poetry, a poetry that is predominantly oral and informed by new media." In addition to slam poetry, one of these poetries is rap, and the debates about authenticity surrounding that form highlight many of the issues that this book raises and call attention to the continuing tradition of the spoken word that harks back to Whitman.[1]

In 1993 Eric Michael Dyson argued that the rap concert "creates space for cultural resistance and personal agency," but with the commercial success of hip hop, questions about the oppositional force of hip hop and the attendant issue of authenticity have arisen. He reflects on this matter of authenticity in a 2006 interview where he addresses the previous year's film *Hustle & Flow,* which features a pimp named Djay who creates his own music at home, in a less-than-advanced technological situation: the film makes "an argument," he says, "for an old-school approach to recording. This is about the culture of the tape, this is about recalling the myth of hip hop origins. The iconography of the tape in an era of digital technology is like the ghetto version of Walter Benjamin's 'The Work of Art in the Age of Mechanical Reproduction.' It's about recording technology in the hands of those who control its content and reproduction." We have seen the ways in which technologies of sound recording carry a political charge for many performance poets, with a lo-fi feel often symbolic of a return to auratic ori-

230

gins, to a time before the mechanics of repetition and (often) popular success set in. As Dyson expounds, again with respect to the poetics and politics of *Hustle & Flow*, "Producing a tape in the age of the CD is . . . about the
quixotic politics of nostalgia linked to the authentic. This is about what's
real. . . . Despite newfangled technologies and forms like the CD and MP3,
what this is about—this production of a tape—is a man and his voice and
his desire, and the people who conspire with him to create art that makes
a difference to the soul." The cassette tape thus serves "to contest the dis-
tancing and destabilizing and deracinating forces of technology," to pro-
tect against "a certain loss of community and identity," with the voice of
the artist presented in a way that is direct, unenhanced, "original"—the
model being Whitman, whom Ferlinghetti hails as "greatest soul speaker."[2]

Dyson credits the Black Arts movement for instructing this sense of
community and identity in early hip hop, explaining that those earlier
artists felt that "politics is central to artistic vision" and that there must exist a "strong tie between artist and community, spurning the heroic indi-
vidualism of European models of artistic endeavor in favor of the collective
roots of artists who express the values, beliefs, ideals, and perceptions of
the communities to which they belong." He imagines as parallel the live
poetry readings of the Black Arts movement and the performance of rap,
which, he believes, is "fueled by the same energy and purpose": "Like their
Black Arts Movement predecessors, [socially] conscious rappers insist that
politics, art, and life are intricately intertwined." When Dyson comments
on the rhetorical skill of hip hoppers, he notes their esteemed lineage,
which, he says, includes Hughes, Giovanni, Sanchez, and Whitman.[3]

One of the principal elements of rap performance is its liveness; it is on
stage in front of an audience "where rappers turn into MCs" or not. As the
artists attest, "Hip-hop is all about performing live," and "is more important than having good records," as liveness serves as a means of certifying
your authenticity ("It seems like you're fake or something if you sound
good on record with Auto-Tune and all of that but onstage you sing horri-
ble"). Getting the crowd amped, connecting with fans, through a strong interactive performance (a "deeply embodied participatory involvement") is
key.[4] The ability to "freestyle," that is, to improvise, on stage is further
proof of the hip hop poet. As with the art of other poets who flow from
Whitman, the MC's stylings (layering, deconstructing, reassembling, su-
perimposing) refute the idea of the work as fixed aesthetic object; as
Richard Shusterman finds, rap exists in a state of change, operating "with-

out the pretense that its own work is inviolable, that the artistic process is
ever final, that there is ever a product that should be so fetishized that it
could never be submitted to appropriative transfiguration. . . . In contrast
to the standard view that 'a poem is forever,' rap highlights the artwork's
temporality and likely impermanence, not only by appropriative decon-
structions, but by explicitly thematizing its own temporality in its lyrics.
For example, several songs by BDP [hip hop group Boogie Down Produc-
tions] include lines like 'Fresh for 88, you suckers' or 'Fresh for 89, you suckers.'"[5] Of course, such updatings are perfectly in line with those that Whitman and his heirs made to their poems.

Rapper Saul Williams, the 1996 winner of the title of Nuyorican Poets
Cafe's Grand Slam Champion, one of the performers in the documentary
SlamNation, and cowriter and star of the 1998 feature film *Slam,* shines a
light on Whitman in *The Dead Emcee Scrolls: The Lost Teachings of Hip-Hop*
(2006), which imagines his discovery of a mystical ancient text with these
teachings on them rolled up in a can of spray paint in the New York City
subway system and his subsequent translation and performance of them.
Williams notes that the book "was written with the intent of being the best
hip-hop album never recorded," and, according to Williams, "The reader
should be able to feel the beats off the page," as he imagines print and orality seamlessly constructing each other.[6] Some reviewers, though, questioned just how seamless that construction was—"But here comes the mil-
lion-dollar question: does it actually hold up on the page?"—reminding us
of the questions that have been asked of performance poetry in print going
back more than a century.[7]

In his prefatory "A Confession" Williams describes his first recital of the
poetry on the scrolls at an open mic reading at a café: "I had already experienced a huge surge of energy while reciting the poem to myself, but I was
by no means expecting the feeling that came with reciting this poem to an
audience. I could practically see the words exiting my mouth. The image of
the open mouth came to mind. I was becoming the manifestation of that
image." The audience responds emotionally, and his performance career
takes off, as he is immediately invited to read with the Last Poets and Gil
Scott Heron, with Sonia Sanchez and Amiri Baraka, and with Allen Ginsberg and the Roots. He quickly gains a reputation as a vessel through which
these lost teachings of hip hop—teachings that he imagines were planted
long ago by African shamans to be unleashed at just this moment in history—speak. In the poem "Co-Dead Language" he cites, among others,

Whitman, Ginsberg, and the black beat poet Bob Kaufman as guiding spirits, and calls us all to a new self-awareness:

> We enlist every instrument: acoustic, electronic,
> every so-called race, gender, sexual preference
> every per-son as beings of sound to acknowledge
> their responsibility to uplift the consciousness
> of the entire fucking world!

The activist Williams reflects on these teachings, acknowledging that "The power of the spoken word is very much a part of the power of hip-hop. The emcee stands in direct lineage to the African griot. . . . The spoken word movement in connection to hip-hop has become a place where the youth have stripped away the beat of the drum to simply focus and sharpen the attention paid to the word"; he also comes to see that "through the simple act of reciting their poem they [young slam poets] are adding their voice to telling of his/story, which was once linear and exclusive of them and the particularities of their story, their perspective." The hip hop emcee, he adds, must learn, as these poets have, that expressing vulnerability is a strength, not a weakness, and use their "newfound voice of independence" audaciously to begin to build, from scratch, a new history, and not fall prey to the misdirected materialism of gangsta rap.[8]

As the incredible vitality of "Whitman's wild children" shows, extending even into the province of hip hop, there exists a long tradition of American performance poetry, though its trajectory has been hidden. For 150 years, "the people's poetry" has performed American culture and cultural identity within it, awakening us to the multiplicity of subjectivities in ourselves and our publics. In the last sentence of his 1855 Preface to *Leaves* Whitman observes that "The proof of a poet is that his country absorbs him as affectionately as he has absorbed it." Revamping that statement the next year in his 1856 poem "Poem of Many in One," in light of slow first-edition book sales, he claims, "The proof of a poet shall be sternly deferred till his country absorbs him as affectionately as he has absorbed it." In this chiasmic expression, Whitman announces his belief—and the belief of the artists in his wake—that no poet in America can be great without first penetrating the people, who through the poet's eloquence shall be "melted into one mass" and "have but one voice."

Notes

Introduction

Federico García Lorca, "Play and Theory of the Duende," in *Deep Song and Other Prose,* ed. and trans. Christopher Maurer (New York: New Directions, 1980), 47. Lorca delivered this lecture in 1933.

Elin Diamond, *Performance and Cultural Politics* (New York: Routledge, 1996), 4.

   1. Walt Whitman, *Poetry and Prose,* ed. Justin Kaplan (New York: Library of America, 1996), 1082. Hereafter cited parenthetically in the text as *PP.*

   2. Ezra Pound and Harriet Monroe, *Poetry* 5 (1914): 29–32.

   3. Karl Shapiro, "The Three Hockey Games of T. S. Eliot," *Antioch Review* 22.3 (1962): 285.

   4. Sterling A. Brown, *A Son's Return: Selected Essays of Sterling A. Brown* (Boston: Northeastern University Press, 1996), 139, 140.

   5. Louis Simpson, "On Being a Poet in America," *Noble Savage* 5 (1962): 24–33.

   6. David Groff, "The Peril of the Poetry Reading: The Page Versus the Performance," http://www.poets.org/viewmedia.php/prmMID/5913 (accessed January 10, 2011). Howard's remarks are quoted in this article.

   7. Dennis Tedlock, "Toward a Poetics of Polyphony and Translatability," in *Close Listening: Poetry and the Performed Word,* ed. Charles Bernstein (New York: Oxford University Press, 1998), 178. Peggy Phelan, *Unmarked: The Politics of Performance* (New York: Routledge, 1993), 146, 148.

   8. Philip Auslander, *Liveness: Performance in a Mediatized Culture* (New York: Routledge, 1999), 5.

   9. Auslander, *Liveness,* 40.

   10. Auslander, *Liveness,* 47, 40.

   11. Auslander, *Liveness,* 4, 2–3.

   12. Bernstein, *Close Listening,* 9.

   13. Elizabeth Fine, *The Folklore Text: From Performance to Print* (Bloomington: Indiana University Press, 1984), 4–11.

   14. Nancy Fraser, "Rethinking the Public Sphere: A Contribution to the Critique of

Actually Existing Democracy," in *Habermas and the Public Sphere*, ed. Craig Calhoun (Cambridge: MIT Press, 1992), 123.

15. Gerard Hauser, "Prisoners of Conscience and the Counterpublic Sphere of Prison Writing," in *Counterpublics and the State*, ed. Robert Asen and Daniel Brouwer (New York: State University of New York Press, 2001), 36–37.

16. Walter Benjamin, "The Work of Art in the Age of Mechanical Reproduction," in *Illuminations*, ed. Hannah Arendt, trans. Harry Zohn (1968; rpt. New York: Schocken Books, 1986), 224.

17. Roland Barthes, "The Death of the Author," in *Image, Music, Text*, trans. Stephen Heath (New York: Hill and Wang, 1977), 142.

18. Mark Eleveld, ed., advised by Marc Smith, *The Spoken Word Revolution: Slam, Hip Hop, and the Poetry of a New Generation* (Naperville, IL: Sourcebooks MediaFusion, 2003), 141. Hereafter cited parenthetically in the text as *SWR*. See my book *Robert Frost and the Politics of Poetry* (Hanover, NH: University Press of New England, 2001) for a discussion of the ways in which intonational ambiguity accrues significance in Frost's poetry.

19. Richard Kostelanetz, *The Avant-Garde Tradition in Literature* (Buffalo, NY: Prometheus Books, 1982), 15, 16.

20. Walter Ong, *Orality and Literacy: The Technologizing of the Word* (New York: Methuen, 1982), 3.

21. Joyce A. Joyce, ed., *Conversations with Sonia Sanchez* (Jackson: University Press of Mississippi, 2007), 108.

22. Bob Holman, liner notes to his poetry slam CD anthology *Grand Slam: Best of the San Francisco National Slam* (NuYo Records, 1994).

23. Alan Ackerman, *The Portable Theater: American Literature and the Nineteenth-Century Stage* (Baltimore: Johns Hopkins University Press, 1999), 47.

24. Tenney Nathanson, *Whitman's Presence: Body, Voice, and Writing in "Leaves of Grass"* (New York: New York University Press, 1992), 8.

25. Walt Whitman, *Notebooks and Unpublished Prose Manuscripts*, ed. Edward F. Grier, 6 vols. (New York: New York University Press, 1984), 6:2224, 2234. Hereafter cited parenthetically in the text as *NUPM*.

Chapter 1

These are the title, wording, and punctuation of the line from the 1881–82 edition of *Leaves of Grass* on. See Sculley Bradley, Harold W. Blodgett, Arthur Golden, and William White, eds., *Leaves of Grass: A Textual Variorum of the Printed Poems*, 3 vols. (New York: New York University Press, 1980). Hereafter cited parenthetically in the text as *LGV*.

Horace Traubel, *With Walt Whitman in Camden*, 9 vols., vols. 1–3 (1906–14; rpt. New York: Rowman & Littlefield, 1961); vol. 4, ed. Sculley Bradley (Philadelphia: University of Pennsylvania Press, 1953); vol. 5, ed. Gertrude Traubel (Carbondale: University of Southern Illinois Press, 1964); vol. 6, ed. Gertrude Traubel and William White (Carbondale: University of Southern Illinois Press, 1982); vol. 7, ed. Jeanne Chapman and Robert MacIsaac (Carbondale: University of Southern Illinois Press, 1992); vols. 8–9, ed. Jeanne Chapman and Robert MacIsaac (Oregon House, CA: W. L. Bentley, 1996), 1:414. Hereafter cited parenthetically in the text as *WWWC*.

1. *Walt Whitman's Workshop: A Collection of Unpublished Manuscripts*, ed. Clifton Joseph Furness (Cambridge: Harvard University Press, 1928), 27.

2. On *Gems from Walt Whitman*, see Ed Folsom, "Leaves of Grass, Junior: Whitman's Compromise with Discriminating Tastes," *American Literature* 63 (1991): 641–63; on the Haldeman-Julius "Little Blue Books," see Kenneth M. Price, "Whitman in Selected Anthologies," *Virginia Quarterly Review* 81 (Spring 2005): 147–62.

3. Walt Whitman, "Walt Whitman and His Poems," http://www.whitmanar chive.org/criticism/reviews/leaves1855/anc.00176.html (accessed January 10, 2011).

4. [Anonymous], rev. of *Leaves of Grass*, http://www.whitmanarchive.org/criti cism/reviews/leaves1855/anc.00024.html (accessed January 10, 2011).

5. Henry B. Rankin, from *Personal Recollections of Abraham Lincoln* (New York: G. P. Putnam's Sons, 1916), 126.

6. Joann P. Krieg, "Whitman and Sojourner Truth," *Walt Whitman Quarterly Review* 16 (Summer 1998): 32–33.

7. Edith Wharton, *A Backward Glance* (New York: Appleton-Century, 1934), 185. In her autobiography, Wharton reports of James's recitation style, "I had never before heard poetry read as he read it; and I never have since. He chanted it, and he was not afraid to chant it, as many good readers are, who, though they instinctively feel that the genius of the English poetical idiom requires it to be spoken *as poetry*, are yet afraid of yielding to their instinct because the present-day fashion is to chatter high verse as though it were colloquial prose. James, on the contrary, far from shirking the rhythmic emphasis, gave it full expression" (185).

8. Doc Searls, "Footprints of Whitman," May 8, 1996, http://www.searls.com/ whitman.html (accessed January 10, 2011).

9. Phelan, *Unmarked*, 36.

10. Ed Folsom, "Appearing in Print: Illustrations of the Self in *Leaves of Grass*," in *The Cambridge Companion to Walt Whitman*, ed. Ezra Greenspan (Cambridge: Cambridge University Press, 1995), 135ff. As Folsom sees, "the authorizing presence" of the 1855 *Leaves* in the visual image on the frontispiece "gradually worked to transform the way most American poets portrayed themselves on their book jackets and frontispieces" (135).

11. These words appear in an ad for *Leaves* in Whitman's *As a Strong Bird on Pinions Free* (1872).

12. Randall Knoper, *Acting Naturally: Mark Twain in the Culture of Performance* (Berkeley: University of California Press, 1995), 28.

13. John Burroughs noted in October 1862 that "Walt Whitman is at Pfaff's every night" (quoted in Justin Kaplan, *Walt Whitman: A Life* [New York: Simon and Schuster, 1980], 263).

14. Walt Whitman, *The Correspondence*, ed. Edwin Haviland Miller, 7 vols. (New York: New York University Press, 1969), 7:209.

15. Quoted in *Walt Whitman's Workshop*, 31.

16. Maurice Bucke, *Walt Whitman* (Philadelphia: D. McKay, 1883), 53–54.

17. Bucke, *Walt Whitman*, 127, 126. Contrarily, some Whitman biographers have stated that Whitman's voice was "high-pitched," perhaps as a result of his stroke (see Larry D. Griffin, "Walt Whitman's Voice," *Walt Whitman Quarterly Review* 9.3 [1992]: 125–33). The poet Jack Foley wonders whether that description is a result of homophobia (*O Powerful Western Star: Poetry & Art in California* [Oakland, CA: Pantograph Press, 2000], 144). The contents of Whitman's "Reading Book," the book of poems that he used as text in public readings, are enumerated in *Walt Whitman's Workshop*, 204–6.

18. J. B. Pond, *Eccentricities of Genius* (New York: G. W. Dillingham, 1900), 497.

19. Quoted in David Haven Blake, *Walt Whitman and the Culture of American Celebrity* (New Haven: Yale University Press, 2006), 189, 192–93.

20. Whitman's corrected proof sheet and note to the publishers is available at http://www.loc.gov/ammem/today/feb09.html (accessed January 10, 2011).

21. George M. Beard, *American Nervousness: Its Causes and Consequences* (1881; New York: Arno Press, 1972), 80–81.

22. See Christopher Looby, *Voicing America: Language, Literary Form, and the Origins of the United States* (Chicago: University of Chicago Press, 1996).

23. Jay Fliegelman, *Declaring Independence: Jefferson, Natural Language, and the Culture of Eloquence* (Stanford: Stanford University Press, 1993).

24. C. Carroll Hollis, "Rhetoric, Elocution, and Voice in Leaves of Grass: A Study in Affiliation," *Walt Whitman Quarterly Review* 2.2 (1984): 1–21. Also see C. Carroll Hollis, " 'Tallying, Vocalizing All': Discourse Markers in *Leaves of Grass*," in *Walt Whitman: The Centennial Essays*, ed. Ed Folsom (Iowa City: University of Iowa Press, 1994), 61–67. The preface to the variorum edition of *Leaves* states that "If we look at 'Song of Myself,' we find that in the 1855 version of the poem, in the first 600 lines alone, there are over 150 uses of ellipsis. In 1856, all of these are changed to dashes or commas. But by the final edition, most of the dashes that replaced ellipses become commas" (*LGV*, 1:28).

25. Fliegelman, *Declaring Independence*, 26.

26. Phelan, *Unmarked*, 146.

27. Auslander, *Liveness*, 58; Phelan, *Unmarked*, 148.

28. As Eric Lott affirms, Bowery theater "was indeed a 'manly' preserve, a sphere of traditional male prowess and bravado whose turf loyalties were as likely to result in individual or gang violence as in the camaraderie of the saloon" (*Love and Theft: Blackface Minstrelsy and the American Working Class* [New York: Oxford University Press, 1995], 86).

29. David Porter, *Emerson and Literary Change* (Cambridge: Harvard University Press, 1978), 107.

30. Quoted in B. L. Packer, *Emerson's Fall: A New Interpretation of the Major Essays* (New York: Continuum, 1982), 1.

31. Ralph Waldo Emerson, *Emerson in His Journals*, ed. Joel Porte (Cambridge: Belknap/Harvard University Press, 1984), 340.

32. Quoted in F. O. Matthiessen, *American Renaissance* (New York: Oxford University Press, 1968), 559.

33. Quoted in David S. Reynolds, *Walt Whitman's America: A Cultural Biography* (New York: Vintage, 1995), 173.

34. Mark Bauerlein, *Whitman and the American Idiom* (Baton Rouge: Louisiana State University Press, 1991), 15, 158. See also Mark Bauerlein, "The Written Orator of 'Song of Myself': A Recent Trend in Whitman Criticism," *Walt Whitman Quarterly Review* 3.1 (1986): 1–14. On Whitman's expressive uses of typography, see Megan L. Benton's "Typography and Gender: Remasculating the Modern Book," in *Illuminating Letters: Typography and Literary Interpretation,* ed. Paul C. Gutjahr and Megan L. Benton (Amherst: University of Massachusetts Press, 2001), 71–93.

35. Michael Moon, *Disseminating Whitman: Revision and Corporeality in "Leaves of Grass"* (Cambridge: Harvard University Press, 1991), 124–25, 126. Whitman refers to editions before 1860 as "little pittance-editions" and as "inchoates": see [Walt Whitman], "All about a Mocking-Bird," http://www.whitmanarchive.org/criticism/ reviews/a_child/anc.00140.html (accessed January 10, 2011).

36. Judith Butler, *Gender Trouble: Feminism and the Subversion of Identity* (New York: Routledge, 1990), 18.

37. Reynolds, *Walt Whitman's America,* 87.

38. Betsy Erkkila, *Whitman the Political Poet* (New York: Oxford University Press, 1989), 132.

39. Luke Mancuso, *The Strange Sad War Revolving: Walt Whitman, Reconstruction, and the Emergence of Black Citizenship, 1865–1876* (Columbia, SC: Camden House, 1997), 28.

40. Ed Folsom and Kenneth M. Price, *Re-scripting Walt Whitman: An Introduction to His Life and Work* (Malden, MA: Blackwell, 2005), 52.

41. Moon, *Disseminating Whitman,* 210, 167, 151.

42. [Anonymous], rev. of *Leaves of Grass,* http://www.whitmanarchive.org/ criticism/reviews/leaves1855/anc.00015.html (accessed January 10, 2011).

43. This is as the lines appear in the 1856 *Leaves.*

44. Fredson Bowers, ed., *Whitman's Manuscripts: Leaves of Grass (1860)* (Chicago: University of Chicago Press, 1955), 156–58.

45. Griffin, "Walt Whitman's Voice." See also Ed Folsom, "The Whitman Recording," *Walt Whitman Quarterly Review* 9.4 (1992): 214–16; and William Grimes, "On Tape, Scholars Think They Hear Walt Whitman Reading," *New York Times,* March 16, 1992: B:1–2.

46. The audio recording is available at http://www.whitmanarchive.org/multime dia/index.html (accessed January 10, 2011).

47. Quoted in Erkkila, *Whitman the Political Poet,* 262.

48. John M. Picker, *Victorian Soundscapes* (New York: Oxford University Press, 2003), 117.

49. Picker, *Victorian Soundscapes,* 111–12, 116.

50. Quoted in Auslander, "Live from Cyberspace," *PAJ* 24.1 (2002): 16.

51. Bob Perelman, *The Marginalization of Poetry: Language Writing and Literary History* (Princeton, NJ: Princeton University Press, 1996). In conversation with Jack Fo-

ley, Allen Ginsberg surmises that it is Whitman on the recording based on the Brooklyn accent given to the word *ample* (Foley, *O Powerful Western Star*, 144).

52. Laura Swinton, "Levi's Rebrand for Independence Day," July 2, 2009, http://www.drapersonline.com/news/news-headlines/levis-rebrand-for-independence-day/5004067.article (accessed January 10, 2011); Levi's, "Go Forth," http://www.goforthnow.com/newamerican (accessed January 10, 2011); to see the television ads go to http://www.youtube.com/watch?v=FdW1CjbCNxw; http://www.youtube.com/watch?v=HG8tqEUTlvs (accessed January 10, 2011).

53. Fergus M. Bordewich, "Manhattan Mayhem," http://nvsocioman.com/Manhattan%20Mayhem.pdf (accessed January 10, 2011).

54. The poem first appears on the title page of the 1876 "Centennial Edition" of *Leaves* (a reissue of the fifth edition). The full copyright notice is available at http://www.whitmanarchive.org/published/LG/1891/whole.html.

55. Martin T. Buinicki, "Walt Whitman and the Question of Copyright," *American Literary History* 15.2 (2003): 269, 270.

56. Phelan, *Unmarked*, 150.

57. Harrison S. Morris, *Walt Whitman: A Brief Biography with Reminiscences* (Cambridge: Harvard University Press, 1929), 96.

58. Interview of Kenneth M. Price by Georgetown University's American Studies *Crossroads Project*, 1996, http://www.whitmanarchive.org/about/articles/anc.00005.html (accessed January 10, 2011).

59. [Anonymous], rev. of *Leaves of Grass*, http://www.whitmanarchive.org/criticism/reviews/leaves1860/anc.00041.html (accessed January 10, 2011).

Chapter 2

Amy Lowell, *A Critical Fable* (Boston: Houghton Mifflin, 1922), 407.

Letters of Vachel Lindsay, ed. Marc Chénetier (New York: Burt Franklin, 1979), 213. Hereafter cited parenthetically in the text as *L*.

1. Harriet Monroe, *Poets and Their Art* (New York: Macmillan, 1926), 21.

2. Cary Nelson, *Repression and Recovery: Modern American Poetry and the Politics of Cultural Memory, 1910–1945* (Madison: University of Wisconsin Press, 1989), 69. Also see John Chapman Ward's essay "Vachel Lindsay Is 'Lying Low'" (*College Literature* 12 [1985]: 233–45) for a full measure of how far Lindsay's stock has fallen as registered by his disappearance from poetry anthologies and curricula.

3. Vachel Lindsay, "Walt Whitman," *New Republic*, December 5, 1923, 4.

4. See Robert K. Nelson and Kenneth M. Price, "Debating Manliness: Thomas Wentworth Higginson, William Sloane Kennedy, and the Question of Walt Whitman," *American Literature* 73 (2001): 497–524. In a *Women's Journal* article entitled "Unmanly Manhood" published in February 1882, Higginson compares Whitman to Oscar Wilde and berates him for refusing to enlist as a soldier in the Civil War.

5. The rebellion against urban-industrial culture also could attract scorn, particularly if the poet appeared as a beggar; as Lindsay reported overhearing after one of his

poetry recitals in exchange for a night's lodging on a 1912 walking tour: "'That was a hot entertainment that young bum gave us last night,' said one man. 'He ought to get to work, the dirty lazy loafer,' said another" (*The Prose of Vachel Lindsay*, ed. Dennis Camp, 2 vols. [Peoria, IL: Spoon River Poetry Press, 1988], 1:174).

6. Anthony E. Rotundo, *American Manhood: Transformations in Masculinity from the Revolution to the Modern Era* (New York: Basic Books, 1993), 232.

7. In *Modernist Quartet* (Cambridge: Cambridge University Press, 1994), Frank Lentricchia examines the gender anxieties of a range of modernist poets, including Ezra Pound, T. S. Eliot, Robert Frost, and Wallace Stevens, in light of the feminine coding of the poetic profession in the early twentieth century.

8. Quoted in John Higham, "The Reorientation of American Culture in the 1890s," in *Writing American History: Essays on Modern Scholarship* (Bloomington: Indiana University Press, 1978), 82.

9. In 1904 Jessie B. Rittenhouse complained that "Poetry grows more and more an intellectual pleasure for the cultured classes, less and less a possession of the people" (*The Younger American Poets* [Freeport, NY: Books for Libraries Press, 1968], 34).

10. Vachel Lindsay, *The Congo and Other Poems* (New York: Macmillan, 1915), 1.

11. In *Vachel Lindsay: A Poet in America* (New York: Biblo and Tannen, 1969), Edgar Lee Masters laments Lindsay's efforts to "peddle poems," concluding that "it could come to nothing": "A man of twenty-six years, soon to write great poems, was playing a strange rôle thus to spend time and energy on so profitless a venture. . . . The conclusion is inescapable that Lindsay was feeding his vanity on these Quixotic jaunts at night about the streets of New York, and betraying something of an exhibitionism. . . . Many will wish that he [Lindsay] had kept to his vision on the subject of not trying to please the mob. If he had done so he would not have taken to the lecture field, there to recite poems which audiences called for, not that they had any appreciation of poetry, but on account of having heard that certain of his poems were exciting" (132–33).

12. *The Poetry of Vachel Lindsay*, ed. Dennis Camp, 3 vols. (Peoria, IL: Spoon River Poetry, 1984–86), 1:105. Hereafter cited parenthetically in the text as *PVL*.

13. The celebrated music scholar and journalist Henry Edward Krehbiel claimed to perceive similarities between ragtime and the African music he had heard some years earlier at the World's Columbian Exposition (Edward A. Berlin, *Ragtime: A Musical and Cultural History* [Berkeley: University of California Press, 1980], 21). Robert W. Snyder has observed that vaudeville, which featured ragtime musicians, helped popularize the new music, which debuted on the commercial entertainment scene in 1896 (*The Voice of the City: Vaudeville and Popular Culture in New York* [New York: Oxford University Press, 1989], 136).

14. Lindsay, *Congo*, vi.

15. Quoted in Jessie B. Rittenhouse, "Vachel Lindsay," *South Atlantic Quarterly* 32 (1933): 274, 275.

16. Rittenhouse, "Vachel Lindsay," 275.

17. Quoted in Edward A. Berlin, *King of Ragtime: Scott Joplin and His Era* (New York: Oxford University Press, 1994), 43.

18. T. E. Hummer states that "'The Congo' is surely well-intentioned, meant as a compliment to what Lindsay, and America, would have perceived as the 'primitive' energy of African culture," but concludes, "Still, it is poetry in blackface" ("Laughed Off: Canon, Kharakter, and the Dismissal of Vachel Lindsay," *Kenyon Review* 17.2 [1995]: 66). Rachel Blau DuPlessis also has pointed up the racist nature of "The Congo": "The popular appeal of the poem may well lie in its reduction of blacks to a repetitive beat, its judgmental participation in primitivist behavior that entertains whites by arousing them with the rhythms to which they feel superior" ("'HOO, HOO, HOO': Some Episodes in the Construction of Modern Whiteness," *American Literature* 67 [1995]: 675).

19. Randolph S. Bourne, "Sincerity in the Making," *New Republic*, December 5, 1914, 27.

20. Lott, *Love and Theft*, 52.

21. Masters, *Vachel Lindsay*, 316.

22. A columnist for the *New York Tribune* (1853) noted of one such act, "'Lucy Long' was sung by a white negro as a male female danced" (quoted in Lott, *Love and Theft*, 49).

23. See Lott, *Love and Theft*, 52–53. Lindsay told his contact at his publisher Macmillan, "I am so glad you consider the Booker Washington trilogy alive and not dead. As to the suggestion of an entire book of this nature, if it comes, it will have to come after more experience and observation with the colored folks" (*L* 128).

24. Quoted in Ann Massa, *Vachel Lindsay: Fieldworker for the American Dream* (Bloomington: Indiana University Press, 1970), 169–70.

25. W. E. B. Du Bois, "The Looking Glass: Literature," *Crisis* 12.4 (1916): 182–83; Vachel Lindsay and Joel E. Spingarn, "A Letter and an Answer," *Crisis* 13.3 (1917): 113–14. Du Bois remarks: "Mr. Vachel Lindsay knows two things, and two things only, about Negroes: The beautiful rhythm of their music and the ugly side of their drunkards and outcasts. From this poverty of material he tries now and then to make a contribution to Negro literature. It goes without saying that he only partly succeeds. His 'Booker Washington Trilogy,' published in *Poetry*, shows his defects as well as his genius. . . . Mr. Lindsay knows little of the Negro, and that little is dangerous" (182).

26. Lindsay notes that A. Joseph Armstrong encouraged him "to teach the John Brown Chorus to Black and White alike, and there has not been a murmur or ripple of protest" (*L* 183). After tramping with Lindsay through the Rockies and returning on foot to Springfield, Stephen Graham, who was to speak about Russia to the students at Springfield High School, was preceded by the students' rehearsal of the school-yell, which "visibly affected" Lindsay and Graham, the latter of whom remarked, "I was borne along by a rapturous enthusiasm which had been started by the yells. The whole school, boys and girls, white and coloured, were fused in one glowing whole. And Vachel said to me once more, 'There is America'" (*Tramping with a Poet in the Rockies* [New York: D. Appleton, 1922], 172–73).

27. M. Alison Kibler, *Rank Ladies: Gender and Cultural Hierarchy in American Vaudeville* (Chapel Hill: University of North Carolina Press, 1999), 31, 46.

28. Kibler, *Rank Ladies*, 47.

29. Kibler, *Rank Ladies,* 46.

30. "Poet Drops Club Women," *New York Times,* December 29, 1925: 8.

31. Quoted in Elizabeth Ruggles, *The West-Going Heart: A Life of Vachel Lindsay* (New York: Norton, 1959), 274; Conrad Aiken, *Scepticisms: Notes on Contemporary Poetry* (New York: Knopf, 1919), 156–57; quoted in S. Foster Damon, *Amy Lowell: A Chronicle* (Boston: Houghton, 1935), 300.

32. Henry Seidel Canby, *American Memoir* (Boston: Houghton, 1947), 295.

33. Quoted in Ruggles, *West-Going Heart,* 237.

34. This statement appears on the cover of the Caedmon audiocassette *Vachel Lindsay Reading* (CDL 51041).

35. John T. Flanagan, ed., *Profile of Vachel Lindsay* (Columbus, OH: Charles E. Merrill, 1970), 31.

36. Louis Untermeyer, *Modern American Poetry: An Introduction* (New York: Houghton, 1919).

37. Quoted in Anthony Slide, *Selected Vaudeville Criticism* (Metuchen, NJ: Scarecrow, 1988), 213.

38. Untermeyer, *Modern American Poetry,* 20.

39. Aiken, "Vachel Lindsay," in Flanagan, *Profile of Vachel Lindsay,* 5; Aiken, *Scepticisms,* 158.

40. *New York Times,* April 11, 1915: BR133.

41. Lindsay, *Congo,* vi. As Ann Massa has noted, "Yeats commended to Lindsay the half-sung, half-spoken delivery of such acts as Tambo and Bones dialogues, which had an apparent spontaneity and a quick-fire incantatory rhythm" (*Vachel Lindsay,* 231).

42. Lindsay, *Congo,* viii–ix. Lindsay's printed voice is in keeping with certain transcriptions of American Indian poetry during the early modernist period. For instance, in *Poetry* magazine (November 1918) the performance poet Lew Sarett scores his translation of "The Blue Duck" (what he calls "A Chippewa Medicine Dance") through marginal recital directions similar to those in Lindsay's chant-poems: "To be read with a vigorous / lilt emphasizing the drum-beats"; "More slowly and quiet- / ly verging on a chant"; "Slower—chant ris- / ing to a wail"; "Melancholy wailing from / this point on—higher and / higher in pitch" (59–61).

43. T. S. Eliot, "Marie Lloyd," in *Selected Essays,* new ed. (New York: Harcourt, 1960), 407.

44. T. S. Eliot, "Durkheim," *Saturday Westminster Gazette,* August 19, 1916, 14.

45. T. S. Eliot, *The Use of Poetry and the Use of Criticism* (Cambridge: Harvard University Press, 1933), 147–48, 240.

46. In Lindsay's "John L. Sullivan, the Strong Boy of Boston," one passage bears the marginal note, "*To be sung. Let the audience join in softly on this tune, wherever it appears*" (*PVL,* 1:341). Ruggles reports: "To make communication complete, he [Lindsay] had begun to call on audiences to join in certain poems. They were to strike the palms together, nod or shake the head, exclaim, 'No!' 'Yes!' 'We will!'" (*West-Going Heart,* 243).

47. Eliot, *Selected Essays,* 7.

48. Eliot, *Selected Essays*, 7, 11, 10.

49. Quoted in Ruggles, *West-Going Heart*, 237.

50. Quoted in Hummer, "Laughed Off," 60.

51. Eliot, "Marianne Moore," *Dial* 75.6 (December 1923): 595.

52. Eliot, *The Sacred Wood* (1920; London: Methuen, 1950), 69.

53. *The Letters of Ezra Pound*, ed. D. D. Paige (London: Faber, 1959), 54.

54. Quoted in Humphrey Carpenter, *A Serious Character: The Life of Ezra Pound* (Boston: Houghton Mifflin, 1988), 212.

55. Marianne Moore, *The Complete Prose of Marianne Moore*, ed. Patricia C. Willis (New York: Viking, 1986), 89–90.

56. *Letters of Wallace Stevens*, ed. Holly Stevens (Berkeley: University of California Press, 1966), 226.

57. Joan Richardson, ed., *Wallace Stevens: The Later Years, 1923–1955* (New York: William Morrow, 1988), 225.

58. *Letters of Wallace Stevens*, 326–27.

59. Lindsay, *General William Booth Enters Into Heaven and Other Poems* (New York: Mitchell Kennerley, 1914), xi.

60. Lindsay, *General*, vi. Mark Morrison has documented the importance of the cultural practice of verse recitation in modernist London, arguing that a premium was placed on "the performance of the pure voice," that is, the voice produced by education and professional training and, thus, one unattainable to the working class ("Performing the Pure Voice: Elocution, Verse Recitation, and Modernist Poetry in Pre-War London," *Modernism/Modernity* 3.3 [1996]: 36). The proponents of verse recitation demanded an untheatrical delivery of the poem, simultaneously insisting on impersonality and authorial presence, and decried any attempt to emulate the artificiality of British music-hall spectacle, a spectacle related to vaudeville, the form to which Lindsay was working hard to pin his aesthetic.

61. Quoted in Massa, *Vachel Lindsay*, 229.

62. Ruggles describes Lindsay's stage performance in the following way: " 'Every day a circus da-ay!' he would cry like a carnival barker halfway through *The Kallyope Yell*, then, breaking his strut across the stage to cock his head and cup his ear, ask 'What?' and answer himself, 'Well, al-most every day!' Eight lines farther on it was the turn of his friends out front. 'Bands a-play-ing every da-ay,' shouted the poet. 'What?' roared his hundreds, sometimes thousands, of new friends. 'Well, al-most every day.' The communion was intoxicating" (*West-Going Heart*, 243).

63. Lindsay tempered the acoustics of the poem upon republication: In *Adventures While Preaching the Gospel of Beauty* (New York: Mitchell Kennerley, 1914) it runs with the headnote, "Loudly and rapidly with a leader, College yell fashion." In his 1925 *Collected Poems*, after turning his back on a poetics of loudness, he observes, "It is to be noted that this song is marked 'College Yell fashion.' But, judged by the best 'Yells,' that does not mean strain, speed or racket. The best yells prophecy great music. The University of Kansas 'Jay Hawk' yell is slowly and beautifully whispered by four thousand students" (*PVL*, 3:860).

64. Quoted in Massa, *Vachel Lindsay*, 243.

65. *Prose of Vachel Lindsay,* 1:157.

66. Harold Holzer, in *Lincoln at Cooper Union: The Speech that Made Abraham Lincoln President* (New York: Simon and Schuster, 2004), recounts: "Sadly, Lincoln was apparently not as careful with his original as he was with his adaptation [the galleys at the newspaper office]. While reading proof, Cummings [*Tribune* proofreader] testified, Lincoln tossed his handwritten manuscript aside, page by page, whenever he was satisfied that each had been faithfully reproduced in type. The thought occurred to neither man to preserve the original. That night, so the old story goes, those now priceless pages were swept out with the trash, never to be seen again" (154–55).

67. Lindsay wrote to Armstrong: "I hope to develop such a system of recital visits that everyone is debarred from the hall that cannot pass a reasonable examination on the Village Magazine or one of my books! But that puts it arrogantly" (*L,* 205).

68. In May 1912 in his pamphlet *Rhymes To Be Traded for Bread* Lindsay states that one of the rules he will observe on his tramp-journey is to "Keep away from the railroads" (*PVL,* 1:105).

69. The ad appeared in *Ladies Home Journal,* February 1900.

70. Vachel Lindsay, "Beauty of Word in the United States," unpublished. The essay is in the University of Virginia Vachel Lindsay archive (Box 16).

71. This article clipping is in the University of Virginia Vachel Lindsay archive (Box 57).

72. *New York Times,* December 6, 1931: 31.

73. After his death, Lindsay's performance style was imitated by his son, Nicholas Cave Lindsay, and his sister, Olive. Olive was handled by the Redpath Bureau, and promotional materials stated that she made Lindsay's "books come alive and walk down from their shelves" in her recital of her brother's work. One review of Olive's performance quoted in those materials noted, "By some almost uncanny power she seemed to let through the voice and concept of the poet himself—to act unconsciously as a medium for his expression, and do it while retaining her own personality and individuality." This brochure is available at http://sdrc.lib.uiowa.edu/traveling_culture/chau1/pdf/lindsay/2/brochure.pdf (accessed January 10, 2011).

74. Nancy Milford, *Savage Beauty: The Life of Edna St. Vincent Millay* (New York: Random House, 2001), 367, 368, 486, 93.

75. John Crowe Ransom, "The Poet as Woman," in *The World's Body* (New York: Scribner's, 1938), 76–110.

76. Lindsay, "Beauty of Word in the United States."

77. Milford, *Savage Beauty,* 259–60.

78. Milford, *Savage Beauty,* 261, 272, 388. In April 1941 Millay began making the only recording of her reading her own poems for RCA Victor, although her voice by then was "thin, uncertain, and forced" (*Savage Beauty,* 458).

79. In 1932, just after Lindsay's death, an article titled "The Ordeal of Vachel Lindsay" was published in the *Bookman.* My echo of it tropes in a fashion the economy of repetition in which Lindsay was ensnared.

Chapter 3

James Weldon Johnson, *God's Trombones: Seven Negro Sermons in Verse* (1927; New York: Penguin, 1990). Hereafter cited parenthetically in the text as *GT.*

Langston Hughes, *The Collected Poems of Langston Hughes,* ed. Arnold Rampersad (New York: Knopf, 1994). Hereafter cited parenthetically in the text as *CPLH.*

1. Quoted in Arnold Rampersad, *The Life of Langston Hughes* (New York: Oxford University Press, 1988), 1:146. Hereafter cited parenthetically in the text as *LLH.*

2. *The Collected Works of Langston Hughes,* ed. Christopher C. De Santis (Columbia: University of Missouri Press, 2002), 9:484–85.

3. Langston Hughes, *The Big Sea: An Autobiography* (New York: Knopf, 1940), 212. Lindsay read to his audience that night the three poems that Hughes handed him, and Hughes felt the effect of his endorsement. Referring to Lindsay as a "great, kind man," he observes in the chapter "Poetry Is Practical" that "the widespread publicity resulting from the Vachel Lindsay incident was certainly good for my poetic career" (213–14). Upon Lindsay's death, Hughes wrote eulogistically: "His work was a living encouragement of the original and the American in the creation of beauty. Thousands feel now a sense of personal loss. We miss him as we miss a friend. A fine poet, and a great heart, has left us for the universe of stars" (quoted in *LLH,* 1:229).

4. Sterling Brown, *Negro Poetry and Drama and The Negro in American Fiction* (1937; New York: Atheneum, 1969), 95; quoted in Joanne V. Gabbin, *Sterling Brown: Building the Black Aesthetic Tradition* (Charlottesville: University of Virginia Press, 1994), 31.

5. Sterling Brown, *The Collected Poems of Sterling A. Brown* (New York: Harper and Row, 1980), 175.

6. Quoted in Gabbin, *Sterling Brown,* 31.

7. Quoted in Mark A. Sanders, *Afro-Modernist Aesthetics and the Poetry of Sterling Brown* (Athens: University of Georgia Press, 1999), 38.

8. James Weldon Johnson, *Writings* (New York: Library of America, 2004), 306.

9. Lorenzo Thomas, "Neon Griot: The Functional Role of Poetry Readings in the Black Arts Movement," in Bernstein, *Close Listening,* 303.

10. Max Bennett Thrasher, *New York Evening Post,* May 12, 1900.

11. Henry H. Mitchell, *Black Preaching* (Philadelphia: Lippincott, 1970), 17, 14, 18, 15–16. Martin Luther King, Jr., stated that a "sermon is not an essay to be read but a discourse to be heard. It should be a convincing appeal to a listening congregation. Therefore, a sermon is directed toward the listening ear rather than the reading eye" (*Strength to Love* [1963; Philadelphia: Fortress Press, 1981], 11–12).

12. William H. Pipes, *Say Amen, Brother! Old-Time Negro Preaching: A Study in American Frustration* (Westport, CT: Negro Universities Press, 1970), 4, 23.

13. Pipes, *Say Amen,* 43, 44.

14. Charles V. Hamilton, *The Black Preacher in America* (New York: William Morrow, 1972), 29; Charles Fager, *Uncertain Resurrection* (Grand Rapids, MI: William B. Erdmans, 1969), 102–3.

15. Pipes, *Say Amen,* 162, 164.

16. Pipes, *Say Amen*, 14.

17. Edward C. L. Adams, *Congaree Sketches*, ed. Robert G. O'Meally (1927; Chapel Hill: University of North Carolina Press, 1987), 45, 46.

18. As Robert G. O'Meally reports, "Adams's home was well known as a place where whites could enjoy such ritualized 'Negro entertainment'—not by professionals but by local blacks who knew how to put on an unprettified Congaree show. Adams must have gathered much of his material from just such parties. In the plantation tradition, too, he hosted all-black affairs (except for Adams himself) to celebrate holidays or special events like the end of harvest. At these more private sessions, 'Dr. Ned' (as blacks called him) stood within the circle of tale-tellers around the big fireplace in his country lodge and heard certain tales, songs, and pieces the blacks thought too risque or otherwise inappropriate for the white general public. These would have certainly been unavailable to most whites in his time" (Edward C. L. Adams, *Tales of the Congaree*, ed. Robert G. O'Meally [1928; Chapel Hill: University of North Carolina Press, 1987], xiii, xvi).

19. Adams, *Tales of the Congaree*, xxx, xvi.

20. Carla Kaplan, ed., *Zora Neale Hurston: A Life in Letters* (New York: Doubleday, 2002), 302.

21. Hurston, *The Sanctified Church* (New York: Marlowe, 1981), 98, 100.

22. Hurston, *Mules and Men* (1935; New York: Harper, 1990), 249.

23. Kaplan, *Zora Neale Hurston*, 302–3, 304.

24. Johnson, *Along This Way*, 335–36, 377–78. In *The Autobiography of an Ex-Coloured Man* (1912; New York: Hill and Wang, 1960), Johnson depicts the popular black preacher John Brown in performance at a southern "big meeting" (similar to a camp-meeting) along similar lines: Brown "possessed magnetism" and "knew all the arts and tricks of oratory, the modulation of the voice to almost a whisper, the pause for effect, the rise through light, rapid-fire sentences to the terrific, thundering outburst of an electrifying climax. . . . He convinced me that, after all, eloquence consists more in that manner of saying than in what is said. It is largely a matter of tone pictures" (173, 175–76).

25. James Weldon Johnson, "The Poor White Musician" (1915), in *The Selected Writings of James Weldon Johnson*, ed. Sondra Kathryn Wilson (New York: Oxford University Press, 1995), 1:284. See Katherine Biers, "Syncope Fever: James Weldon Johnson and the Black Phonographic Voice," *Representations* 96 (Autumn 2006): 99–125.

26. See Eric J. Sundquist, *The Hammers of Creation: Folk Culture in Modern African-American Fiction* (Athens: University of Georgia Press, 1992).

27. Jean Wagner, *Black Poets of the United States: From Paul Laurence Dunbar to Langston Hughes*, trans. Kenneth Douglas (Urbana: University of Illinois Press, 1973), 378, 383, 384. The study was published originally in French in 1963.

28. Joseph Moncure March, "Is Negro Exhorting High Art, Too?" *New York Evening Post*, August 6, 1927, 3:9.

29. Joseph Auslander, "Sermon Sagas," *Opportunity* 5 (1927): 274.

30. Brown, *Negro Poetry and Drama*, 68.

31. Brown, *Negro Poetry and Drama*, 95.

32. Johnson, *Selected Writings*, 2:409, 412.

33. Joan Shelley Rubin, *Songs of Ourselves: The Uses of Poetry in America* (Cambridge: Harvard University Press, 2007), 217, 219–20.

34. Johnson, *Along This Way*, 336.

35. Johnson, *Along This Way*, 377.

36. Carl Van Vechten, *Keep A-Inchin' Along: Selected Writings of Carl Van Vechten about Black Art and Letters*, ed. Bruce Kellner (Westwood, CT: Greenwood, 1979), 117. Johnson's recording of "The Creation" is commercially available on the CD *Our Souls Have Grown Deep Like the Rivers: Black Poets Read Their Work* (Rhino, 2000).

37. *Collected Works of Langston Hughes*, 7:356. In "Sunday Morning Prophecy" Hughes probably had the evangelist George Becton in mind. In *The Big Sea*, he says that "Dr. Becton was a charlatan if there ever was one, but he filled the huge church—because he gave a good show" (275).

38. Hughes was hailed in California upon being introduced to an audience as "The first Negro poet in America to span the continent, coast to coast, with his poetry!" (*I Wonder as I Wander: An Autobiographical Journey* [1956; New York: Thunder's Mouth Press, 1986]), 63. Hughes remarks: "I found no colored colleges in California, but Negro churches and clubs gave me audiences" (*I Wonder*, 63). Like Lindsay, Hughes complained about the exhaustion that touring caused; as Rampersad reports, " 'This tour m'en fiche!' he groaned to Prentiss Taylor in New York" in March 1932 (*LLH*, 1:234).

39. Hughes, *I Wonder*, 41.

40. Hughes, *I Wonder*, 48, 54; Hughes, *Big Sea*, 212. In 1923, Hughes made some money reading at the local "colored" YMCA, and he had his first "white" reading in 1925, just before his encounter with Lindsay (*LLH*, 1:81, 115).

41. Hughes, *I Wonder*, 56–57.

42. Hughes, *I Wonder*, 57, 59.

43. Quoted in Thomas, "Neon Griot," 303.

44. *Remember Me to Harlem: The Letters of Langston Hughes and Carl Van Vechten, 1925–1964*, ed. Emily Bernard (New York: Knopf, 2001), 95. Hughes persuaded Knopf to issue a special one-dollar edition of *The Weary Blues* for him to sell on tour along with *Negro Mother* (*Remember Me to Harlem*, 91). In *I Wonder* Hughes reflects, "Few white people bought our book [*Negro Mother*], but to Negroes I sold three large printings" (47–48).

45. Langston Hughes, *The Negro Mother and Other Dramatic Recitations* (1931; Salem, NH: Ayer, 1971), 6.

46. Hughes, *Negro Mother*, 18.

47. Hughes, *Negro Mother*, 11.

48. Hughes, *I Wonder*, 47–48.

49. Langston Hughes, *Shakespeare in Harlem* (New York: Knopf, 1942), n.p.

50. Edward J. Mullen, ed., *Critical Essays on Langston Hughes* (Boston: G. K. Hall, 1986), 69.

51. Hughes, *Shakespeare in Harlem*, 125.

52. *Langston Hughes: The Contemporary Reviews,* ed. Tish Dace (New York: Cambridge University Press, 1997), 281.

53. Dace, *Langston Hughes,* 280.

54. Mullen, *Critical Essays,* 71, 72.

55. Quoted in Meta DuEwa Jones, "Listening to What the Ear Demands: Langston Hughes and His Critics," *Callaloo* 25.4 (2002): 1151.

56. Mullen, *Critical Essays,* 88. Rampersad states that "For each section [of the poem], consciously taking his lead from Vachel Lindsay's *The Congo: A Study of the Negro Race,* he [Hughes] carefully fashioned musical cues integral to his poetic meaning" (*LLH* 2:317).

57. Dace, *Langston Hughes,* 640, 645.

58. Hughes included blues and instrumental jazz on his reading programs as early as 1926 and wanted to be credited as the "original jazz poet" in a blurb on his *Selected Poems* (*LLH* 2:280).

59. Liner notes to *Weary Blues* (Polygram Records, 1991).

60. Nat Hentoff, "Langston Hughes: He Found Poetry in the Blues," *Mayfair,* August 1958, 27, 43.

61. Jones, "Listening to What the Ear Demands," 1156.

62. Liner notes to *The Poetry of Sterling Brown* (Folkways, 1995). The *Poetry of Sterling Brown* represents a selection from three previous Folkways albums: *Langston Hughes and Sterling Brown Read from Their Work* (1952) (recorded in 1946); *An Anthology of Negro Poets* (1966); and *Sixteen Poems of Sterling Brown* (1973).

63. Hughes and Van Vechten, *Remember Me to Harlem,* 97.

64. Hughes, *A New Song* (New York: International Workers Order, 1938), n.p.

65. Hughes, *A New Song,* 24.

66. Hughes, *Big Sea,* 56.

67. Hughes, *Big Sea,* 58.

68. Karen Ford, "Making Poetry Pay: The Commodification of Langston Hughes," in *Marketing Modernisms: Self-Promotion, Canonization, Rereading,* ed. Kevin J. H. Dettmar and Stephen Watts (Ann Arbor: University of Michigan Press, 1996), 278, 282, 321, 279. James Smethurst believes that both Hughes's 1950s "political quietude" and the degree to which he withdrew in the 1950s from the Left and its organizations have been "overstated." He contends that the structure of *The Panther and the Lash* "created a dialogue between the left of the 1930s and 1940s with the new radicalism of the 1960s," thus pointing up the historical continuum of black political struggle ("'Don't Say Goodbye to the Porkpie Hat': Langston Hughes, the Left, and the Black Arts Movement," *Callaloo* 25.4 [2002]: 1226, 1232).

69. Ford, "Making Poetry Pay," 281–89. Contemporary reviews of the book insisted on Hughes as a "militant," claiming his poems as "of our times" on account of their "aggressiveness" (Mullen, *Critical Essays,* 89, 90).

70. Ford, "Making Poetry Pay," 284.

71. Langston Hughes, *The Panther and the Lash: Poems of Our Times* (1967; New York: Knopf 1989), 104.

72. Langston Hughes, *The Langston Hughes Reader* (New York: George Braziller, 1958), 147–48.

73. Hughes, *A New Song,* n.p.

74. Hughes, *A New Song,* 7, 8.

75. Robert Shulman, *The Power of Political Art: The 1930s Literary Left Reconsidered* (Chapel Hill: University of North Carolina Press, 2000).

76. See Langston Hughes, "My Adventures as a Social Poet," *Phylon* 8.3 (1947): 205–12.

77. *Arna Bontemps–Langston Hughes Letters, 1925–1967,* ed. Charles Nichols (New York: Dodd, Mead, 1980), 405.

Chapter 4

Lawrence Ferlinghetti, "Note on Poetry in San Francisco," *Chicago Review* 12.1 (1958): 4.

Anne Waldman, *Fast Speaking Woman* (San Francisco: City Lights, 1975). Hereafter cited parenthetically in the text as *FSW*.

1. Allen Ginsberg, *Journals: Early Fifties, Early Sixties,* ed. Gordon Ball (New York: Grove, 1977), 91.

2. Allen Ginsberg, *Deliberate Prose: Selected Essays, 1952–1995,* ed. Bill Morgan (New York: HarperCollins, 2000), 287.

3. Gary Snyder, *The Real Work: Interviews and Talks, 1964–1979,* ed. William Scott McLean (New York: New Directions, 1980), 75.

4. Allen Ginsberg, *Cosmopolitan Greetings: Poems 1986–1992* (New York: Harper-Collins, 1994), xiv.

5. Bill Morgan, *I Celebrate Myself: The Somewhat Private Life of Allen Ginsberg* (New York: Viking, 2006), 272.

6. Ginsberg's remarks about Lindsay are transcribed from his July 23, 1976, lecture on "aboriginal poetics" at Naropa Institute (now University), which is available at http://www.archive.org/details/naropa_allen_ginsberg_class_on (accessed January 10, 2011).

7. Jack Spicer, *The House that Jack Built: Collected Lectures of Jack Spicer,* ed. Peter Gizzi (Hanover, NH: Wesleyan University Press, 1998), 229–30.

8. Lawrence Ferlinghetti, *The Populist Manifestos* (San Francisco: Grey Fox Press, 1976), 21–24.

9. Lawrence Ferlinghetti, *Wild Dreams of a New Beginning* (New York: New Directions, 1988), 63–64. For publication history, see *Wild Dreams,* 125–26. The poem also was published in *Rolling Stone.*

10. Quoted in Barry Silesky, *Ferlinghetti: The Artist in His Time* (New York: Warner, 1990), 262.

11. Gary Snyder, *The Real Work,* 165.

12. Ferlinghetti, "Note on Poetry in San Francisco," 4. The poet Diane Wakoski has stated that "It's that idealistic, post World War II interest in—whatever you want to call it—socialism, Marxism, some kind of communal democratic politics . . . that

made Ferlinghetti decide that he wanted these pocket books with the, to me, hilariously idealistic idea that they were small enough that a workman, a factory worker, could stick them in his pockets so he could be reading them in between work on the line at Boeing or wherever. . . . We're right back to Whitman. Whitman thinks he's doing it even if he's not doing it. Factory workers are in fact going to hate the Beats more than they would hate something that's more elitist. And Ferlinghetti is right there in the center of it" (quoted in Silesky, *Ferlinghetti*, 263).

13. Snyder, *The Real Work*, 5.

14. *Howls, Raps, and Roars: Recordings from the San Francisco Poetry Renaissance* (Berkeley, CA: Fantasy, 1993), 29.

15. Michael McClure, *Scratching the Beat Surface* (San Francisco: North Point Press, 1982), 29.

16. Kenneth Rexroth, *American Poetry in the Twentieth Century* (New York: Herder and Herder, 1971), 141.

17. Ginsberg, *Deliberate Prose*, 240, 241. Kerouac's fictionalized description of the event in his 1958 novel *The Dharma Bums* locates the reading at the Six Gallery as "the night of the birth of the San Francisco Poetry Renaissance": "I was the one who got things jumping by going around collecting dimes and quarters from the rather stiff audience standing around in the gallery and coming back with three huge gallon jugs of California Burgundy and getting them all piffed so that by eleven o'clock when Alvah Goldbook [Allen Ginsberg] was reading his, wailing his poem 'Wail' drunk with arms outspread everybody was yelling 'Go! Go! Go!' (like a jam session) and old Rheinhold Cacoethes [Kenneth Rexroth] the father of the Frisco poetry scene was wiping his tears in gladness" (*The Dharma Bums* [New York: Penguin, 1986], 13–14).

18. Lewis Hyde, ed., *On the Poetry of Allen Ginsberg* (Ann Arbor: University of Michigan Press, 1984), 24.

19. Ferlinghetti, *Populist Manifestos*, 31.

20. McClure, *Scratching the Beat Surface*, 12–13, 15.

21. Hyde, *Poetry of Allen Ginsberg*, 314–15, 314, 316.

22. Lawrence Lipton, *The Holy Barbarians* (New York: Julian Messner, 1959), 196.

23. Joyce Johnson, *Minor Characters: A Young Woman's Coming of Age in the Beat Orbit of Jack Kerouac* (New York: Penguin, 1999), 116.

24. Jason Shinder, ed., *The Poem That Changed America: "Howl" Fifty Years Later* (New York: Farrar, 2006), 231.

25. Allen Ginsberg, *Holy Soul Jelly Roll: Poems and Songs 1949–1993* (Los Angeles: Rhino, 1994), 13. Ginsberg explains that the quality of his vocal delivery of poetry shifted over time: "There's an audible difference in my intonation & poetic style between the 1949 Holmes session and 1954 at Neal's house. . . . The voice changes from the singsong crooning style of academic poetry to a more lively style of conversation, but still has an overlay of weltschmerz and literary slow-down, not as quick as regular speech. I'm head-trip musing to myself in only two or three tones, not yet with full range of vernacular pitch, actual talk, developed by the late '50s or early '60s." He goes on: "John Clellon Holmes had an apartment in central Manhattan,

mid-block 56th Street three flights up, facing Lexington Avenue. Kerouac and I and Neal Cassady and many others used to visit him, intelligent & hospitable. He had a little tape machine, wire or paper tape perhaps, and made a few recordings of Kerouac and myself during parties or after" (9–10).

26. Ginsberg, *Holy Soul Jelly Roll*, 7.

27. *Howls, Raps, and Roars*, 13.

28. Hyde, *Poetry of Allen Ginsberg*, 374.

29. In *The Jew's Body* (New York: Routledge, 1991) Sander Gilman has documented the feminizing rhetoric of anti-Semitic discourse in western Europe around the turn of the twentieth century. As Ann Pellegrini notes, "the feminization of the Jewish male body was so frequent a theme in this period that Jewishness—more precisely the Jewishness of Jewish men—became as much a category of gender as of race" ("Whiteface Performances: 'Race,' Gender, and Jewish Bodies," in *Jews and Other Differences: The New Jewish Cultural Studies*, ed. Daniel Boyarin and Joshua Boyarin [Minneapolis: University of Minnesota Press, 1997], 108). In *Tough Jews: Political Fantasies and the American Dilemma of American Jewry* (New York: Basic Books, 1990), his study of images of Jews in American culture since the 1967 Arab-Israeli War, Paul Breines explicitly links representations of Jews killed in the Holocaust with a long history of associations between the weak, defective, feminized body and the Jew.

30. Leland S. Meyerzove, "Allen Ginsberg: Poet of Hebraic Mysticism," *Burning Bush* 2 (September 1964): 49.

31. *Harper's*, October 1966, 134–35. Ginsberg explains that the Brandeis audience was "sympathetic and encouraging," that he had "drunk a little wine," and "so for self-dramatic historic reasons I decided to open up my soul and read *Kaddish* complete" (*Deliberate Prose*, 235–36).

32. Luc Sante, "The Ballot of Eternity," in Shinder, *Poem That Changed America*, 221; Paul Blackburn, "Writing for the Ear," *Big Table* 1.4 (1960): 128–29; *Evergreen Review* 1.2: 139, 140.

33. Mikhail Bakhtin, *Rabelais and His World*, trans. Hélène Iswolsky (Bloomington: Indiana University Press, 1984), 10, 8, 67, 49, 9.

34. Marjorie Perloff, *Poetic License: Essays on Modernist and Postmodernist Lyric* (Evanston, IL: Northwestern University Press, 1990), 210.

35. Bakhtin, *Rabelais and His World*, 12.

36. Hyde, *Poetry of Allen Ginsberg*, 367–69.

37. Robert Polito, "Holy the Fifth International," in Shinder, *Poem That Changed America*, 226.

38. David Bergman, *Gaiety Transfigured: Gay Self-Representation in American Literature* (Madison: University of Wisconsin Press, 1991), 111, 113. Bergman also observes that "Allen Ginsberg is not usually associated with camp, yet *Howl* is a supremely campy poem, and as time has gone on, Ginsberg has recited it with greater and greater emphasis on its comically carnivalesque tone" (120).

39. Hyde, *Poetry of Allen Ginsberg*, 361–62.

40. Foley, *O Powerful Western Star*, 150. In his interview with Foley, Ginsberg states that everyone enjoys a "multiple identity": "The notion of a single, fixed identity goes along with monotheism and the notion of a fixed selfhood which goes to

heaven and is preserved for ever (along with the body nowadays). . . . It's just a limiting thing to say you've only got one identity when you've got fifty. And your ultimate identity is totally open space."

41. Ginsberg, *Holy Soul Jelly Roll*, 12, 13.

42. Hyde, *Poetry of Allen Ginsberg*, 384.

43. Anne Waldman, "Premises of Consciousness," in Shinder, *Poem That Changed America*, 269. As Waldman notes, censorship of Ginsberg's mediatized "Howl" remains in force on the radio by FCC decree: "Even as he [Ginsberg] died, readings or recordings of 'Howl' could not—and still can't—be broadcast on daytime radio in the United States of America. The struggle continues on many fronts."

44. Ginsberg, *Deliberate Prose*, 231.

45. Ginsberg, *Deliberate Prose*, 236. First published as liner notes to *Allen Ginsberg Reads Kaddish* (Atlantic, 1966).

46. Quoted in Bill Morgan and Nancy J. Peters, *Howl on Trial: The Battle for Free Expression* (San Francisco: City Lights, 2006), 47.

47. Norman Mailer, "The White Negro," in *Advertisements for Myself* (1959; Cambridge: Harvard University Press, 1992), 375.

48. Allen Ginsberg, *Allen Verbatim: Lectures on Poetry, Politics, Consciousness*, ed. Gordon Ball (New York: McGraw-Hill, 1975), 161.

49. Quoted in Paul Portugés, *The Visionary Poetics of Allen Ginsberg* (Santa Barbara: Ross-Erikson, 1978), 80.

50. Ginsberg, *Deliberate Prose*, 277.

51. Ginsberg, *Holy Soul Jelly Roll*, 26. Ginsberg wrote Part III of "Wichita Vortex Sutra" while driving south across Kansas, February 4, 1966 (*Holy Soul Jelly Roll*, 56).

52. Allen Ginsberg, *Composed on the Tongue*, ed. Donald Allen (Bolinas, CA: Grey Fox Press, 1980). Bob Dylan gave Ginsberg the money to buy the tape recorder.

53. Ginsberg, *Deliberate Prose*, 259–60.

54. Quoted in Hyde, *Poetry of Allen Ginsberg*, 294. Ginsberg says that he "realized . . . that it was possible in a poem to reproduce some body rhythm which if inserted in other peoples' [*sic*] bodies might catalyze a similar experience, 'cause that's what happened to me" (*Talking Poetics from Naropa Institute*, ed. Anne Waldman and Marilyn Webb, 2 vols. [Boulder, CO: Shambhala, 1979], 382).

55. Liner notes to the CD *Wichita Vortex Sutra* (Artemis Records, 2004); Michael Davidson, *Ghostlier Demarcations: Modern Poetry and the Material Word* (Berkeley: University of California Press, 1997), 204.

56. *Wichita Vortex Sutra* liner notes; Cary Nelson, *Our Last First Poets: Vision and the History in Contemporary American Poetry* (Urbana: University of Illinois Press, 1982), 15; Hyde, *Poetry of Allen Ginsberg*, 312.

57. Ginsberg, *Cosmopolitan Greetings*, 89.

58. Ginsberg, *Holy Soul Jelly Roll*, 32.

59. Ginsberg, *Holy Soul Jelly Roll*, 32.

60. A description of the reading project and instructions on how to help create the performance are online at http://archives.obs-us.com/obs/english/books/ginsberg/atp.htm (accessed January 10, 2011).

61. Gloria G. Brame, "An Interview with Poet Allen Ginsberg," 1996, http://www.gloria-brame.com/glory/ginsberg.htm (accessed January 10, 2011).

62. Waldman and Webb, *Talking Poetics* 2:384, 388; Ginsberg, *Allen Verbatim*, 21; Waldman and Webb, *Talking Poetics*, 2:383.

63. Jack Kerouac, "The Origins of Joy in Poetry," *Chicago Review* 12:1 (1958): 3.

64. These remarks are transcribed from Allen Ginsberg and Anne Waldman's audiocassette *Beauty and the Beast*, Naropa Recordings, Boulder, CO, August 9, 1975.

65. Waldman and Webb, *Talking Poetics*, 2:279.

66. Interview of Anne Waldman, with Jim Cohn, "Illuminati in the Void," October 17, 1994, http://www.poetspath.com/waldmanimages/illuminati.html (accessed January 10, 2011).

67. Waldman and Webb, *Talking Poetics*, 2:315.

68. Transcribed from Ginsberg and Waldman, *Beauty and the Beast*.

69. Interview of Anne Waldman, *Whole Earth Review*, Winter 1988.

70. Waldman, *Vow to Poetry: Essays, Interviews and Manifestos* (Minneapolis: Coffee House Press, 2001), 269, 331.

71. Roland Barthes, *The Pleasure of the Text*, trans. Richard Miller (New York: Hill and Wang, 1975), 66.

72. Interview of Anne Waldman, *Whole Earth Review*, Winter 1988.

73. Lipton, *Holy Barbarians*, 216, 222.

74. Quoted in Larry Smith, *Lawrence Ferlinghetti: Poet-at-Large* (Carbondale: Southern Illinois University Press, 1983), 28–29.

75. Kenneth Rexroth, "Jazz Poetry," in *World Outside the Window: The Selected Essays of Kenneth Rexroth*, ed. Bradford Morrow (New York: New Directions, 1987), 68. A version of this article appeared on the back cover of the LP *Kenneth Rexroth: Poetry and Jazz at the Blackhawk* (Fantasy, 1960).

76. This is from the text on the back cover of *Poetry and Jazz at the Blackhawk*.

77. This statement appears in the notes to the 1958 Fantasy LP recording *Poetry Readings in the Cellar* that was the result of a series of jazz and poetry readings Rexroth and Ferlinghetti had done in North Beach in San Francisco at a club called The Cellar with the Cellar Jazz Quintet.

78. Lawrence Ferlinghetti, *A Coney Island of the Mind* (New York: New Directions, 1958), 48.

79. Quoted in Neeli Cherkovski, *Ferlinghetti: A Biography* (Garden City, NY: Doubleday, 1979), 88.

80. *Howls, Raps, and Roars*, 17.

81. Liner notes to *Poetry Readings in the Cellar*. These notes are reprinted on the cover of the CD reissue by Fantasy Records in 2004.

82. Quoted in Smith, *Lawrence Ferlinghetti*, 29.

83. Smith, *Lawrence Ferlinghetti*, 56.

84. Greg Beets, rev. of Lawrence Ferlinghetti's *A Coney Island of the Mind* (Rykodisc), December 31, 1999, http://www.austinchronicle.com/music/1999-12-31/75326/ (accessed January 10, 2011).

85. Smith, *Lawrence Ferlinghetti*, 84, 209.

86. Alan Dugan, "Three Books, a Pamphlet and a Broadside," rev. of Lawrence Ferlinghetti's *Starting from San Francisco, Poetry* vol. C, no. 5 (August 1962): 314, 315; Smith, *Lawrence Ferlinghetti*, 79.

87. James Schevill, "The Pulsing Voices of the New Poets," *San Francisco Sunday Chronicle* (March 25, 1962): 30.

88. Lawrence Ferlinghetti, *Starting from San Francisco* (Norfolk, CT: New Directions: 1961), 66; Smith, *Lawrence Ferlinghetti*, 138.

89. Blackburn, "Writing for the Ear," 130.

90. Ferlinghetti, *Starting from San Francisco*, 36.

91. Lawrence Ferlinghetti, *Americus: Book I* (New York: New Directions, 2004), 11.

92. Quoted in Foley, *O Powerful Western Star*, 70.

Chapter 5

Sonia Sanchez, *We a BaddDDD People* (Detroit: Broadside, 1970), 55.

Sanford Pinsker, "A Conversation with Etheridge Knight," *Black American Literature Forum* 18.1 (1984): 12.

1. Larry Neal, "The Black Arts Movement," in *Visions of a Liberated Future: Black Arts Movement Writings, with Commentary by Amiri Baraka et al.*, ed. Michael Schwartz (New York: Thunder's Mouth Press, 1989), 62; LeRoi Jones and Larry Neal, *Black Fire: An Anthology of Afro-American Writing* (New York: William Morrow, 1968), 655.

2. Don L. Lee, *Directionscore: Selected and New Poems* (Detroit: Broadside Press, 1971), 67; Ken McCullough, "Communication and Excommunication: An Interview with Etheridge Knight," *Callaloo* 14–15 (February–May 1982): 4.

3. *Conversations with Nikki Giovanni*, ed. Virginia C. Fowler (Jackson: University Press of Mississippi, 1992), 45.

4. Jones and Neal, *Black Fire*, 653.

5. Stephen Vincent and Ellen Zweig, eds., *The Poetry Reading: A Contemporary Compendium on Language and Performance* (San Francisco: Momo's Press, 1981), 75.

6. Quoted in Mark Anthony Neal, "Critical Noir: The Full Moon of Sonia," February 23, 2005, http://newblackman.blogspot.com/2009_10_01_archive.html (accessed January 10, 2011); Sonia Sanchez, *I've Been a Woman: New and Selected Poems* (Sausalito, CA: Black Scholar Press, 1978), 92.

7. *Conversations with Amiri Baraka*, ed. Charlie Reilly (Jackson: University Press of Mississippi, 1994), 209.

8. Don L. Lee, *Dynamite Voices I: Black Poets of the 1960's* (Chicago: Broadside, 1971), 30; D. H. Melhem, *Heroism in the New Black Poetry: Introductions and Interviews* (Lexington: University Press of Kentucky, 1990), 208.

9. Neal, "The Black Arts Movement," 78; Charles Rowell, "An Interview with Etheridge Knight," *Callaloo* 19.4 (1996): 979. Knight asserts that: "If he is honest, a

black artist can't help directing his art to a black audience" ("An Interview with Etheridge Knight," 972).

10. *Conversations with Nikki Giovanni,* 48.

11. *Conversations with Amiri Baraka,* 154. Ginsberg introduced Baraka to Whitman, but Baraka says that Whitman "didn't really inspire me that much" (*Conversations with Amiri Baraka,* 173).

12. *Conversations with Amiri Baraka,* 169, 209.

13. Steven C. Tracy and Etheridge Knight, "A MELUS Interview: Etheridge Knight," *MELUS* 12.2 (1985): 19.

14. Quoted in Thomas, "Neon Griot," 307; Kaye McDonough, "Bob Kaufman Reading at Vesuvio's, 1973," *Umbra 5: Latin/Soul Anthology* (1974): 78.

15. Jim Perlman, Ed Folsom, and Dan Campion, eds., *Walt Whitman: The Measure of His Song* (Minneapolis: Holy Cow! Press, 1981), 345, 346.

16. McCullough, "Communication and Excommunication," 4.

17. Jones and Neal, *Black Fire,* xvi.

18. Lee, *Dynamite Voices,* 26.

19. Lee, *Dynamite Voices,* 27, 28–29.

20. Lee, *Dynamite Voices,* 144; Amiri Baraka and Amina Baraka, *The Music: Reflections on Jazz and Blues* (New York: William Morrow, 1987), 330, 331, 332.

21. Giovanni states: "Broadside didn't publish me. They distributed my books. I published myself. *Black Feeling / Black Talk* and *Black Judgement* were published by me" (*Conversations with Nikki Giovanni,* 59); Marshall McLuhan and Quentin Fiore, *The Medium Is the Massage: An Inventory of Effects* (New York: Random House, 1967), 123.

22. Interview of Sonia Sanchez by Lock Haven University of Pennsylvania, January 18, 2006, http://www.lhup.edu/pr/releases/012006%20Sanchez%20answers.htm (accessed January 10, 2011).

23. Neal, *Visions of a Liberated Future,* 78.

24. Stephen Henderson, *Understanding the New Black Poetry: Black Speech and Black Music as Poetic References* (New York: William Morrow, 1973), 30.

25. Lee, *Dynamite Voices,* 74.

26. Houston A. Baker, Jr., and Patricia Redmond, eds., *Afro-American Literary Study in the 1990s* (Chicago: University of Chicago Press, 1989), 38–39.

27. Charles Olson, *Collected Prose,* ed. Donald Allen and Benjamin Friedlander (Berkeley: University of California Press, 1997), 246.

28. Patricia L. Hill, *San Francisco Review of Books,* 3.9 (1978): 10.

29. Etheridge Knight, *Poems from Prison* (Detroit: Broadside Press, 1968), 17.

30. *Conversations with Nikki Giovanni,* 183.

31. Alvin Aubert, "Book Reviews," *Black Academy Review* (Winter 1970): 65; Houston A. Baker, Jr., on the back cover of Sanchez's book *Under a Soprano Sky* (Trenton, NJ: Africa World Press, 1987); Lee, *Dynamite Voices,* 50; Liz Gant, rev. of *We Walk the Way of the World* and *We a BaddDDD People, Black World,* April 1971, 86. On the back cover of *Under a Soprano Sky* Houston Baker also remarks, "It is impossible to hear this [Sanchez's] sound and not recognize its authenticity."

32. Carolyn M. Rodgers, "Uh Nat'chal Thang—The WHOLE TRUTH—US," *Black World*, September 1971, 5.

33. Quoted in Melba Joyce Boyd, *Wrestling with the Muse: Dudley Randall and the Broadside Press* (New York: Columbia University Press, 2003), 236.

34. Don L. Lee, *Black Pride* (Detroit: Broadside Press, 1968), 8.

35. Boyd, *Wrestling with the Muse*, 173; Don L. Lee, *Think Black*, rev. ed. (Detroit: Broadside Press, 1969), 16; Don L. Lee, *Don't Cry, Scream* (Detroit: Broadside Press, 1969), 16, 15.

36. Lee, *Don't Cry, Scream*, 32–34.

37. Julius E. Thompson, *Dudley Randall, Broadside Press, and the Black Arts Movement in Detroit, 1960–1995* (Jefferson, NC: McFarland, 1999), 170.

38. Thompson, *Dudley Randall*, 99.

39. Lee, *Don't Cry, Scream*, 16, 17.

40. Boyd, *Wrestling with the Muse*, 174–75. In a 1973 interview Randall said that he thought he would try the new format since "phonograph records are more popular with the public than cassettes or reel recorders" (quoted in Thompson, *Dudley Randall*, 104).

41. Interview with Dudley Randall, *Black World*, December 1971, 31.

42. Quoted in Thompson, *Dudley Randall*, 99.

43. Thompson, *Dudley Randall*, 178.

44. Randall, *Broadside Memories: Poets I Have Known* (Detroit: Broadside Press, 1975), 13; Boyd, *Wrestling with the Muse*, 233.

45. Rowell, "Interview with Etheridge Knight," 974.

46. Tracy, "A MELUS Interview," 9, 10. Knight notes in this interview that "my primary audience is first to Black males" (13).

47. Virginia C. Fowler, *Nikki Giovanni* (New York: Twayne, 1992), 15. Fowler reports that "The album was a phenomenal success, staying for weeks on the hit charts and receiving the National Association of Television and Radio Announcers (NATRA) award for the Best Spoken Word Album" (15).

48. *Conversations with Nikki Giovanni*, 35, 40, 41.

49. *Conversations with Nikki Giovanni*, 41, 35.

50. Fowler, *Nikki Giovanni*, 156.

51. *Conversations with Nikki Giovanni*, 41, 35; Fowler, *Nikki Giovanni*, 156; *Conversations with Nikki Giovanni*, 34.

52. Fowler, *Nikki Giovanni*, 15–16, 148, 149. *Truth Is on Its Way* was criticized for its commercialism, and Giovanni herself was criticized for being "a kind of nationalistic Rod McKuen": she "exploited her appeal" and "employed publicity agents and top photographers who took good advantage of her photogenic qualities" (quoted in Evans, *Black Women Writers*, 213–14, 218). Giovanni responded to the disparagement by Baraka (then LeRoi Jones), saying, "LeRoi, you know, bitched about *Truth Is On Its Way,* and I said to somebody, . . . I don't know what he's upset about. I'm only doing what he did. . . . He recorded an album, and it's not my fault nobody bought it" (quoted in Fowler, *Nikki Giovanni*, 148).

53. Kalamu ya Salaam, rev. of Sanchez's *My House* and *Like a Ripple on a Pond, Black World*, July 1974, 70.

54. Thomas Lask, "Soul Festival: A Cool Nikki Giovanni Reads Poetry," *New York Times*, July 26, 1972: 21. Lask further finds that Giovanni "controlled the reading with her presence and her reading gave the evening its character of informality and joyousness. . . . It may not have been a poetry reading in the conventional sense, but it was a great night."

55. *Conversations with Nikki Giovanni*, 105, 104; quoted in Fowler, *Nikki Giovanni*, 60.

56. *Conversations with Nikki Giovanni*, 119.

57. Melhem, *Heroism*, 153–54, 154; quoted in Fowler, *Nikki Giovanni*, 150.

58. Sonia Sanchez, *A Sun Woman for All Seasons Reads Her Poetry* (Folkways, 1971), n.p.

59. Dudley Randall alleges that the prosodic device of the slash is not as "black" as some Black Arts poets think, descending as it does from E. E. Cummings and white corporate-speak: "they [young black poets] would be quite shocked if you told them that they were, in fact, imitating a white poet. When poets use the slash (/), for example, they may think it's new and revolutionary, but, in actuality, this method is taken from white business reports that read, 'He/she must do this' or, 'This sum should be paid to him/her.' Young Black poets adopted this method thinking that it was a 'Black thang' when, in reality, it was a 'white thang'" (*Black World*, December 1971, 30).

60. Sanchez, *Sun Woman*, n.p.

61. Sanchez, *Sun Woman*, 8.

62. Randall, *Broadside Memories*, 18.

63. Bernstein, *Close Listening*, 309.

64. Melhem, *Heroism*, 158, 154.

65. Larry Neal, *Black Boogaloo (Notes on Black Liberation)* (San Francisco: Journal of Black Poetry Press, 1969), 43.

66. Sonia Sanchez, *Under a Soprano Sky*, 51.

67. Etheridge Knight, *Poems from Prison* (Detroit: Broadside Press, 1968).

68. Larry Neal, *Hoodoo Hollerin' Bebop Ghosts* (Washington, DC: Howard University Press, 1974), 37, 56.

69. Houston A. Baker, Jr., "Critical Memory and the Black Public Sphere," in *The Black Public Sphere: A Public Culture Book,* ed. Black Public Sphere Collective (Chicago: University of Chicago Press, 1995), 17, 21.

70. Lee, *Directionscore*, 77.

71. Don L. Lee, *We Walk the Way of the New World* (Detroit: Broadside, 1970), 20.

72. *Conversations with Amiri Baraka*, 176.

73. Amiri Baraka, *Black Magic: Collected Poetry, 1961–1967* (Indianapolis: Bobbs-Merrill, 1969).

74. Neal, *Black Boogaloo*, i.

75. Neal, *Black Boogaloo*, i. Baraka states: "The question to me of a poet writing in silence for people who will read in silence and put it in a library where the whole thing is conceived in silence and lost forever is about over. And I think it didn't really influence many people. I mean if you conceive of how many people are in the

world and how many people ever learned how to read" (*Conversations with Amiri Baraka*, 177).

76. Amiri Baraka, *Transbluecency: The Selected Poems of Amiri Baraka/LeRoi Jones (1961–1995)*, ed. Paul Vangelisti (New York: Marsilio, 1995), 175.

77. Amiri Baraka, "The Wailer," *Callaloo* 8.1 (Winter 1985): 249; Baraka, *Transbluecency*, 188.

78. Werner Sollors, *Amiri Baraka/LeRoi Jones: The Quest for a "Populist Modernism"* (New York: Columbia University Press, 1978), 204; Kalamu ya Salaam, *Black World*, July 1971, 28.

79. Sollors, *Amiri Baraka/LeRoi Jones*, 202; Imamu Amiri Baraka, ed., *African Congress: A Documentary of the First Modern Pan-African Congress* (New York: William Morrow, 1972), 101.

80. Baraka, *It's Nation Time* (Chicago: Third World Press, 1970), 22.

81. Meta DuEwa Jones, "Politics, Process, and (Jazz) Performance: Amiri Baraka's 'It's Nation Time,'" *African American Review* 37.2/3 (Summer–Fall 2003): 246, 249.

82. Nathaniel Mackey, *Discrepant Engagement: Dissonance, Cross-Culturality, and Experimental Writing* (Cambridge: Cambridge University Press, 1993), 29.

83. LeRoi Jones [Amiri Baraka], *Blues People: Negro Music in White America* (New York: William Morrow, 1963), 172.

84. Kalamu ya Salaam, *Black World*, November 1973, 90, 91.

85. Quoted in Theodore R. Hudson, *From LeRoi Jones to Amiri Baraka: The Literary Works* (Durham: Duke University Press, 1973), 139.

86. Amiri Baraka, "I Will Not 'Apologize,' I Will Not 'Resign'!" October 2, 2002, http://www.amiribaraka.com/speech100202.html (accessed January 10, 2011).

Chapter 6

Miguel Algarín and Bob Holman, eds., *Aloud: Voices from the Nuyorican Poets Cafe* (New York: Holt, 1994), 225. Hereafter cited parenthetically in the text as *Aloud*.

"Holy Kid: An Interview with Edwin Torres," with Bob Holman, http://www.brainlingo.com/html/about/interview1.htm (accessed January 10, 2011).

1. Eleveld, *The Spoken Word Revolution*, 167.

2. Roger Ebert, rev. of *SlamNation*, http://rogerebert.suntimes.com/apps/pbcs.dll/article?AID=/19981023/REVIEWS/810230305/1023 (accessed January 10, 2011).

3. Lisa Martinovic, "SlamMania," December 18, 2008, http://slaminatrix.com/?p=84 (accessed January 10, 2011). An abbreviated version of the essay ran in the *San Francisco Chronicle* on February 24, 2000.

4. Michael Ingrassia, "A Sudden Turn for the Verse," *Newsweek*, April 19, 1993, 61.

5. Quoted in Kurt Heintz, "An Incomplete History of Slam," 1994, http://www.e-poets.net/library/slam/ (accessed January 10, 2011).

6. Bob Holman, "Performance Poetry," in *An Exaltation of Forms: Contemporary Poets Celebrate the Diversity of Their Art*, ed. Annie Finch and Kathrine Varnes (Ann Arbor: University of Michigan Press, 2002), 344.

7. Jessica Care Moore, "Poetic License," *Black Issues Book Review*, March 1, 2002, http://www.thefreelibrary.com/Poetic+license.a083553093 (accessed January 10, 2011).

8. Yusef Komunyakaa, "Foreword: Necromancy," in *Listen Up! Spoken Word Poetry*, ed. Zoë Anglesey (New York: Ballantine, 1999), xi.

9. Tracie Morris, *Intermission* (N.p.: Soft Skull Press, 1998), 50.

10. Quoted in Jeannine Amber, "Poetry Revival—Young African American Poets," *Essence* 25.5 (September 1994): 58.

11. Sonia Sanchez, "Foreword," *Bum Rush the Page: A Def Poetry Jam*, ed. Tony Medina and Louis Reyes Rivera (New York: Three Rivers Press, 2001), xv.

12. *Grand Slam*, n.p.; Gary Glazner, *Poetry Slam: The Competitive Art of Performance Poetry* (San Francisco: Manic D Press, 2000), 11. Hereafter cited parenthetically in the text as *PS*.

13. Heintz, "Convergence" (section of "An Incomplete History of Slam"), http://www.e-poets.net/library/slam/converge.html (accessed January 10, 2011).

14. Heintz, "Convergence."

15. *Grand Slam*, n.p.

16. Michael R. Ball, *Professional Wrestling as Ritual Drama in American Popular Culture* (Lewiston, NY: Edwin Mellen Press, 1990), 33, 75.

17. Heintz, "Convergence."

18. Kenneth J. Bindas, "'The Future is Unwritten': The Clash, Punk, and America, 1977–1982," *American Studies* 34.1 (Spring 1993): 76.

19. "The Man in the Back Row Has a Question VI," *Paris Review* 154 (Spring 2000): 379.

20. Slam organizer Gary Mex Glazner also likens the slam to the world of carnival: http://www.e-poets.net/library/slam/ (accessed January 10, 2011).

21. Bakhtin, *Rabelais and His World*, 11, 93, 92, 7.

22. Bakhtin, *Rabelais and His World*, 444, 12.

23. Caryl Emerson, *The First Hundred Years of Mikhail Bakhtin* (Princeton: Princeton University Press, 1997), 105.

24. Bob Holman, "Report from the Poetry Wars: Slam's 10th Anniversary, a NYC Perspective," June 29, 1999, http://poetry.about.com/library/weekly/aa062999.htm (accessed January 10, 2011).

25. Anglesey, *Listen Up!* xi, xiii.

26. Regie Cabico and Todd Swift, eds., *Poetry Nation: The North American Anthology of Fusion Poetry* (Montréal: Véhicule Press, 1998), 23–24. Hereafter cited parenthetically in the text as *PN*.

27. Roger Bonair-Agard, et al., *Burning Down the House: Selected Poems from the Nuyorican Poets Café's National Poetry Slam Champions* (N.p.: Soft Skull Press, 2000), ii. In "Was That 'Different,' 'Dissident,' or 'Dissonant'? Poetry (n) the Public Spear: Slams, Open Readings, and Dissident Traditions" (in Bernstein, *Close Listening*), Maria Damon contends that "The world of poetry slams and open-mike readings, while not directly politically interventionist, perhaps, creates a public sphere that is healthily contestatory" (327). See Susan B. A. Somers-Willett's *The Cultural Politics of Slam Po-*

etry: Race, Identity, and the Performance of Popular Verse in America (Ann Arbor: University of Michigan Press, 2009) for further discussion of identity politics and the slam.

28. *Bum Rush the Page,* xx, xxi.

29. Bakhtin, *Rabelais and His World,* 195, 10, 17.

30. Bakhtin, *Rabelais and His World,* 11.

31. Butler, *Gender Trouble,* 141.

32. Butler, *Gender Trouble,* 138.

33. Bakhtin, *Rabelais and His World,* 453.

34. Martinovic, "SlamMania."

35. Heintz, "What Did Slam Poets Do with the Internet" (section of "An Incomplete History of Slam"), http://www.e-poets.net/library/slam/internet.html (accessed January 10, 2011).

36. John Giorno, liner notes to the box set *The Best of William Burroughs: From Giorno Poetry Systems,* 1998.

37. Jordan Trachtenberg and Amy Trachtenberg, eds., *Verses That Hurt: Pleasure and Pain from the POEMFONE Poets* (New York: St. Martin's Press, 1997), xxi, xxii.

38. Bob Holman, *Panic DJ!* (New York: University Arts Resources, 1987).

39. Bob Holman to Canadian dub poet Clifford Joseph, 1994, on T.V. Ontario's *Have You Heard the Word;* transcribed by Julie Schmid in her dissertation, "Performance, Poetics, and Place: Public Poetry as a Community Art."

40. Mark Eleveld, ed., *The Spoken Word Revolution Redux* (Naperville, IL: Sourcebooks MediaFusion, 2007), 214–15.

41. Quoted in "'The United States of Poetry': A Series by PBS," http://www .poets.org/viewmedia.php/prmMID/5708 (accessed January 10, 2011).

42. *Bum Rush the Page,* xxii.

43. Ben Brantley, "Untamed Poetry, Loose Onstage," *New York Times,* November 15, 2002: E1.

44. Quoted in Julie Schmid, "What's Going On: Poetics, Performance, and Patricia Smith's *Close to Death,*" in Martina Pfeiler, *Sounds of Poetry: Contemporary American Performance Poets* (Tübingen, Germany: Gunter Narr Verlag, 2003), 145.

45. Holman, "Performance Poetry," 344; Patricia Smith, "Persona Poem," in *PS,* 73.

46. Caryn James, "Poetry Gets Real, Flashing Its Form on MTV," *New York Times,* July 25, 1993: H28.

47. Kathleen Crown, "'Sonic Revolutionaries': Voice and Experiment in the Spoken Word Poetry of Tracie Morris," in *We Who Love To Be Astonished: Experimental Women's Writing and Performance Poetics,* ed. Laura Hinton and Cynthia Hogue (Tuscaloosa: University of Alabama Press, 2002), 216.

48. Auslander, *Liveness,* 93, 108.

49. Christine Hume, "Improvisational Insurrection: The Sound Poetry of Tracie Morris," in *American Poets in the 21st Century: The New Poetics,* ed. Claudia Rankine and Lisa Sewell (Middletown, CT: Wesleyan University Press, 2007), 9, 210, 211, 213, 216.

50. Transcribed from conversation between Tracie Morris and Charles Bernstein, http://writing.upenn.edu/pennsound/x/Morris.php (accessed January 10, 2011).

51. Tracie Morris, "Hip-Hop Rhyme Formations: Open Your Ears," in Finch and Varnes, *An Exaltation of Forms*, 223, 225.

52. Tracie Morris, "Project Princess," on the CD *Our Souls Have Grown Deep like the Rivers* (Rhino Records, 2000).

53. The audio of the PBS recording is available at http://www.worldofpoetry.org/usop/land4.htm (accessed January 10, 2011).

54. "Holy Kid: An Interview with Edwin Torres."

55. Edwin Torres, "The Limit Is Limitless," August 26, 2003, http://poetry.about .com/cs/reviewsessays/a/perfpoetorres.htm (accessed January 10, 2011).

Afterword

SWR, 169.

1. Dana Gioia, *Disappearing Ink: Poetry at the End of Print Culture* (St. Paul, MN: Graywolf Press, 2004), 3, 6–7.

2. Michael Eric Dyson, *Know What I Mean? Reflections on Hip Hop* (New York: Basic Civitas Books, 2007), 62, 29, 31, 32.

3. Dyson, *Know What I Mean?* 44, 62, 64, 65.

4. Paul Edwards, *How to Rap: The Art and Science of the Hip-Hop MC* (Chicago: Chicago Review Press, 2009), 289, 290, 464.

5. Murray Forman and Mark Anthony Neal, eds., *That's the Joint! The Hip-Hop Studies Reader* (New York: Routledge, 2004), 462.

6. Quoted in Felicia Pride, rev. of *The Dead Emcee Scrolls: The Lost Teachings of Hip-Hop, Baltimore City Paper*, April 12, 2006. This review is available at http://www2 .citypaper.com/arts/review.asp?rid=10167 (accessed January 10, 2011).

7. Modern Pea Pod, rev. of *The Dead Emcee Scrolls*, February 6, 2006, http://blog critics.org/books/article/book_review_the_dead_emcee_scrolls/ (accessed January 10, 2011).

8. Saul Williams, *The Dead Emcee Scrolls: The Lost Teachings of Hip-Hop and Connected Writings* (New York: MTV Books, 2006), xxii, 104–5, 108–9, 107. In an interview, Williams told DJ Matt Werner that Whitman "opened a door for me," reflecting that "the writing itself and the reading of the writing in my case often is a form of ritual. So that I look at much of my writing as a form of incantation. Or I'm aiming to essentially call on or release a certain amount of energy, of power through the recitation of this piece. And so quite simply I guess sometimes I go there in the writing in trying to crack open the vortex. I think Whitman for example is someone who's kept that really in perspective and kept very grounded in his perspective, and I really admire him for that" ("Saul Williams Interview with DJ Matt Werner on Fresh Air: The Alternative," recorded on November 21, 2008, and aired on December 9, 2008, http://djmattwerner.blogspot.com/2009/04/saul-williams-interview-with-dj-matt.html.

Index

When a poem has been performed under more than one title, the index reflects the most recent title only.

May Day," 115; "Chant for Tom Mooney," 113–15; "Christ in Alabama," 118; "The Colored Soldier," 106–7; "Cross," 104; "Dark Youth of the U.S.A.," 108–9; *The Dream Keeper and Other Poems* (book), 120; *The Dream Keeper and Other Poems* (recording), 112; "Freedom [2]," 119; "Freedom [3]," 119; "I, Too, Sing America," 104; *I Wonder as I Wander,* 103; "Justice," 122; *Langston Hughes Reader,* 105, 117, 120; *Langston Hughes Reads and Talks about His Poetry,* 113; "Militant," 119; "Negro," 119; "The Negro Mother," 107; *The Negro Mother and Other Dramatic Recitations,* 105–9, 113; "A New Song," 115, 116, 120–21; *A New Song,* 115, 121, 122; *The Panther and the Lash,* 118, 119–20; *The Poems of Langston Hughes,* 112; "The Poet and the Public," 122; *Scottsboro Limited,* 105, 122; *Selected Poems,* 117, 119; *Shakespeare in Harlem,* 109–10; "Sunday Morning Prophecy," 101; "Ten Ways To Use Poetry in Teaching," 112; *The Voice of Langston Hughes,* 113; "Walt Whitman's Darker Brothers," 89; *The Weary Blues,* 101–2, 120; *The Weary Blues and Other Poems Read by Langston Hughes,* 112; "Words Like Freedom," 118; "Youth," 120
Hume, Christine, 227
Hurston, Zora Neale, 13, 93–94, 97, 102
Hussein, Saddam, 145
Hustle & Flow, 230–31
Hymes, Dell, 7–8

Iman, Yusef, 194
Industrial Workers of the World. *See* I.W.W.
Iraq War, 144, 145
I.W.W. (Industrial Workers of the World), 121

James, Caryn, 224–25
James, Henry, 19, 237n7
Jihad Productions, 168
Jihad Singers, 194
Joans, Ted, 165
Johns, Jasper, 219
Johnson, Barbara, 169
Johnson, Freddie, 194
Johnson, James Weldon, 13, 93, 97–98; 178; works: *The Autobiography of an Ex-*

Coloured Man, 247n24; "The Creation," 95, 98, 99–100, 164; "The Crucifixion," 96; *God's Trombones,* 94–101, 112; "The Judgment Day," 96; "Let My People Go," 100–101; "Lift Every Voice and Sing," 90; "Listen, Lord—A Prayer, 88, 95–96, 100
Johnson, Joyce, 131
Johnson, Tom, 121
Jones, LeRoi. *See* Baraka, Amiri
Jones, Meta DuEwa, 113, 195
Jordan, Harry, 70
Jordan, June, 165–66
Judson Dance Theatre, 219

Kaplan, Justin, 22
Kaufman, Bob, 165, 233
Keillor, Garrison, 19
Kennedy, John F., Jr., 10
Kerouac, Jack, 126, 128, 131, 137, 138, 139, 146, 164, 251n17, 252n25
Kibler, Alison M., 70
Kill Rock Stars, 228
King, Martin Luther, Jr., 101, 130, 163, 177, 191, 246n11
Knight, Etheridge, 162, 164–65, 166, 172, 180, 255–56n9, 257n46; works: "The Idea of Ancestry," 172; *Poems from Prison* (book), 172, 191; *Poems from Prison* (recording), 179–80
Komunyakaa, Yusef, 200
Korean War, 129
Kostelanetz, Richard, 10
Kreymbourg, Alfred, 109

Lacan, Jacques, 155
Last Poets, The, 178, 201, 226, 232
Laughlin, James, 156
Leadbelly, 153
Lee, Don L., 14, 162, 167; works: "Assassination," 177; *Black Pride,* 164, 166, 176; *Directionscore,* 190, 191; *Don't Cry, Scream,* 176, 191; "DON'T CRY, SCREAM," 176–77; *Dynamite Voices: Black Poets of the 1960's,* 166–67, 169; "Malcolm Spoke / who listened?" 177; *Rappin' and Readin',* 178; "Re-Act for Action," 176; "'Stereo,'" 190; *Think Black,* 176; *We Walk the Way of the New World,* 177, 178, 191
Leonard, Eddie, 109
Leopold II, King (of Belgium) 59

Moore, Jessica Care, 200
Moore, Marianne, 76
Morphine, 157
Morris, Harrison, 52
Morris, Tracie, 200–201, 226–28, 229
Mos Def, 222
Moses (biblical), 100, 101, 191
MTV, 203, 228
MTV Unplugged, 224–26, 228
Muhammed, Idris, 195

Naropa Institute, 134, 148, 151
National Poetry Slam, 223
Neal, Larry, 162, 163, 164, 166, 189, 191,
    192, 193, 251–52n25; works: *Black
    Boogaloo,* 189, 192; *Black Fire,* 166–67;
    "Morning Raga for Malcolm," 191
Nelson, Cary, 55, 141
New Negro, 13, 88, 90, 91
New Negro, The, 98
Newport Jazz Festival, 110
New York Community Choir, 181, 183
Nine Inch Nails, 3
Norris, Clarence, 116–17
Nuyorican Poets Cafe, 199, 204, 207, 232

O'Hara, Frank, 189
Olson, Charles, 139, 171–72
Ong, Walter, 11

Page, Thomas Nelson, 97
Pan African Congress (1970), 194–95
Parry, Milman, 154
Patchen, Kenneth, 152, 153
Perelman, Bob, 44–46
Perloff, Marjorie, 134
Pfaff Beer Cellar, 22, 237n13
Phelan, Peggy, 5, 6, 20, 28, 48–49, 50
Picker, John, 44
Pinsky, Robert, 4
Pipes, William H., 92
Plato, 221
Poemfone, 220
poetry slam, 3, 10, 14–15, 54, 161,
    199–220, 224, 226–27, 229, 230, 233,
    260n20, 260–61n27
Poetry Systems, 220
Pond, James, 24–25, 80
Porter, David, 29

Pound, Ezra, 1–2, 3, 124, 127, 155, 171,
    241n7
Presley, Elvis, 167
Price, Abby, 23
Price, Kenneth M., 35, 53
Prirogine, Ilya, 146–47
professional wrestling, 202–3
Public Broadcasting Service. *See* PBS
public sphere, 8–9, 13, 22, 56, 70, 78, 103,
    106, 111, 161, 180, 182, 229, 260n27
punk, 203
Pyramus and Thisbe, 68

Radio Corporation of America. *See* RCA
Raleigh, Sir Walter, 71
Rambolina, 202
Rampersad, Arnold, 89, 102, 103
Randall, Dudley, 166, 168, 170, 176, 178,
    179, 188, 257n40, 258n59
Randolph, John, 57
Ransom, John Crowe, 85
Rauschenberg, Robert, 219
RCA (Radio Corporation of America), 157,
    245n78
Reagan, Ronald, 143
Reed, Edward Bliss, 60
Rexroth, Kenneth, 127–28, 139, 152–53,
    251n17, 254n77
Rexroth, Martha, 139
Reynolds, David, 33
Reznor, Trent, 3
Riley, James Whitcomb, 12, 61
Rittenhouse, Jessie B., 61–62, 241n9
Roach, Max, 189
Robinson, Smokey, 194
Rocky Flats (Boulder, Colorado), 142, 151
Rodgers, Carolyn, 174
Roots, The, 232
Ross, Diana, 195
Rothenberg, Jerome, 148
Rotundo, E. Anthony, 57–58
Rubin, Joan, 99
Russell, Irwin, 97
*Russell Simmons Def Poetry Jam on Broad-
    way,* 223
Rutgers University-Camden, 126

Sabina, Maria, 148–49
Salaam, Kalamu ya, 194, 196
Salla, Jerome, 201–2, 203
Sanchez, Sonia, 11, 14, 54, 162, 201, 226,
    231, 232, 256n31; and audio recording,

Town Hall Theater (Berkeley, California), 131
Traubel, Horace, 16, 17, 25, 32, 43, 50, 51, 52–53
Troupe, Quincy, 226
Turner, Lorenzo Dow, 89
Turner, Nat, 163
Twain, Mark, 22, 59, 86–87
Tzara, Tristan, 137

University of California, Berkeley, 158
Untermeyer, Louis, 62, 73, 85

Van Doren, Carl, 72
Van Vechten, Carl, 100, 102, 105
Verve Records, 112
Vesuvio's (San Francisco), 165
Vietnam War, 140, 144–45
Voice of America, The, 159

Wagner, Jean, 97–98
Waldman, Anne, 14, 54, 124, 137, 151, 201, 253n43; works: "Crack in the World," 149–51; "Fast Speaking Woman," 148–49; *Fast Speaking Woman,* 146–49; "Uh Oh Plutonium!" 151
Walker, George, 63
Wallace, George, 194
Warhol, Andy, 219
Wasson, R. Gordon, 148
Wayne State University, 178
Webster, John, 125
Werner, Matt, 262n8
Wesley, Carter, 104
Wharton, Edith, 19, 237n7
Whistler, James M., 81
White, Walter, 102
Whitman, Walt, 142, 152, 160, 193, 199–200, 220, 222, 227, 230, 231, 233; and audio recording, 21, 42–46, 124; and celebrity, 50–52; and copyright, 46–49, 54; and gender, 18–19, 22, 28–30, 92; and hypertext, 52–54; and nationality, 26, 30, 32–34, 38, 43, 54, 192; and photography, 20–21; and popularity, 2–3, 121, 124–25, 126–27, 165–66, 168, 222, 233; and race, 26, 35–36, 39; and revision of poems, 30–42, 49, 143, 195, 232; works: "Amer-

ica," 43–44, 124; *As a Strong Bird on Pinions Free,* 49, 237n11; "As I Ebb'd with the Ocean of Life," 36; "As I Sat Alone by Blue Ontario's Shore," 16, 23, 30, 34, 37; "Beat! Beat! Drums," 22; "A Boston Ballad," 33; "Chants Democratic. 12," 41; "Come, said my soul," 48; *Complete Poems and Prose,* 21; "Crossing Brooklyn Ferry," 44; *Drum-Taps,* 37; "Election Day, November, 1884," 54; "A Font of Type," 25; *Gems of Walt Whitman,* 18; "L. of G.," 54; "Mediums," 40; "My Legacy," 49–50; "Mystic Trumpeter," 23; "Note at End of Complete Poems and Prose," 54; "Now Precedent Songs, Farewell," 19; O Captain! My Captain!" 24–25; "On Journeys through the States," 38; "One's Self I Sing," 126; "Passage to India," 38; "Pioneers! O Pioneers!" 46; "Poem of the Dead Young Men of Europe, the 72d and 73d Years of These States," 33; "Poets To Come," 124; "Respondez!" 36; "Salut au Monde!" 39–40; "The Sleepers," 35–36; "A Song for Occupations," 19, 49; "Song of Myself," 32–33, 37, 40; "Song of the Banner at Daybreak," 37; "Song of the Broad-Axe," 30; "Song of the Exposition," 24, 38; "Song of the Open Road," 19; "Song of the Universal," 38; *Specimen Days and Collect,* 1, 21, 23; "Starting from Paumanok," 160; "Vocalism," 41–42; "A Voice Out of the Sea," 16; "Walt Whitman's Last," 49; "Who Learns My Lesson Complete?" 33–34
Wilkins, Roy, 195
Williams, Bert, 62–63, 109, 110
Williams, Saul, 3, 262n8; works: *The Dead Emcee Scrolls: The Lost Teachings of Hip-Hop,* 232–33; *Slam,* 232
Williams, William Carlos, 171
Wills, Elizabeth Mann, 56
Wilner, Hal, 131
Winters, Yvor, 207
Wordsworth, William, 154
wrestling. *See* professional wrestling

Yeats, William Butler, 71, 74, 76, 243n41